The Ravaged Bridegroom

Marie-Louise von Franz, Honorary Patron

**Studies in Jungian Psychology
by Jungian Analysts**

Daryl Sharp, General Editor

The
Ravaged Bridegroom

Masculinity in Women

MARION WOODMAN

To my parents, Andrew D. Boa and Ila J. Phinn.
With much gratitude to Ross Woodman, Daryl Sharp,
Katherine Anne Skinner and my analysands.

Canadian Cataloguing in Publication Data

Woodman, Marion
    The ravaged bridegroom: masculinity in women

(Studies in Jungian psychology by Jungian analysts; 41)

Includes bibliographical references.

ISBN 0-919123-42-2

1. Women—Psychology.   2. Masculinity (Psychology).
3. Women's dreams.   4. Jung, C.G. (Carl Gustav), 1875-1961.
I. Title.   II. Series.

HQ1206.W66 1990   155.6'33   C89-090542-8

INNER CITY BOOKS
Box 1271, Station Q, Toronto, Canada M4T 2P4
Telephone (416) 927-0355

Honorary Patron: Marie-Louise von Franz.
Publisher and General Editor: Daryl Sharp.
Senior Editor: Victoria Cowan.

INNER CITY BOOKS was founded in 1980 to promote the
understanding and practical application of the work of C.G. Jung.

Cover: "Pluto and Persephone," watercolor by Tennessee Dixon.
(© 1988; used by permission)

Index by Daryl Sharp

Printed and bound in Canada by Webcom Limited

Contents

See final page for descriptions of other Inner City Books

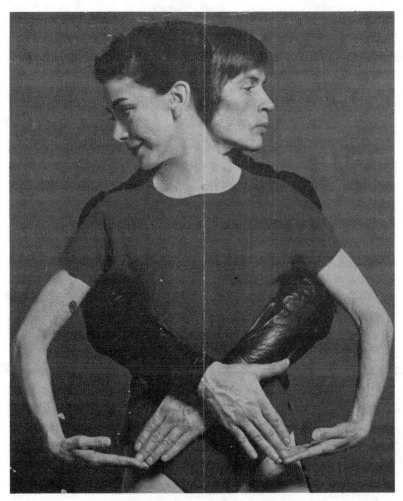

Margot Fonteyn and Rudolf Nureyev

Introduction

Is the battle of the sexes becoming more bitter? How has patriarchy compounded the distance between men and women? Why do our efforts to bridge the gap fail? Why is an understanding of unconscious dynamics important? How can our dreams guide us in healing ourselves, our relationships, our planet? These are a few of the questions addressed in this book.

As an analyst I work with many dreams every week. While my analysands struggle with what seem to them to be isolated images, I see the same or similar images repeating from hour to hour in my practice and in the dreams of workshop participants from coast to coast. When I see a theme emerging, I study twenty or thirty dreams revolving around that particular issue. I try to analyze where the energy is blocked (and, therefore, unavailable to the ego), how it can be released, and where it is trying to go. When I see what seems to be a pattern, I choose one dream that epitomizes the shifting energy lines, concentrate on it, and check my conclusions against similar dreams. While every dream is unique to the dreamer, archetypal patterns emerge that reveal evolving energies in the collective unconscious of the culture. They point the way in which consciousness may eventually move.

All but one of the dreamers in this book have been in analysis and some type of body work for at least five years. They understand the importance of meditating on an image in order to mine its healing power and its potential for guiding them in their outer life. They are developing the skills for interpreting their own dreams. Like everyone else, they sometimes need the outer eye that clears the mote from their own; generally they are able to feel and fathom what can be revealed in a dream and honor the mystery that cannot.

Many dreams, especially those that come from the archetypal depths, are rather like classical dramas. True art also comes from these depths and has certain similarities to the structure, imagery and language of dreams—like photographs of the conscious situation taken from the unconscious point of view.

It can be argued, of course, that many modern dreams, like modern artistic creations, are a "heap of broken images" coming from a fragmented archetypal field where the pattern, as in a poem like *The Waste Land* or a novel like *Ulysses,* operates at a more subliminal level. It can be argued that in bringing the dream forward from the unconscious into consciousness something of its subliminal power is lost, even as Eliot's notes on *The Waste Land* tend, if read too scrupulously, to encumber the poem rather than illuminate it.

It can also be argued that analyzing a dream is like tearing a Shakespearean sonnet to pieces in the classroom. If, however, we value a sonnet enough to spend hours understanding how the basic image works, how the alliterations are holding the music of the vowels in a phrase like "sessions of sweet silent thought," how those tones are affecting our feeling, how all of this and much more is orchestrating fourteen lines into a magnificent totality, then we are able to read the poem aloud and be silenced in the presence of genius.

The same is true of dreams. Who is this incredible genius we sleep with every night? What is this realm in which exact images reveal our inner world and connect it to the outer? However we wish to name the genius, one basic pattern emerges. Jung called it a natural gradient toward wholeness, guided by the Self (god-image within and regulating center of the personality).

It is as if life, when it is truly being lived, were a series of birth canals. We go along for a period of time, then suddenly or gradually we are no longer satisfied. Our job is no longer challenging, our partner is no longer exciting, the old ways no longer suffice. If we relate to the natural rhythms of the psyche, we find ourselves in a womb, withdrawn from the world, no longer sure who we are or where we are going. If we can stay with the pain of the death of the old, and bear the crucifixion of the transition, eventually we are born anew. We may enjoy the new plateau for a few years, then the opposites begin to break apart again, forcing us to new levels of consciousness. Sometimes we feel we are moving up, sometimes down —whichever way is both up and down. The lotus flower that opens to the sun has its roots deep in the nourishing mud.

This book focuses on evolving masculinity and femininity as two energies within each individual, both striving toward an inner harmony. So long as these energies are projected onto others, we rob ourselves of our own maturity and our own freedom. Until we take responsibility for these projections, genuine relationship is impossible because we are entangled in our own images instead of relating to new possibilities that expand our boundaries.

The anguish of broken relationships is increasingly forcing individuals to come to some understanding of what liberated masculinity and liberated femininity could be. How do we release them from the outworn mythologies in which they are entombed?

*

That question became frighteningly immediate the night I turned on the television to learn of the tragedy that had struck the University of Montreal. A gunman shouting, "You're all a bunch of feminists!" had walked into a classroom, separated the men from the women, and before the carnage was over had shot and killed fourteen female students, wounded thirteen others (including one man), then turned the gun on himself. Our nation grieves for the dead, for their families, for the society in which such mindless violence can happen. Certainly it was the action of a severely disordered mind, but such minds pick up what is consciously or unconsciously in the collective. Deep-rooted hatred of women, blasting out of a semi-automatic weapon, blasts open other arsenals of fear, bitterness and rage in both men and women.

Our shared grief can initiate the consciousness that would transform the murderous act into a meaningful sacrifice—a sacrifice profound enough to revolutionize our society. Our sentimental glasses have been ripped off. Thoughtful questions are being asked: Has this tragedy enacted something endemic in our society? Is femininity in

both sexes in jeopardy? The images on the screen recall contemporary dream images that clearly reveal a similar situation in the unconscious of many men and women. This tragedy, this *human* tragedy,
summons every one of us to look at our own power shadow.

A wind is sweeping across the whole world. It left perhaps hundreds of Chinese students dead when they tried to confront the old
regime. Their deaths were not in vain. When the same wind struck in
Czechoslovakia, the citizens saw their students pummelled by their
own police and rose up and said, "No more." They stood in their
thousands in Wenceslas Square, jaws firm, eyes bright, demanding
freedom. In Poland, Lech Walesa put his Black Madonna button on
his lapel and led his people in orderly revolt. This very day, as I
write these lines, the army in Romania has joined the people in their
bid for a just society. The grassroots humanity of Eastern Europe has
risen up against stifling dictatorships. By its very numbers and vision, it is bringing the old order down. The same wind is blowing in
South Africa, Central America and countless other areas on the
planet. The global village is in the chaos of rebirth.

The same wind is blowing in America. We dare not tuck ourselves
into our warm duvets, smugly happy that those in the Old World are
at last finding the freedom we have found. Freedom for what? To
dream of being kicked into a concentration camp, or running for our
lives from the muzzle of a gun? Freedom to drug our femininity out
of her frenzy? To bury our soul child in a pile of garbage?

The Berlin Wall is down. The Wall of Mirrors through which men
and women fail to see each other is still up. It stands invisible in the
streets, in our institutions and in personal relationships. It stands
most dangerously in the unconscious of the sons and daughters of
patriarchy. Subtle, frosted with illusions and projections, it betrays.
Now as we try to plumb its illusive depths, we, both men and
women, are facing our anguished femininity and her ravaged masculine partner, both victims of obsolete ideals. She will no longer be a
silent victim, nor will he remain ostracized.

Breaching that wall is going to take patience and total dedication.
It cannot be done from outside. The unconscious dynamics that keep

the feminine a prisoner of patriarchy are in the marrow of our bones. Yet if we could each take responsibility for our own inner victim and tyrant, we could truly depotentiate the old parental complexes. Released from their power, we would be free to love.

Freedom is not license, nor is it selfish egoism. To be psychologically free is to be confident in our own inner world, responsible for our own strengths and weaknesses, consciously loving ourselves and, therefore, able to love others. Dreams guide us in that direction, however crooked the path may be. The insights and dreams presented in this book are our contributions, my analysands' and mine, to breaching the wall that blocks our path to freedom.

Toronto, December 1989

Brew us the magic in which all limits dissolve,
spirit forever bent to the fire!
The fathomless limit of evil, first, which revolves
also around those who are resting and do not stir.

Dissolve with a few drops whatever excludes in the limit
of the ages, which makes our past wisdom a fraud;
for how deeply we have absorbed the Athenian sunlight
and the mystery of the Egyptian falcon or god.

Don't rest until the boundary that keeps the sexes
in meaningless conflict has disappeared.
Open up childhood and the wombs of more truly expectant

generous mothers so that, shaming all that is empty,
and not confused by the hindering wood,
they may give birth to future rivers, augmenting the sea.

—Rainer Maria Rilke, from *The Sonnets to Orpheus.*

So here we have a three-fold universe: an intelligible universe, a sensory universe, and between the two a universe for which it is difficult in our language to find a satisfactory term. If we use the word *Imaginable,* we risk suggesting the idea of eventuality, possibility. The word must be given all the force of a technical term as designating the object proper to the *imaginative perception,* everything that can be perceived by the Imagination, with as much reality and truth as the sensory can be perceived by the senses, or the intelligible by the intellect.
    —Henry Corbin, *Spiritual Body and Celestial Earth.*

1
Dragon Slaying:
Murder or Sacrifice?

If men and women are to be equal partners in the outer world, the foundations for that partnership must first be laid within themselves. As within, so without. Nothing can be achieved without, if the foundations are not firmly established within. Negotiations between the sexes are bound to collapse into misunderstandings or remain suspended in compromises that satisfy neither, so long as men and women remain strangers to their inner reality.

Each sex is beginning to hear within itself what the other is demanding. More than that, each sex is beginning to recognize what is heard as an inner need essential to wholeness. Only in this way can a partnership between the sexes be forged that completes and enhances both. In the forging of such a relationship, human society on all its interacting levels will become the beneficiary.

In the Book of Revelation, John of Patmos is granted a vision of such a society when he sees the new Jerusalem descending as a bride adorned to meet her bridegroom.

> And I saw a new heaven and a new earth: for the first heaven and the first earth were passed away; and there was no more sea.
> And I John saw the holy city, new Jerusalem coming down from God out of heaven, prepared as a bride adorned for her husband.[1]

What John witnesses is a vision of the inner marriage in a new creation. "Behold, I make all things new," declares the voice.

No one who is conscious of the transformation of the planet Earth into a global village can doubt that, whether we like it or not, with or without our cooperation, we are caught up in a revolutionary movement that cannot be halted. Forces have been released which inspire

---

[1] Revelation 21:1-2.

13

in us a sense of helplessness and vulnerability even as they fill us with the exhilaration of a creative challenge. The realization that the earth is now one country with all humanity its citizens is less a nightmare from which we hope to awake than the fulfillment of a prophetic dream. Some already experience the global community more as John's visionary city so ardently described throughout the Bible than as an armed camp with every neighbor a potential enemy. For three world religions, Jerusalem today epitomizes the longing for a new creation still held in the paralyzing grip of the old. It is from this adolescent state that humanity is now struggling to emerge.

How we view the global village in which we now live makes a considerable difference to the way we conduct our lives. In forging a partnership of equals between the sexes—a partnership that belongs to the new creation—we need to be very sure whether we are negotiating a partnership as enemies whom our inherited prejudices have taught us to fear or as bride and bridegroom, each coming forth to greet the other.

"Be fruitful and multiply," God's command to "male and female created he them," no longer has an exclusive biological connotation in a world already dangerously overpopulated. The fruits of union belong to every sphere of human creativity and constitute in the largest sense a genuinely new creation, understood as the coming of age of the entire human race. Lest such a hope lose its inherent potency to impotent fantasy, we need to recognize the degree to which a vision of the new Jerusalem and her bridegroom, understood as the creative partnership of the sexes on every level, has been a propelling force. It has governed the evolution of Western civilization from its most primitive tribal stages to its present global integration. Today we confront the fact, not the fantasy, of one world. And it is with this in mind that we shall explore the dynamics that have as their goal a creative and abiding partnership between the sexes.

The first task that confronts us is to raise the feminine to a new level of consciousness so that matter (always associated with the feminine), instead of being experienced as dark and opaque, will be suffused with its own inner light, a radiant container strong enough to relate with vibrancy and creativity to the emerging masculine consciousness.

A major impetus toward the emergence of the conscious feminine came from the German and English Romantic poets. They were aware of the overdeveloped excesses of an obsolete patriarchy which, even in the nineteenth century, was experiencing the oppressive and destructive death throes of an old order fighting the inevitability of its own extinction. This left us, in Matthew Arnold's phrase, "Wandering between two worlds,/ One dead, the other powerless to be born."[2]

John Keats tried twice to write about it. His unfinished *Hyperion* is an epic for which he martyred his heart in an effort to forge, along with his fellow Romantics, a new creation based upon a feminine consciousness as the receiver of a newly emergent masculine, which Keats identified with the sun god Apollo. His intense search brought forth in the figure of Moneta a feminine image very like the broken-hearted woman who appears in many modern dreams, sometimes as the Black Madonna.

> As I had found
> A grain of gold upon a mountain side,
> And twing'd with avarice strain'd out my eyes
> To search its sullen entrails rich with ore,
> So at the view of sad Moneta's brow,
> I ach'd to see what things the hollow brain
> Behind enwombed: what high tragedy
> In the dark secret chamber of her skull
> Was acting, that could give so dread a stress
> To her cold lips, and fill with such a light
> Her planetary eyes; and touch her voice
> With such a sorrow.[3]

Keats' insight into feminine consciousness was far ahead of its time. The effort he expended pioneering a new inner path, with his

---

2 "Stanzas from the Grande Chartreuse," lines 85-86.
3 "The Fall of Hyperion," canto 1, lines 271-282.

concept of life as a "vale of Soul-making,"[4] opened channels of sensibility that may have precipitated his early death at twenty-five.

The search for the lost feminine that continued into the twentieth century in poetry, dance and art has now become a conscious search in the lives of countless men and women who are committed to their psychic and spiritual growth. The fact remains, however, that the masculine bound to an obsolete patriarchal tradition experiences the emergence of the feminine as a threat. To disarm the masculine of its patriarchal fear of the feminine is thus crucial to releasing the creative dynamics of partnership. Equally the oppression of the feminine within a patriarchal tradition renders the masculine shaped by that tradition its natural enemy. It is therefore also necessary to disarm the feminine of its fear of the patriarchal masculine in order to release the dynamics of the new relationship. Overcome by these fears, neither sex is in a position to forge a new creation. Their negotiations are rather like wine merchants discussing prohibition. Instead, a disarmed honesty must precede or at least accompany negotiations.

Crucial to a discussion of the conscious feminine is the liberation of the word from its bondage to gender. While I am deeply concerned with forging a new relationship between the sexes, I am more immediately concerned with the inner basis of that new relationship through the coming together of masculine and feminine within the individual of either sex. The term "conscious feminine" applies as much to men as to women, even as the term "conscious masculine" applies to both sexes. In the age now emerging, the same dynamics operate in both sexes to create thereby what has not yet been sufficiently recognized: a genuine meeting ground between them.

Mature men and women of the new age will be bound together less by the attraction of opposites than by their shared humanity. This shared humanity does not neutralize sexual attraction. Differentiated masculinity in a woman attracts strong men; differentiated femininity in men attracts strong women. The energy at work in a male body functions differently from the energy at work in a female body.

---

[4] "Letter to George and Georgina Keats," Feb. 14—May 3, 1819.

Gender, which is a matter of biology, is a desirable distinction absolutely essential to the survival of the human race. But survival on psychic and spiritual levels carries us beyond biology into the area Jung called individuation. The unity of the human race dictated by the global village we anxiously inhabit—while still looking for a safer place to settle—is a unity that far transcends the sexual attraction of opposites. It is rather a unity that issues from a profound identity that needs urgently to be understood.

So long as we fail to do the hard work of bringing our own masculine and feminine sides to consciousness, we fall back upon those ancient parental figures who have long since hardened into the established forms which reinforce a patriarchal order. Passively to submit to that order is unconsciously to relate to society as children relate to their parents, projecting onto them archetypal powers which reinforce parental authority and inflate their actuality.

Though children obviously require the security archetypal projections create, adults cannot continue to submit to that authority without undermining their own psychic growth. At their worst, infantile projections onto parents, if not withdrawn, become the foundation upon which any dictatorial system depends, particularly when the tyranny of that system is never fully experienced because the security it provides outweighs the cost of submission.

In *The Brothers Karamazov*, Dostoyevsky's Grand Inquisitor, when confronted by the return of Christ, assures him in a manner that contains the threat of a second crucifixion that there is no room for him in the Catholic Church. The security offered to Christendom by an authoritarian church, at once matriarchal and patriarchal, satisfies human needs in a manner that can only be threatened by the freedom offered by Christ. To crucify freedom in the name of the security bestowed by the authority of omnipotent parents is, the Inquisitor suggests, the very foundation of human society.

The old petrifying mother is like a great lizard lounging in the depths of the unconscious. She wants nothing to change. If the feisty ego attempts to accomplish anything, one flash of her tongue disposes of the childish rebel. Her consort, the rigid authoritarian father, passes the laws that maintain her inertia. Together they rule with an iron fist in a velvet glove. Mother becomes Mother Church, Mother Welfare State, Mother University, the beloved Alma Mater, defended by Father who becomes Father Hierarchy, Father Law, Father Status Quo. We unconsciously introject the power inherent in these archetypal figures which, in the absence of the individuation process, remain intact at an infantile level. So long as they remain intact, uninterrupted by the consciousness that can disempower them, the inner dictators enslave more cruelly than the outer.

In my understanding of patriarchy, these outworn parental images wield the power that inhibits personal growth. So long as they are in control, conscious masculinity and conscious femininity are merely words. Men and women who are unconsciously trapped in power drives have no individual freedom, nor can they allow freedom to others. Women can be worse patriarchs than men. The myth of the sun hero fighting the dragon and winning his way to consciousness has suffered from overkill. The energies of that myth have been exhausted and we are now struggling with the abuses of its excess. In killing the dragon, we are now in danger of killing nature herself on whom we depend for life. Moreover, the tunnel vision that has been so focused on conquering the unconscious mother has been blind to her conquering through the back door: the effort of centuries to kill the dragon has ended in the worship of mother in concrete materialism. The sons and daughters of patriarchy are, in fact, motherbound.

The symbolic meaning of killing as sacrifice which leads to transformation has been lost. Transformation moves energy from the unconscious to consciousness. When dragon slaying is concretized, mother becomes concrete matter, and unconsciously her children continue to worship the outworn mother because the consciousness that would lead to transformation is not present. Without it, killing the mother only leads to bringing her back in a stronger form, since she feeds on the energy of the killer—as many an addict has discovered. In the myth, death is followed by resurrection, but in our concretized culture, there is only death. We could die in our own garbage. Somewhere along the line, slaying became simply an act of murder instead of a means to transformation.

Patriarchy originated in one of the oldest myths of humankind: the hero's journey. In this myth, the hero is the descendant of the sun god, that symbol of absolute authority upon which all life depends. The sun god continuously reasserts his absolute authority by the conquest of the forces of darkness that challenge his reign. "Let there be light" is the divine fiat which constitutes creation. Arming himself in the name of the sun god, his shield a symbol of the sun, the son hero goes forth in the name of his father god to perform that essential patriarchal act which identifies him with the creator himself. The supreme male action is then to repeat the eternal act of creation. Against the hero stand arrayed the forces of darkness that in themselves can shed no light save as they receive it from the sun.

One symbol of this darkness is the moon with its lunar, as opposed to solar, cycle. This cycle, essentially feminine, rules the night even as the sun rules the day, though not by shedding its own light, but rather by reflecting the light of the sun. The relationship of sun and moon thus comes to symbolize the relationship between the sexes themselves. The feminine, standing for the forces of darkness and chaos, is brought within the orbit of a masculine light-bringing creation as a reflection of its power.

Milton sums it up in describing the Biblical figures of Adam and Eve:

He for God only, she for God in him.[5]

Closely aligned to the feminine imaged as a lunar cycle is the figure of the dragon or serpent to whom woman is traditionally related, subsequently coming under the domination of masculine power. Usually in the hero myth, the dragon must be slain. Where the slaying of the dragon is not understood as a symbolic process of transformation, then the feminine is separated from its own source of life and power in matter *(mater)*. Then woman becomes what Freud de-

---

[5] *Paradise Lost,* Book 4, line 299.

clared her to be: a castrated male, her vagina an open wound that strikes terror into a man when he first perceives it.

The slaying of the dragon, as heroically idealized, particularly in Romance literature, includes the rescuing of the maiden who is held captive by the dragon. Deeply embedded in this solar myth is the conviction that the feminine must be rescued from its own darkness. The solar hero, who stands for spirit and light, the penetrating power of rational insight, cannot comprehend this darkness, which comes down to us as the feminine mysteries. Historically, as celebrated in the Eleusinian rituals, the participants were forbidden to articulate them. The process of creation enacted in the darkness of the womb is inaccessible to the light of the sun though it is not inaccessible to the moon. Crucial, therefore, to the equality of the sexes is a transformation in the male fear of the feminine process. What has yet to replace the slaying of the dragon by the solar hero, still considered by many men a sacred obligation, is the development of a feminine consciousness that the slaying of the dragon too often precludes. It is the discriminating integration of the unconscious feminine, rather than its rejection, that leads to transformation. The dragon, akin to the alchemists' *deus absconditus* (the god hidden in matter),[6] must not be slain. The dragon must, as in Jung's "Answer to Job," become the living redeemer.[7]

The mutation in consciousness which is here suggested would reconstruct the foundations upon which the male ego has for centuries rested. Still it is clear in our evolving consciousness that slaying is at best an arrested act of transformation. The characteristic male response to the rejection of the dragon-slaying myth in favor of transformation is the ancient fear that the forces of darkness may then overtake the forces of light, leaving the man in the condition of the woman, denied his phallic power. Here we come face to face with what is involved in a man's response to his own inner feminine as anything other than a threat to his hard-won masculinity. Almost

---

6 See Jung, *Alchemical Studies*, CW 13, pars. 138-139.
7 See *Psychology and Religion*, CW 11, par. 619.

nothing in his social experience prepares him to view it in any other way.

How then can such a leap in consciousness come about? How can men lose their fear of the feminine so as to bring it fully to consciousness rather than repressing it into an abysmal darkness? The answer may lie in an understanding of the psychic dynamics of creativity itself, dynamics which men have traditionally seen as a threat to their manhood. Poetry making, even the study of it, is still considered by many to be a less than manly activity.

Those dynamics were consciously explored by the Romantic poets. What struck them most forcibly was the responsibility of every human being for the growth and nourishment of his or her own soul. They therefore identified the psychic dynamics of the creative process with what Keats described as "Soul-making." Both sexes share this common and essential activity. Both are deeply involved at the psychic level with giving birth to themselves, knowing that the father of the child being shaped in the dark womb of creativity is a supernatural rather than natural being. The myth of the virgin birth applies equally to men and to women when it is perceived in terms of the psychic dynamics governing the making of soul.[8] The science of soul making is called psychology. Psychology is neither male nor female, but both. Significantly, Freud finally felt it was his patriarchal responsibility to sacrifice the soul to the reality principle.

If men fear the feminine, so also do women. But the basis of that fear is different in a woman. She is biologically creative. The leap from the physical to the psychic, a leap epitomized by the Virgin Mary confronted by the Archangel Gabriel, is a leap of consciousness which her own biology not only resists but often denies because the body is confronted by a psychic reality that appears to usurp the apparent omnipotence of its power. The male fear of the feminine is deeply rooted in the dark mystery of the female body, a mystery women have secretly worshiped for centuries in rites traditionally

---

[8] See Marion Woodman, *The Pregnant Virgin: A Process of Psychological Transformation*.

identified with underground caves and equated with the Mother Goddess who in Christianity becomes the Mother of God himself.

Women have not been immune to the temptations of body power. The elaborate rites dedicated to the enhancement of that power—the cosmetics industry is one of the most competitive in the world—still constitute the worship of the bewitching shadow of the unconscious feminine. Men bound to the solar myth are particularly susceptible to this shadow because it is the essential target of the dragon-slaying initiation.

Jung called the soul-making process an *opus contra naturam,* a work against nature, by which he meant one had to work against the unconscious pull of nature in order to release the soul essence. The inclination of the masculine spirit in this *opus* is to transcend the body, to go against the unconsciousness of nature by ignoring it, to reach for the perfection of disembodied soul. Conversely, the feminine, already bonded to nature by biology, tends to fall even deeper into the concretization of matter and fails to distill the soul essence. The soul, the essence which I understand as conscious femininity, is endangered equally by disembodied spirit and by concretized matter, but her distillation is imperative in laying the foundations for a new partnership between the sexes.

Dragon Slaying, Soul Making and Metaphor

Perhaps enough has been said to expose the trap into which we fall when we settle for obsolete mythologies. What we see is the shadow of the unconscious feminine luring with her ancient rituals of mystification the solar hero who simultaneously finds in her the object of his constellated desire and the target of his initiating rite. He must slay the thing he thinks he loves, the very love striking and igniting terror in his heart in which union becomes destruction. The highest expression of Othello's love of Desdemona emerges when he sees himself as the noble upholder of a cause, killing his wife as an act of sacrifice. She glows before him with the chastity of stars and the smoothness of monumental alabaster. About to strangle her, he says, "It is the cause, it is the cause, my soul."[9]

Rarely has the slaying of the dragon been more closely identified with the murder of the beloved than in Shakespeare's treatment of *liebestod*, dying together for love. So long as we remain moved by it, so long as it is in our imagination as an icon of highest tragedy, we remain in the grip of a mythology that may yet succeed in destroying us for what we still consider the highest and noblest end.

The "cause" that Othello refused to name ("Let me not name it to you, ye chaste stars")[10] is the dragon-slaying myth of the solar hero. It finds its energized source in the alluring shadow of the unconscious feminine symbolized by the powers of darkness. When Desdemona declares that Othello is innocent, she is admitting to her unconscious collusion in his divinely dictated crime. Love in the service of murder is what the solar myth has become in its arrested form, a form which I would identify with patriarchy.

This reading of the dragon-slaying myth that so powerfully plays into the shadow of the unconscious feminine is a revisionary interpretation of one of the most pervasive myths in world mythology. So long as patriarchy was identified with the order of the cosmos itself, the myth was not open to question. It was as self-evidently true as the rising and the setting of the sun. To call into question its arrested or killing form (the devastation of nature, for example), as I and many others are now doing, is to bring down upon us the wrath of patriarchal power raging against the dying of its light. To invoke such rage is not my intention. Nor do I wish to appease it. I prefer not even to address it because I want to look ahead. I want to put my energy into working on an alternative model of soul making. The new model, as I have suggested, owes much to the Romantic poets, whose major contribution was not, as many believe, a celebration of romantic love, but a profound critique of it. That critique, too long unrecognized, becomes self-evident in Shakespeare's tragedy when

---

[9] *Othello,* act 5, scene 2, line 1.
[10] Ibid., line 2.

Othello is at last forced to see that what he had romantically idealized as a sacrifice was, in fact, a murder.

Crucial to an understanding of dragon slaying is an opposition between matter and spirit, where matter not only resists the light of the spirit but seeks to destroy it in the name of eternal darkness. The forces of light and the forces of darkness are eternal enemies which together enact a primitive power struggle in which murder, rather than sacrifice, remains the imperative form of action. No matter how idealized that action may appear in order to enhance the status of the primitive epic hero, it remains in its essence a murderous act whose redemptive power has become, with time, a delusion that can no longer be rationally or spiritually upheld. Blood cannot bridge the gap of spirit and matter which dragon slaying attempts in vain to achieve. The present struggle toward a feminine consciousness is a rejection of the murder of its fully energized identity. It is not a rejection of the sacrifices which consciousness demands.

In turning now to soul making, we need first to discuss the role of metaphor in bridging the apparent gap between matter and spirit. Metaphor yokes them together without bloodshed. It reveals consciousness holding matter and spirit together by the linguistic transformation *(meta-phor* in Greek means a carrying across) of the realm of matter into symbols of the spirit.

All language is, in fact, metaphor—words standing for something. Much of our daily talk is metaphor: She chewed me out. I can't stomach him. Let's make a clean breast of it. She's a peach, a princess, a Pollyanna. He's a prick, a prince, a paragon. Metaphor is colorful language because it carries an emotional and imaginative charge as well as a meaning. Take, for example, the familiar lines of Macbeth when he learns that his wife, once his "dearest love," is dead:

> To-morrow, and to-morrow, and to-morrow,
> Creeps in this petty pace from day to day
> To the last syllable of recorded time,
> And all our yesterdays have lighted fools

> The way to dusty death. Out, out, brief candle!
> Life's but a walking shadow, a poor player
> That struts and frets his hour upon the stage
> And then is heard no more.[11]

Like many, you may have wondered why Shakespeare was not smart enough to say what he meant, as you probably wonder why your dreams don't say what they mean. Suppose Macbeth had said, "I'll end my empty, short life." Would those words capture the total collapse of everything a great man once was and ever hoped for? Would the imagination be fed with the image of the spark suddenly disappearing into nothing? Would the heart resonate with the keening of Lady Macbeth sleepwalking with a candle, groping in a world in which "Twas lighter—to be Blind"?[12] Would we see the candle of her life, like the candle of our own lives, flicker into darkness?

A metaphor is by definition the imaging of spirit in matter, or even spirit *as* matter. That world in which the two are joined is the intermediate world identified as soul. The continuous intercourse between matter and spirit is thus apparent in the very nature of language, which originates in metaphor. Language, therefore, presents us with a world in which matter and spirit are intimately linked. This is the mysterious realm of the subtle body.

The subtle body, an expression Jung took over from alchemy, is the body in which we live, move, and have our being. It is through the subtle body that we experience and relate to ourselves and to others on every level of existence. The subtle body is, in Wordsworth's phrase, "the world/ Of all of us, the place where, in the end,/ We find our happiness or not at all."[13] It is a body whose soul affirmation of itself releases it from its primitive identification with those powers of darkness which have for too long treacherously lured the deluded dragon slayers into the murderous performance of a pseudo-redemptive act.

---

[11] Act 5, scene 5, lines 19-26.
[12] Emily Dickinson, *The Complete Poems,* no. 761.
[13] "The Prelude," book 2, lines 142-144.

To illustrate the transformation of matter into spirit, let us recall an event which, thanks to television, many of us experienced. Within this event, I would like to locate the subtle body which has nothing to do with gender, nothing to do with dragon slaying or unconscious feminine allure. It applies equally to the humanity of men and of women. More than that, because it was a genuinely global event, involving an experience in space which contained the globe as a globe, I see it as an emblem of that oneness of humankind which the inner marriage celebrates.

On February 11, 1986, President Reagan quoted the following lines from a sonnet written by a nineteen-year-old Canadian airman who was killed in the Second World War:

> Up, up the long, delirious, burning blue
> I've topped the wind-swept heights with easy grace,
> Where never lark, or even eagle, flew;
> And while with silent, lifting mind I've trod
> The high, untrespassed sanctity of space,
> Put out my hand, and touched the face of God.[14]

President Reagan was addressing the stricken families of the seven astronauts who had confidently lifted off in Challenger and seventy-three seconds later ceased to exist in this reality. Before the incredulous eyes of their loved ones and millions of television viewers, they disappeared. The word "space" took on new meaning. Instantaneously, the astronauts were translated from matter into spirit. Those who were watching, consciously or unconscious, felt their own light go out.

How do human beings deal with the brutality of sudden, silent end? As individuals they repeatedly tell their story, listen to music, read poetry, walk in nature. After a national tragedy, television does a similar thing for the masses. Interspersed between replays of the tragedy—the unfathomable reality—are music, poetry, scripture, the only language that at that moment means anything. The imagination, through metaphor, makes the bridge that at once separates and joins

---

[14] John Gillespie Magee, Jr., "High Flight."

matter and spirit. Because the soul is eternal essence living in matter, the images of matter bestowed by the five senses carry within them the food of the soul.

Spirit yearns with limitless aspirations; matter imposes limitations on spirit. Soul mediates between them. When spirit is brought down by nature, soul suffers. When opaque matter is brought into consciousness, soul suffers. The function of soul growth is suffering and sacrifice. In confronting the disasters of spirit, instead of rejecting spirit, we come to terms with limitations. That is the intermediate world. In confronting disasters of matter, instead of rejecting body, we come to terms with its limitations. That too is the intermediate world. Soul dwells in the intermediary world, in the subtle body. Patriarchal fear of the feminine can be overcome by building a conscious feminine container—a receptive soul that no longer needs to fear either spirit or matter.

Journeying between earth and heaven, joining one to the other, the soul understands the language of poetry, the language of metaphor, which integrates the image with feeling, mind and imagination. The metaphor, or the symbol, heals because it speaks to the *total* person. For this reason, Jung believed that the contemplation of dream images was the pathway to wholeness.

The explosion of Challenger was on one level the explosion of disembodied spirit, intelligence divorced from human limitations and natural laws, hubris that overvalued technological ascendancy. In one flash, the microcosm revealed the macrocosm. Challenger became a metaphor for the individual and the planet. The fatal gap between spirit and matter is too often filled by the annihilation of consciousness. The way to avert tragedy is to recognize that the soul is huddling in the gap.

Without the metaphor, the mind may be fed, but the imagination and heart go hungry. Without the pondering in the soul, the banquet table in dreams may be laden, but the food is not assimilated and so the soul starves. There is nothing sadder in analysis than to see dreams rich with healing images, but the dreamer is unable to eat; that is, consciousness either is unable or refuses to take the time to bite into, chew, swallow, digest, and integrate what is represented by the images.

So long as the meaning of a dream is not brought to consciousness, the metaphors we are dreaming are enacted either in our bodies or in our relationships. If, on the other hand, we work hard on associations to the dream images and allow the feelings, imagination and mind to move in and through and around the symbol, inevitably we are silenced by the rightness of the metaphor. There is a moment of YES! or OH NO! when the truth resonates through body, soul and mind, sometimes a painful truth, but nevertheless a truth that leads toward freedom.

The raw honesty of an image from the unconscious can strike us dumb with tears or laughter, often with both, because the image moves on that fine edge of the absurd between tragedy and comedy. If the ego can assimilate the point of view presented by the unconscious and see itself *objectively*, then it can find a new standpoint. It can observe itself suffering, but at the same time experience the suffering as pangs of birth. The ego that is relating to the soul (right-brain thinking, if you like) is motivated to reflect the dream images in painting, dancing, singing, sculpting, writing, thus allowing the healing process to transform what would otherwise be dead images into life energy.

Transformation takes place through metaphor. Without metaphor, energy is locked in repetitive patterns; Medusa traps energy in stone. In the creative matrix, the symbol flows between spirit and matter, healing the split.

In children, the split has not yet taken place; thus for them the world is still magical. Their imaginations light up their bodies. They play. With total concentration, they play. Uncanny wisdom slips out of their mouths, but it is not conscious. In the growing-up process in our culture, rational thinking supersedes imaginative perception to such a degree that imagination is stifled. Without it, spontaneity and creativity petrify. When eternal essence is no longer perceived in daily living, life becomes a repetitive treadmill. The feminine container, the receiver, is so shut down that nothing new registers. The contraries (spirit/matter, masculine/feminine) cease to be perceived as living paradox; without their tension, humor, wit, playfulness, the salt that gives life its savor is not there. Laughter explodes when two different realities collide, and if we are to live the divine comedy, we have to be holding the tension of the paradox between those two worlds.

Samuel Beckett, one of the greatest playwrights of our century, is a master of that tension. His plays are stark. With basic stage sets, colloquial dialogue and simple characters, his unforgettable images cut through to the naked truth. In *Endgame,* for example, blind Hamm reigns over his one-room kingdom from his wheelchair, sardonically ridiculing his no-legged parents whom he imprisons in garbage cans beside him. At the same time he tyrannizes his servant, Clov, who no longer savors Hamm.

From the beginning of the play to the end, Clov stands with his suitcase packed, paralyzed, forever on the brink of leaving but unable to go. From his opening line—"Finished, it's finished, nearly finished, it must be nearly finished"[15]—to Hamm's closing words—

> Since that's the way we're playing it . . .
> . . . let's play it that way . . .
> . . . and speak no more about it . . .
> . . . speak no more.[16]

—the four characters do their best to "play" with all the innuendoes on that word.

To love Beckett is to find yourself looking for your false teeth without your glasses and suddenly hearing Nell's elegiac, "Ah, yesterday!" swirl up from your gut until you collapse in a chair laughing until you cry. That's paradox, resonance, life and death and new energy—all in a flash. If, however, your feminine receptor, your soul in matter, is shut down, you will receive nothing, no flash of insight, no fun. You'll just go on cursing your blindness and chew-

---

[15] *Endgame, a Play,* p. 1.
[16] Ibid., p. 84.

ing your wrinkled lips. Without a strong conscious container in which to receive, the moment that contains finite and infinite does not happen. Without light in matter, the corresponding light of spirit cannot penetrate. Without attunement to baseball, the game looks crazy. Without attunement to Mozart, the music is noise. Without attunement to dreams, they are meaningless.

Manic activity, the predominant rhythm in our society, denies soul. Driven by ambition, competition, perfectionist ideals or the sheer necessity of keeping a job that demands a frenetic pace, people hurtle into space. In their dreams, they leave their soul impounded with Nazi torturers and their body filled with vacant rooms. Because they are separated from their source, they want a "high." They want it fast, and they want it concrete—drugs, gambling, shopping, drinking, eating, sex. In other words, they want to transcend their ego, get out of a boring, humdrum existence.

But we are human beings and transcending our humanness cannot come through a fast escape into an altered state of consciousness that cannot be integrated into daily living. Escape compounds the split between spirit and matter. We may fall into a bliss state, a timeless, spaceless world—the womb of the Great Mother—or we may become possessed. Possession by stupor, ecstasy, frenetic energy, is unconsciousness. The ego is not functioning and therefore the treasure cannot be brought back. In other words, our standpoint and attitude toward life remain unchanged; we are impaled on our own fascist sword, still locked in the old dragon-slaying myth. Genuine transcendence involves a container strong enough and flexible enough to surrender to another reality and to bring back into consciousness the treasures it has experienced; then daily living takes on rich and textured meaning.

The treasures of the sacraments which once incorporated daily life into a divine plan brought grace to millions of believers. Many can no longer experience those treasures, let alone bring them back. The projection which once went onto a great and loving father-God with a flowing white beard has been withdrawn. God is dead. Many find god talk not only meaningless but offensive. What is dead is the projection. Goddess talk can become equally meaningless and stupidly sentimental if there is no inner experience to validate the theorizing.

God and Goddess can no longer be projected. They are inner experiences through which we discover ourselves, nature, relationships and the imperial moments that are gifts we cannot understand. Soul making goes on in the body.

Since, to quote William Blake, the body is "a portion of Soul discern'd by the five Senses, the chief inlets of Soul in this age,"[17] we children of the patriarchy have to learn to love the body—the goddess in her mother aspect. We do not naturally surrender to the comfort of her womb. We do not hear her slow heartbeat. We take only a fleeting glance at the dying fingers of winter clutching at the triumphant buds. We don't pause for a lung full of spring, for skin saying thank you for sun or the taste of rain. So warped are our sensitivities that we have to learn to honor nature, to honor our own bodies. We have to reconnect with the primal wisdom that assures us that we are loved, that life is our birthright, that we need not prove ourselves nor justify our existence. Knowing in our bones that life is the supreme gift, we can accept paradox. Life is no longer broken into right and wrong, light and dark, birth or death. Everything is part of the awesome mystery.

Consciously relating to the Great Mother is coming back to the garden and recognizing the place for the first time, recognizing that it is a garden and that we have dishonored it. Consciousness takes an ego stand and refuses to identify with devouring appetites for food, drink, sexuality. It refuses to fall into compulsive behavior. By disciplining the power drives of instincts that are damaged because they have been abused, consciousness opens the way for love, rather than the compulsion of the dragon-slaying vow to kill the mother in order to be free of her dark womb.

As opposed to the shadow of the unconscious feminine identified with the forces of darkness, what begins to emerge when the femi-

---

[17] "The Marriage of Heaven and Hell," *The Selected Poetry and Prose of William Blake*, p. 123.

nine finds its own voice and is released from its identification with
the dragon can be seen in Leonardo da Vinci's cartoon of the Virgin
and her mother Anne. In this drawing, protected against dragon
slayers under bullet-proof glass in a darkened room in London's
National Gallery, the Virgin Mary is shown sitting on the lap of
Anne, who had immaculately conceived her. Matter in this powerful
image is conceived in the redeemed form not only of the virgin,
Mary, but of her mother as well. Matter, that is, has been raised to
the consciousness of Saint Anne and her daughter, which in the
Christian understanding of the myth is the redemption of their Greek
counterparts, Demeter and Kore.

This image is even more strongly present in da Vinci's *Madonna
of the Rocks,* one version of which is in the National Gallery. Here
Anne is absent, replaced by a grotto that powerfully suggests the
dark womb from which the virgin emerged and which still acts as the
container of herself and her divine child. Apparent in these powerful
images of the Christian redemption of matter by the introduction of
an enlightened feminine consciousness into it, a consciousness ultimately identified with the spirit of the divine child, is the introduction
of a feminine consciousness at work in God's redemption of creation.

The introduction of this enlightened feminine consciousness,
identified in the Old Testament with the figure of Sophia, or feminine
wisdom, presents us with a powerful alternative to the patriarchal
dragon-slaying myth. In the Catholic church these two mythologies
existed side by side and at one period, in the eleventh and twelfth
centuries, the matriarchal myth (as opposed to the patriarchal)
achieved a position in which it appeared to encompass and contain,
even to subdue, patriarchy itself.

The loss of the cult of the Virgin in the Reformation served to reinforce patriarchy, liberating it from the containing restraints of a
mother church. What we see in the cult of Mary is the attempt to refine the masculine by the infusion of a feminine consciousness. This
infusion of a feminine consciousness as the container of a transcendent spirit—understood as the masculine light, conquering in its

heavenward ascent the forces of darkness—transforms those forces into soul. The result is a realignment of masculine energy into a creative partnership with the conscious feminine. In that way, the work of soul making not only comes into focus, but its dynamics are triumphantly affirmed as the very ground of creative activity. Thus Milton's epic *Paradise Lost*, traditionally read as perhaps the most severely patriarchal poem in English, is now undergoing a radical reinterpretation as the role of Urania, the female muse who dictated to Milton while he slept, is taken far more seriously.

Indeed, there is in Milton's epic a creative partnership between masculine and feminine of which the patriarchal Milton was still the unconscious agent. Romanticism, focused on the figure of Urania, turned the serpent into an instrument of feminine consciousness and rejected the dragon-slaying action of the patriarchal Milton in the name of a feminine consciousness that served as the announcement of a new creation. This reading of *Paradise Lost* is in fact prefigured in the two works of da Vinci mentioned above. Shelley went so far as to describe Romanticism as a new religion, a rebirth of Christianity itself.[18] It is in this sense that I have, in this book, aligned myself with the Romantic poets—to draw out from them the implications of the role of the conscious feminine in a newly established partnership with conscious masculinity.

To reemphasize, this new partnership is itself a transformer of both the masculine and the feminine that exists only within the creative dynamics of a partnership where neither is controlling or dominating the other. The transformation of relationship can come about through a genuine understanding of the difference between murder and sacrifice. Both kill or suppress energy, but the motives behind them are quite different. Murder is rooted in ego needs for power and domination. Sacrifice is rooted in the ego's surrender to the guidance of the Self in order to transform destructive, although perhaps comfortable, energy patterns into the creative flow of life. Often only in retrospect can we tell one from the other.

---

18 Percy Bysshe Shelley, "A Defence of Poetry."

The virgin soul, if she is embraced, brings light (consciousness) into matter. She is matter in the continual process of becoming more light through the wisdom that is forever being revealed to her through her own matter. She is the personification of the redemption of matter. She becomes the ravished bride of the true bridegroom. Essential, therefore, to this understanding of the conscious feminine is a respect for the sacredness of its own creative unfolding. This is what the dragon-slaying myth rejects as an enveloping darkness, even as the shadow of the unconscious feminine demonically parodies it as mystification and satanic allure.

Light in matter is the light that comes to the soul through the medium of the senses. That light is different from the spiritual light that suddenly announces itself and changes the vibration of every cell in the environment. A concert pianist, for example, may have perfected his technique so that his feminine container is exquisitely sensitive. Only if he is receptive to spirit as well can something transcendent happen. When soul opens to spirit, feminine and masculine are creating in the moment. Then musician and audience become music together—the music of the spheres.

The conscious virgin sitting on the lap of the conscious mother is an image of the soul alive to its own values, needs, possibilities, grounded in a body whose cells are attuned to every variation in the harmonics of the soul capable of opening to more subtle variations.

Throughout this chapter I have repeatedly referred to Keats' expression, "Soul-making." I would like to conclude with a portion of the letter in which he first used it, endowing it with the excitement of what he considered a genuine discovery. "Seriously," he wrote, "I think it probable that this System of Soul-making may have been the Parent of all the more palpable and personal Schemes of Redemption among the Zoroastrians, the Christians and the Hindus."[19]

On the basis of his own experience, Keats was convinced that the creative process itself was the parent of those schemes of redemption which characterize the world's religions, thus serving as the unifier

---

[19] See above, note 4.

of them all. Humanity was bound together in a religion of the soul, a global religion to which the word psychology would become attached, designating, as Keats himself insisted, that a knowledge of the soul is better than worship, for in worship lay the danger of deifying human powers in a manner that arrested them in some dogmatic form. Keats' concern is less with the product than with the process, with a partnership rather than a binding.

Here is Keats, one hundred and seventy years ago, tentatively exploring a new consciousness to which I am profoundly indebted. In the following passage the "horn book" he refers to is a child's primer, made of paper attached to wood and covered by transparent horn. Through the transparency of the horn, the child learned to know words by heart, even as the adult learns to know life by heart.

> I will call the *world* a School instituted for the purpose of teaching little children to read—I will call the *human heart* the *horn book* used in that school and I will call the *Child able to read,* the *Soul* made from that *school* and its *hornbook.* Do you not see how necessary a World of Pains and troubles is to school an Intelligence and make it a Soul? A Place where the heart must feel and suffer in a thousand diverse ways! Not merely is the Heart a Hornbook, It is the Mind's Bible, it is the Mind's experience, it is the test from which the Mind or intelligence sucks its identity. . . . And what are proovings of [man's] heart but fortifiers or alterers of his nature? And what is his altered nature but his Soul?—and what was his Soul before it came into the world and had these proovings and alterations and perfectionings? An intelligence—without Identity—and how is this Identity to be made? Through the medium of the Heart? And how is the heart to become this Medium but in a world of Circumstances?[20]

---

[20] Ibid.

But is heaviness truly deplorable and lightness splendid?

The heaviest of burdens crushes us, we sink beneath it, it pins us to the ground. But in the love poetry of every age, the woman longs to be weighed down by the man's body. The heaviest of burdens is therefore simultaneously an image of life's most intense fulfillment. The heavier the burden, the closer our lives come to the earth, the more real and truthful they become.

Conversely, the absolute absence of a burden causes man to be lighter than air, to soar into the heights, take leave of the earth and his earthly being, and become only half real, his movements as free as they are insignificant.

—Milan Kundera, *The Incredible Lightness of Being.*

When fishes flew and forests walk'd
And figs grew upon thorn,
Some moment when the moon was blood
Then surely I was born;

With monstrous head and sickening cry
And ears like errant wings,
The devil's walking parody
On all four-footed things.

The tatter'd outlaw of the earth,
Of ancient crooked will;
Starve, scourge, deride me: I am dumb,
I keep my secret still.

Fools! For I also had my hour;
One far fierce hour and sweet:
There was a shout about my ears,
And palms before my feet.

—G.K. Chesterton, "The Donkey."

Fear *is* matter and matter is ultimately free as light. All human fears and animal fear mechanisms—indeed all living fear in all plant and animal life—are similarly traced to electronic self-annihilations. The only escape is in remembrance of our true source. We are all beings of light from the lowliest to the highest among us, from the slugs to the astronauts.—Fred Alan Wolf, *Star Wave.*

2
Magicians, Tricksters and Clowns:
Masculinity in Addictions

Possession is one with loss.
—Dante, *The Divine Comedy.*

One reason for rationalizing our behavior is to disguise the action itself. Far from explaining the action, we explain it away, even to the point of attributing it to someone else. "The devil," we say, "got into me." The action of an addict is performed by someone the addict does not know but who must be appeased. If the unknown someone is not appeased, the result can be catastrophic. The unknown someone in an addict is almost always a killer.

To stand and face the killer usually results in unconsciousness. The killing takes place while the victim is under the anaesthetic of the addiction. Upon returning to consciousness the addict finds the weapon plunged deeply into the killing place. The used needle is there; the empty bottle is there; tomorrow's cake is eaten. The evidence of the kill is there. Is the addict alive? Has the addict been magically brought back to life? The most difficult problem in treating an addiction is the conviction of addicts that they live a magical life. They are alive, not dead. Being alive, they can try it again. Test the magic. See if it still works. Their confidence increases. The luck of the dice! Each time they are murdered, they magically revive. Addicts live not by nature, but by magic. The magician presides.

In the *Ion,* Plato ironically describes the Bacchantes (the god-intoxicated followers of Bacchus). In the possession induced by the sacred dance, which is the weaving of a magic circle three times around themselves, they draw honey and milk from the rivers only to discover when they return to their senses that it is nothing but simple water.[1] If we are to help addicts return to their senses, we must try to understand the magic which appears to turn water into the milk of Paradise, even though our understanding robs them of their gods, their false sense of the numinous. They are deluded, and so long as we collude with the magic, we encourage the delusion that is driving them to self-destruction.

The question is: "Who is the magician transubstantiating the natural elements into a demonic parody of a sacramental act?" Transubstantiation is a ritual legitimately performed by the Catholic priest standing at the altar: the body of Christ is received by the kneeling believers in the form of a wafer. Although transubstantiation does not occur in an addictive ritual, addicts are drawn to the object of their desire as if it were as sacred as the transubstantiated wafer. Taboo is a better word in this context than sacred, because taboo means both sacred and forbidden, magnetic and repellent at the same time.

The magician who can create such powerful magic has to be uncovered if the addict is ever to be free.

Parents and parental figures—priests and ministers, for example— are naturally deified by children; these adults, therefore, carry magical projections. If the trust that goes with the projections is betrayed, addictions can be the result. Where the relationship between parent and child is one of abuse, physical or psychic, love becomes perversely identified with a taboo object associated with the abusive act. At the center of an addiction is, in one form or another, a radical betrayal of trust.

An addiction reenacts a traumatized relationship to the body. The acts performed by the parental figures can make the body itself the taboo object. The child is then unconsciously possessed by its own body, both imprisoned in it and forbidden to enter it.

In Claude Tardat's *Sweet Death,* a book that can destroy even an addict's faith in "two breasts of vanilla ice cream with candied cherry

---

[1] See Roger Ingpen and Walter E. Peck, eds., *The Complete Works of Percy Bysshe Shelley,* vol. 7, pp. 238-239.

nipples,"[2] a young woman makes a death pact with sugar, and consciously watches her body turn into a monster. This is an act of revenge against her socialite mother, who wants her daughter to be thin and beautiful. What she finally realizes is that "the fundamental insipidity"[3] of her existence was rooted in her conception. She was not the child of the blond man she thought was her father. Her real father was a dark-haired Spaniard.

In the last scene, the woman ceremoniously eats the wedding cake she has ordered for her death marriage. Having described the masterpiece of confection—"spangled with silvery sugar pearls, lacquered with caramel"—she continues:

> Right at the top are the traditional tiny bride and groom, he all in black, she all in white, holding hands and smiling the same frozen plastic smile, rosy-red and inane. Naive image of the greatest human illusion. Because what can they do now, those two, after having climbed up so high, but go back down the sticky mountain side, fall victims to the flypaper of life? . . . I speak the painful truth, the mother's milk of despair: impermanence and falsehood. . . . me, that brown-haired dwarf with the dull and already oily complexion, me, the ignorant little monster . . . with eyes the color of snuff, like a dark, indelible stain.
>
> My inky eyes. And the little packages of pink candies furtively placed by the bedside lamp. And the black venom of scorpions.
>
> And now, twenty years later, the truth finally hits me. Stupid little monster, I was the unwitting incarnation of betrayal. Suddenly I no longer have a name. Anonymous among the nameless, I don't even know the Spaniard's name.[4]

The betrayal of the child's reality turned her body into a controlling tyrant; all her faculties surrendered to its dictates.

The dark mother—opaque matter—has an impressive resistance to the light that would expose the lie. Unawakened to the light of spirit, nature is either out of touch with soul or blindly protecting it from

---

[2] *Sweet Death*, p. 100.

[3] Ibid., p. 95.

[4] Ibid., pp. 114-115

impossible pain. The task is to uncover the betrayal of trust that cut the body off from ego consciousness.

In dreams opaque matter can appear as a crocodile not quite asleep in mud, a huge energy mired in inertia, self-absorbed, rigid, aspiring to nothing. It produces adamantine fatigue in the dreamer. It may appear in dreams anytime, but in the later stages of analysis the dreamer is told in no uncertain terms that the depths must be dealt with before the spiritual eye can open.

In other words, the grounding of the life force in the lowest chakra has to be secure, open to the energies of the earth, before the radiance of the spirit can take up residence.

Here is where an addiction can be the royal road to the unconscious, and while the road is sometimes lost in a barnyard, it may find itself in a stable with a divine child lying in a manger, the cattle hardly distinguishable from the wise men. The danger of falling back into the addiction keeps addicts walking with eyes wide open, knowing now that the addiction has brought the suffering that is forcing them to connect with their body at the deepest level, with the awareness of light in the body, and with the love of Sophia that radiates in all life. At this level of consciousness, they are able to draw on the strength of the Self to face moment by moment the darkest corner of their addiction.

The ability to draw on divine strength is powerfully described in an Islamic tradition concerning the day of judgment. According to that tradition, Fatimah, the daughter of Muhammad, will on that day appear unveiled as she crosses the Bridge Sirat. This bridge is as sharp as the edge of a sword and as thin as a single hair. It joins Earth to Heaven; below it breathes the heaving abyss of Hell. Fatimah *unveiled* symbolizes in Islam the emergence of the conscious feminine which unites the believer to Allah through his prophet Muhammad. That apocalyptic union, like the union described in the Book of Revelation, is the union of bride and bridegroom.

Fatimah, as the unveiled bride united in marriage with the divine, finds its analogue in the image of Christ who, in the parable of his return, is described as the bridegroom who comes at midnight to the

The union of bride and bridegroom (body and spirit).
(Antonio Canova, 1757-1822; Louvre, Paris)

wise virgins, their lamps filled with oil, to take them into his bridal chamber or kingdom. The foolish virgins

> took their lamps and took no oil with them. . . . And while they went to buy, the bridegroom came; and they that were ready went in with him to the marriage: and the door was shut.[5]

In these powerful images of the bride and the bridegroom, the condition of the addict guided step by step by the Self is evocatively suggested. Wisdom or Sophia unveiled is seen as crossing the dangerous Bridge Sirat that will unite her with the true object of her desire, while the abyss below, filled with its false hunger, waits upon a single false step.

Essential to the healing of an addiction is the surrender to a power greater than the ego which the ego, overcoming the childhood betrayal, has learned to trust. As trust builds, consciousness between body and ego increases; sensitivity to poison, psychic or physical, becomes acute, and the body is determined to cleanse itself. As one woman put it, "The Self keeps putting the ante up." Another says, "I used to be able to eat a dozen doughnuts. Now my stomach bloats if I eat one." Another bounces into my office and laughingly announces that she must be becoming quite conscious because whereas she used to be able to drink quantities of alcohol, her body now reacts to one sip. The concentration required to hold the tension is expressed by another woman when she says, "It's not a matter of a mouthful of chocolate. It's my soul that's at stake. I thought I was fighting my lack of will power. Now I realize I am fighting powers and principalities that are out to murder my soul. I can't afford to be smug for one hour."

These women have been doing body/soul work and analysis for over five years and they now perceive their addiction as the Self's way of guiding them to an understanding, an experience of incarnation. In the initial stages, the most painful fact they have to face is that the deeper they go into the body work, the more alienating their

---

5   Matt. 25:3,10.

sense of abandonment becomes and the more compulsively they are driven toward their addiction. If they can hold firm against its magnetic pull, they will experience the full-blown tyrant their body has become. Anyone who stands between it and the milk of Paradise is going to be figuratively killed. If they can endure the tension, they will find the core of the trauma: the body is a tyrant because it is under the spell of a magician, outside the jurisdiction of the conscious ego. Whether the parental figures dominated abusively or graciously, the child's body was treated as an object to be filled or emptied, punished or played with.

Parents may triumph over a child, but ultimately there is no such thing as triumph by force, even if that force is elegantly disguised. Domination is domination and the body that has been tyrannized has learned its lessons well. It becomes a potentate, abandoned, outside the civilizing influence of love. In its desolation, it compensates by becoming possessive, clinging to objects or people, investing them with magical powers. Dependent on these talismans for any sense of vitality, the body becomes ferocious in its demands to possess and control them, trying to perpetuate a phantasm in which it no longer believes.

I do not mean to make parents feel guilty. We are all products of our cultural situation, which encourages competition and dominance. We scarcely understand what love in the body is. We confuse it with sexuality and need. Genuine love, however, permeates every cell of the body. It is immediately recognized by animals, children and even some adults who were either born with it or have found it through suffering and surrender. Gilt-edged guilt merely compounds the abandonment. Our task is to work to change the dynamics.

The overwhelming sense of abandonment which terrorizes so many people is rooted not in the parents' abandonment of the child, but in the abandonment of the child's soul. By projecting their own image of their child, they obliterate the actual child who then goes underground, abandoned not only by the parents, but by the child itself. Out of this habitual abuse arises the sense of shame connected with some unknown crime for which the child feels guilty. Dreams of a murder being committed, or a corpse lying hidden, reveal the betrayal that is perpetuated into adulthood. When a relationship is endangered, for example, the adult again abandons the underground child, who is impossibly honest; then the persona takes over, trying to please, hoping to save the relationship at whatever cost. The guilt is two-fold: "I am guilty for being who I am," and, at a deeper level, "I have abandoned myself."

The abandoned one becomes the victim of the magician who exploits the loneliness, connects with the rejected essence, produces magic in a realm where soul seems to be lived, then shatters the illusion. The dark side of the magician takes the addict deeper and deeper into his or her secret death-dealing world; the light side, as wise old man, can take the released soul into its own creativity. The razor's edge between those two worlds is genuine feeling. "I am wrong, I am guilty, I am a victim, I deserve to be punished," leads to magic and addiction. "I will not abandon myself, I am not guilty, I will be who I am," leads to mystery and creativity.

Julia is an addict whose childhood faith in her father was repeatedly betrayed by, of all things, his laughter. He was the magician who every night at storytime wove spells that made her forget her sadness, but at the same time led her deeper into it.

Lest it be assumed that every father who reads to his young daughter at bedtime is unconsciously drawing her into his own unacknowledged erotic fantasy, something needs to be said about this particular relationship as it gradually came into focus in the analytic process.

The father was a charming puer whose imagination created palaces where others saw poverty. Alienated from his wife, who found his idealism a threat to the material welfare of herself and her family, he turned to his daughter as his chief psychic support. In her infancy he had sought to protect her from the sudden, irrational outbursts of her mother's physical violence. As a result, Julia accompanied him wherever he went and spent the happiest days of her childhood working beside him at her small desk in his study or rocking on his lap to the rhythms of poetry or song. The two of them seemed bonded against a world largely indifferent, if not hostile, to the spiritual splendor which they together brought to it, her imagination fed by his aspirations.

The world the father and daughter shared, while reading together, was a secret, treasured world, associated with a forbidden "high." The father magician was psychically seducing his daughter. The child felt shame, but the shame was compelling because to be in that intimacy with her father was numinous. Together they were caught up in a strange, mysterious rite. Repeatedly, the child tested the magic to see if she could restrain her tears until she was alone. Controlling her body in this way gradually cut her off from body awareness. While Julia has no memory of physical abuse, the psychic betrayal split body from soul as surely as actual incest.

Perhaps alarmed by the intensity of their relationship, the father continually punctured it in a manner that radically betrayed his daughter's boundless trust. Her favorite story reveals, as all favorite stories tend to do, her psychic situation. She loved to hear "The Little Match Girl," which tells the tale of an abandoned child who on New Year's Eve uses her last match to keep warm and to light her fantasies. When it goes out, she freezes to death. This story, which summed up the daughter's relationship to her mother, against whom her father was her sole protection, served a healing function. She believed that in reading this story to her, her father was not only acknowledging her plight but assuring her of his understanding and support. When, therefore, he responded to her tears with explosive laughter, her trust was brutally betrayed. She was the little match girl whose last match went out with her father's laughter. The terror was compounded by the intervention of her mother who slapped her, declaring "I'm not raising a crybaby."

These episodes constituted a childhood trauma that repeated itself in her intimate relationships. As she surrendered to the magical world of unboundaried intimacy, at the same time she anticipated the killing blow that would sever her from the magician and from her own body, frozen in unexpressed emotions. Already fading into unconsciousness, she disappeared when her mother struck. This trauma later manifested itself in her unconscious setting up situations in which she manipulated men into what she experienced as acts of betrayal. Food and sex became for her a box of matches which, if emptied, would lead to starvation. She ate and made love in an attempt to fill a hole—her traumatized body—that, because of its alienation, was always empty.

After Julia had stabilized at a healthy weight, she attended body/ soul sessions in which she encountered overwhelming vulnerability without her fat body and a resultant terror of being abandoned by the man she loved. Repeatedly she had been dreaming of a handsome man dressed in a broad-brimmed black hat and flowing black cape, a magician who had the power to give life and to take it away. In the following dream, it is the father whom she adored and strove to please who finds her guilty for being who she is. The childhood relationship that kept her alive now shows its other face. The projection she had put on men comes home to roost.

> I am on trial. The courtroom is my church. My father is the judge in the pulpit. I am resigned. The verdict is inevitable. I know I will be found guilty for being who I am. I stand dignified before my father-judge, but I am terrified because I can hear the barking of starving dogs in the graveyard and I know the punishment for my crime is to be thrown to the dogs.

We can see in the dream how the father, albeit quite unconsciously, betrayed his child's essence. Trusting him to understand her empathy with the abandoned child in the story, she was totally cut off when he laughed at her tears. Her feelings were repressed in her body, which became the tyrant dogs that threatened to eat her as ravenously as she ate food to try to avoid their rage.

Significantly, the father appears in the dream as a patriarchal principle—judge, bishop, father-god—without personal love for Julia. The outer man has become the inner magician. In reality, the power she once projected onto her father she now projects onto her lover; the lack of grounding in life (abandonment by the mother) now makes her cling to her lover as mother; her terror of loss activates her eating compulsion (sweetness, nourishment from mother). The dogs in the graveyard were hungry for all she had denied herself—feel-ings, tears, sexuality. But were they to come out, what then? To have angered her father would have dismembered her world. Therefore, she took the blame for the bewildering outcome of their magical times together and split off her feeling heart. To anger her lover was once again to watch the dying of the light in what she ex-perienced as her last match. Thus she suppressed her real feelings but anticipated the death sentence.

The punishment the father complex metes out in the dream comes from the place of his, now her, own rejected feelings rampant in the ravenous instincts locked in the church graveyard. At this point, Julia had neither the masculine strength to control the dogs nor the femi-nine ego in a grounded body to contain them. Having dealt with her perfectionist ideals on one rung of the spiral with food, she was once again flying with perfectionist fantasies in her relationship. She was resisting matter, resisting life. Thus her body, instead of being a loving container, counteracted her rejection of herself as an imper-fect, passionate woman by becoming rigid, impervious to light.

In her desire to be "beautiful enough" for her lover, Julia was moving into anorexia. NO to food became an eroticized NO, charged with the euphoric high of starvation. NO to her feelings, NO to her instincts, all produced dreams of passionate love making with the magician or her lover. As long as she was starving, she experienced herself as lovely, healthy, pure, worthy of her beloved. At the height of her fasting, she once heard the demonic laughter of her magician father who was claiming her for his own, taking her into the perfec-tion of death. Just as she once looked to her father to bring the light, she now looked to her lover. In projecting the action of a god onto a human being, she was creating a magician who flung her from infla-tion into despair. Again she was catapulted into binging, uncon-sciously communing with the mother she yearned for, and raping her instead. The rape was the compulsion to possess the loving mother even through death, her own death. Thus the demonic is appeased while the soul, under the anaesthetic of carbohydrate, passes out into the very darkness that through some magic may yet become light.

Any addict knows these extremes. The body-in-control is an unloved tyrant, resistant to light because it exists without love. The starving dogs in the graveyard of her body are rejected instincts trying hard to make themselves heard. Julia needs to connect to them with consistent, loving discipline. Being victimized by rampant instincts can result in promiscuity, which, like insane eating, is a manifestation of instinct cut off from feeling.

The early splitting off of the body in order to survive is revealed in midlife in body/soul work and dreams. Kate, after several years of both, realized that her problems with sexuality were her own responsibility. To take them into her relationship would destroy what she and her partner were so carefully creating. Fortunately, he was a very sensitive man, also working on his own difficulties. He recognized the subtle changes taking place in her and was quick to respond to the shifting changes in himself, as he allowed their new relationship to unfold. Each of them worked alone, integrating their own material, then related to each other from a new place of consolidation. Thus, instead of ranting at each other, they brought consciousness into their partnership. Of course, there were confrontations, but not mindless attacks. The rage in both sexes comes out of centuries of abuse. If it is taken into relationships, it destroys. Attacking each other in a state of possession has nothing to do with liberation.

In body work, while delving into the core of her fear, Kate found her anger. She then realized she was afraid to express it because of the danger of releasing her rage. Therefore, she suppressed her anger, but in exerting that control she was always on her own periphery, a repetitive circle with fear turning back on itself. Until she could experience the fragmenting—the cutting off of her own feelings when her boundaries were invaded by her alcoholic father—there would always be a part of herself she could not know.

"I always avoided whatever would trigger the pain of fragmenting," said Kate. "I have to be able to tolerate that pain. If the ego is to live in a dignified relationship to the Self, it has to be strong enough to heal the fragmenting. The point at the center has to be free for me to inhabit."

Here is how she experienced her fragmenting in a session (with my observations in brackets):

I get a feeling of sickness, a real fear of going crazy. I twist my being, I get tricky and angry. As a child I split in order to survive. *(Breathes, exhales, pushes into the mattress—raises pelvis, lets go)* If I go into this, I will go crazy. Will you be able to put me together again? *(Moonface, no emotion, stillness)* I'll crush you into nothing. *(Hands, feet, torso, face curled; snarling, teeth bared. Spits, jaw shaking)* I'm just as good as you. You won't get me. You won't trick me again, I'm just as good as you are. I'll split into a thousand pieces and you'll never get me. You can't stamp me out. You make me sick into the bottom of myself. You give me a bad taste in myself. *(Springs)* I'm in a million pieces. Find me there?

No. There? No. Who am I? Here? No. Who am I? Here?

No. Let's play pretend. I'm this. This is who I am. You don't know who I am. YOU DON'T WANT TO KNOW WHO I AM. If I could tell you, I would. This is who I am. You think you have me in your pocket. You don't have me. You thought I was a fool—A FOOL. I'm getting out. No one will destroy me. *(Whispering)* I'm first. I won't let you twist me. *(Hands searching, quiet)*

When she returned to herself Kate said, "It appalls me that I could go to that extreme. My back is pulsing."

Centuries of bone-deep rage are in that outcry. If the trauma held in the body can be released in a therapeutic situation, as Kate was able to do, deep cleansing results. Body and psyche are liberated. Once the repressed energies become conscious, they cannot be ignored without endangering physical health. Because they are so primitive, few people allow themselves to touch into that chthonic depth. In dreams, however, a psychotic character, crazed with rage, often bursts from the attic or basement, runs through the house, sometimes attacking and shrieking. When the fear of being possessed by rage is dealt with, a person is more able to express anger. Anger comes from a personal level, rage from an archetypal core.

If a person has never confronted the childhood betrayal that led to trauma, the process of fragmentation can gain such ascendancy that it becomes autonomous. The individual is unable to understand his or her own behavior, particularly when that behavior repeatedly results in actions that are the opposite of the conscious intent. The ego is so undermined that it cannot confront either the incongruous behavior or the original trauma. The childhood betrayal remains unconscious as betrayal.

Keith was a young man whose mother died when he was in puberty. Consciously he did not experience her death as an abandonment of him, nor was he aware of his resultant abandonment of himself. Unconsciously he assumed responsibility for her death, leaving him with feelings of guilt that were as inexplicable as they were unrecognized. His adoration of his mother and his inability to accept her death led to fantasies of being perfect for her sake. The result was a series of failures of his best-laid plans. Without realizing it, he was locked in a twelve-year-old's traumatic experience.

Confronted by that trauma as a possible explanation for his repeated failures, he was able at a fantasy level to describe what was, in fact, his actual behavior. Gradually, he saw the fantasy he was describing as the reality he was living. In that recognition, the two worlds met for the first time. In that meeting of fantasy and fact, he recognized the possibility of healing the fragmentation—fantasy going one way, fact going the other, each cancelling the other out. For the first time, it struck him that the two could work together because they belonged together. The possibility that he could get on with his life became a reality that now had the support of his fantasy. He began to lay practical plans for the future that he now accepted as realizable.

Slowly, Keith felt himself being freed of an unconscious omnipresence that had been robbing him of his life. He sensed that he might be making some contact with the person who, on some level, he knew he was. Here is how he described his situation:

> I set out for my classes in the morning. I have no texts in my bag because I have no texts. There is a loose-leaf notebook but there are no notes in it because I have no notes. What is in it are my running shoes and my Walkman. I leave thinking I am equipped for the day. My equipment is the absence of equipment.

Riding to university I'm not sure I'm going to get there. Getting there is knowing I am not going to get there. I arrive, I do not arrive. I remove the front wheel of my bike, chain and lock it. I am now going to my class which is to say I am not going to my class. The knowing what I am going to do is the not doing it. I arrive at the door of the classroom. I am approximately five minutes late. I am about to push the door and enter which means I know I am not going to enter. The two—the doing and the not doing, which are one—come together. To do and not to do are the same thing. In order to go into the class it is necessary not to go into the class. In order not to go into the class, it is necessary to go into the class. My decision when I set out was to go into the class. The only way I can do this is not to go in. I turn away from the door and walk out of the building. In doing this, I walk into the class.

In fantasy Keith was doing what in reality he didn't do. This behavior is eventually answerable to reality, which threatens or smashes the fantasy. The reality is a class test, the due date of an essay, the term mark for the weekly labs he never attended. On all three accounts he fails and fails completely because he does not write the test, he does not turn in the essay, he receives zero for the lab work. Reality declares he has failed. His fantasy, on the other hand, tells him that he attended the classes by not attending. He wrote the essays by not writing them. And he got a perfect mark in his labs by not doing any of the experiments. He isn't afraid of failure as other people know it; his failure is the failure to achieve the perfection of the fantasy. So long as he doesn't start, he hasn't failed. He is convinced he knows it all, in his mind he has done it all. But is his mind answerable to the reality of the situation? Having failed twice, he says, "No, my mind is not answerable. I do know it all."

He then meets a young woman, and for the first time since the death of his mother he makes genuine human contact. He confronts his own absence not as the fantasized presence of his mother, but in the actual presence of a young woman his own age, intelligent, extraverted, very much in her own body. She embraces everything which is absent in his life. She, therefore, actually fulfills his fantasy through her own immediate person. Sexuality, the linking of his body to hers, the discovery of a genuine other, a body different from his own to which he can positively relate, removes the burden of a hugely overcharged fantasy released by the sickness and death of his mother. The life that stopped at the age of twelve, continuing only in the realm of fantasy, is now returned to reality.

What Keith was reliving in going into the classroom by not going into it was the trauma of his mother's death, which he had never directly confronted. He never said a final farewell to her, so he did not know whether she was alive or dead. He never dealt with his sense of betrayal at being abandoned. The result was that the arrested action repeated itself over and over again—the not saying good-by to his mother. He did not know if he walked through a door whether she would be there or not and he was not prepared to find out. His mother was dead. Unconsciously, he did not know she was dead. He was unable to put it to the test. Loving his young woman, however, his body taught him two things: his mother was dead, his beloved was alive. That is, people die and life goes on. He is now struggling to learn how to walk through a door by walking through a door.

This young man is very like the young masculine of many addicted women who dream that some catastrophe has occurred and carry irrational guilt for something they have unconsciously done. Their repressed aggressiveness makes them docile. Thus, in acting out their addiction, they absent themselves. What has to be done is inhuman, impossible; therefore, although their body is present, they are absent. If they do contact the original trauma, and if the positive masculine energy that can reconnect them to reality does appear, it comes forward at precisely the age at which it was struck down. If it manifests as a pubescent boy, the woman may find herself shaken by her erotic response to adolescents. Few rites of passage are more explosive and demanding than that of puberty. The burgeoning sexuality releases ripple effects that not only spread throughout the body but activate dormant areas of the psyche as well. The bonding the woman yearns for and imagines as an expansion is really a fusion, a coming together as one person, her wholeness depending upon the presence of the other. It is the adolescent longing that characterizes romantic love in which years of unconscious yearning for the lost mother enter a period of apparently insatiable gratification that reinforces rather than overcomes an absence from the world.

Mythically this stage is enacted by Perceval in a romance written by Chrétien de Troyes (circa 1185), one of the first of many versions of the quest for the Holy Grail. The Grail is the chalice of the Last Supper which, according to the legend, was brought to England by Joseph of Arimathea. In Chrétien de Troyes' romance, however, no Christian explanation of the Grail is offered. Perceval stumbles upon the castle of the Fisher King where he witnesses a solemn procession that includes a bleeding lance and the Grail shimmering with golden light. Perceval, whose father and two brothers were slain in knightly combat when he was still a baby, had promised his mother, who feared for the fate of her only surviving son, that he would become a knight on the condition that he would respect all damsels, go daily to church and ask no questions. Thus Perceval's initiation into knighthood is under the aegis of his fearful mother, so his first intimations of the Grail have more to do with the dark womb of the old mother than with the sacredness of the vessel. It then becomes the container for the wounded phallus of her son, the bleeding lance that Perceval sees in his vision. Mindful of his mother's instructions, he fails to ask any questions concerning what he has seen. The next morning, the Fisher King's castle has disappeared.

Jung believed that Perceval embodied an archetypal image of masculinity important for the twentieth century. Perceval enacts a situation similar to that of Keith, who entered classrooms by not entering. What passes before them is both there and not there, existing, if at all, in a "Once upon a time" world. What neither Keith nor Perceval realized, so long as they were lost in adolescent unconsciousness, was that the search for the idealized mother of their childhood, a search secretly governing their behavior, is the wounding of the phallus in the pursuit of a luminous feminine vessel. So long as masculinity is trapped in the fantasy of the mother, puberty rites (at whatever age) are in danger of becoming castration rites.

The failure to ask the question—Whom does the Grail serve?—
leaves Perceval in the unconscious grip of the outworn mother
whose sole desire is to protect him against life, to keep him psychically bonded to her withering womb. The failure also leaves the old
Fisher King impotent. In Chrétien de Troyes' account, Perceval, in
the beginning, is not consciously present in his knightly deeds.
Failing to identify himself with them, he is denied the psychic
growth they potentially contain. Having, for example, pledged himself to the Lady Blanchflor, triumphantly defending her besieged
lands, he is free to claim her hand. The actual claiming of her hand is
the conscious meaning of his exploits. Instead, he goes again in
search of his mother.

The Perceval of Chrétien de Troyes personifies the animus of
many contemporary women whose naive masculinity cannot say NO
to the addiction that is bewitching them into the realm of the unconscious mother. (Circe, the sorceress, bewitched Ulysses' men and
turned them into pigs, the animal of the Earth Mother.) Too often
women confuse their own wounded, therefore sensitive, masculinity
with their longing to be reconciled with the mother who rejected
them. They are then fatally attracted to a man whose unconscious
quest is for the lost mother. They see in him the embodiment of their
own need for reconciliation. The result is that the Perceval lover
inevitably takes them down into the realm of the mothers, the very
mise-en-abyme (the scene of the hidden act) of their addiction.

The adolescent Perceval animus is a mother's son who lacks the
capacity for discrimination in dealing with reality. He is the son
alienated from the father. He probably carries his mother's spirit
projection and is therefore disconnected from his body and grounded
feeling. His shadow side may be the courageous daredevil who repeatedly lures the addict to the verge of the abyss. On one level, life
is so absent that only flirtation with death brings a consciousness of
the gift of life. On another level, the supreme effort to escape the
dark cave of inertia evokes total awareness of life in the moment.

Women with this kind of animus dream of bullfighters, trapeze
artists, race car drivers, jet pilots, astronauts and deep-sea divers.

Their own gypsy shadow is a natural partner for these perfectionist males who care little for their own lives. Together they are in a love/death relationship; their passion is the anesthetic that makes them dare the magic that may destroy them. Their real investment is in the perfection of death together. They are the perpetual cliff-hangers reaching for the peak.

An anorexic often dreams of this kind of demon lover. He personifies tyrannical, disembodied spirit. He may be a homosexual artist who adores her exquisite bone structure and dedicates himself to sculpting her beauty in marble. When the silent perfection is complete, he moves on to find another perfect face. He has no more feeling for her as a woman than she has for the shadow woman in herself. Both are murdering their genuine masculinity and femininity.

In real life, when gypsy shadow meets flying puer, life is recklessly exciting. If they marry and have children, gypsy can flip into a responsible but somewhat resentful mother who requires a dutiful mate. If she clips her flier's wings, she grounds him. If she clips too close, she kills his dream and his spirit. Then she will be bored with him; she may seek refuge in an addiction, or find another playmate. So the wheel goes round and round unless consciousness intercedes.

I do not mean to mock playmates. Many men and women have wept copious tears in my office for the one who has brought new light into their dark cave. "I am alive again," they say. "I cannot go back." Playing as children play, with the concentration that sets the imagination alight, can awaken or reawaken sleeping energy. If the young Perceval can ask the question that brings consciousness, even the clipped flier may sprout new wings.

Consider Anya, attempting to make a new life for herself and her children after a divorce.

Anya fell in love with a man, projected her soul values onto him and put all her trust into what she believed was an ongoing relationship. Suddenly he found another woman. In her despair, Anya concentrated on playing with images. She drew a picture of the cruel face of the magician (see overleaf) who had made her the victim of his whims.

When she brought the picture to my office, she put it on the couch beside us as she poured out her grief and anger. Later, after discussing what it could mean, we chanced to see the painting upside down. Now we saw not the magician but the round face of a clown laughing up at us. We could scarcely believe what we were seeing. Without any conscious awareness of what she was doing while drawing the malicious magician, Anya had at the same time created a merry clown. She was so astounded at the paradoxical viewpoints that she had to laugh.

The potential for this kind of paradox always exists in the unconscious. It only remains for consciousness to see the situation from a different perspective—to move from the personal ego standpoint, in thrall to the magician, to a transpersonal perspective symbolized by the clown, who can feel tragedy and look at it at the same time. The clown knows the pain involved in sacrificing the possessive, ego-centered clutching that makes us vulnerable to loss, but honors the detachment that leads to freedom. Clown energy lives on the fine line between tears and laughter, personal tragedy and divine comedy. Playful concentration that includes and transcends the opposites is the energy that can transform the magician.

Merlin is the archetypal magician who also contains elements of the clown. He was the devil's child born of a virgin. His heritage makes him very important as a transformative figure in addictions because he carries both the Luciferian light and the groundedness characteristic of the mature virgin.

At first glance, his dual or multiple aspect and his knavish and clownish characteristics lend him a Mephistophelian quality, but his knowledge of the past and future betoken a greater degree of consciousness than is possessed by Arthur and his knights who are, indeed, remarkably unconscious and unthinking. It is due to this greater consciousness that Merlin, like the Grail, functions as a form of projected conscience, in that he exposes the mistakes and crimes of the people. As the prophet of hell put into the world by the Devil he is, moreover, clearly distinguishable as the Antichrist. . . . Thanks to his mother's virtue, Merlin's devilish inheritance cannot work itself out. This devilish trait appears most clearly in his magic power and in his enjoyment of playing tricks on others and fooling them. But for the most part neither of these traits has a destructive character.[6]

Merlin is significant, especially in people whose opposites are extreme, because he is close to nature, embodies divine energies and has the consciousness to hold the tension of the opposites. As clown, he compensates the rigidity of the outworn collective consciousness and opens the way to the irrational depths with their wealth of instinctual and archetypal energies. "Merlin thus becomes . . . the whole man . . . in which the ordinary man has become one with the wholeness that transcends him."[7] His clown aspects make him a healing figure breaking open the too one-sided, egotistical, tragic perspective. It is Merlin who shows Perceval the way that leads to the castle of the Fisher King.

Finding a loving relationship between her opposites—disembodied spirit and unconscious body—has been Brigette's most difficult task in her analysis. Tyrannical energy has kept her psychic pendulum swinging from one extreme to the other: light and achievement plummet into darkness and despair.

Brigette is a woman who through a hospital error missed the primary bonding with her mother. When she was born, her mother was given the wrong baby. By the time the error was discovered, the mother had already bonded with the original baby. Brigette thus became for her mother not her real child but the haunting presence of her absent child. As a result, Brigette grew up with a ghostly sense of herself, as if behind or within herself was another person who was her mother's real daughter. That ghostly self dominated with perfectionist standards, dictated by an undifferentiated animus.

Very early in life, her body (which unconsciously she could not embrace as her own because it was not bonded to her mother) forgot how to relax and move with its own energy. She moved from false control to rigid control to loss of control. The pattern manifested in

---

[6] Emma Jung and Marie-Louise von Franz, *The Grail Legend*, p. 355.

[7] Ibid., p. 365.

her eating addiction, her shopping addiction, her ways of spending time and money. In almost every area, her life fluctuated between feast and famine. What distressed her most was alternately gaining and losing thirty-five pounds each year.

Then one weekend she found herself in the hospital. Recalling the shock and the consequent changes in her life, she wrote:

> I had thought my weariness was the accumulated stress I was under. It had numbed my ability to assess my strange symptoms. God knows I had stress! Now in addition I had diabetes! It shattered my belief that my body could take the abuse and neglect I dished out. I realized how I'd treated my body like a donkey, carrying all my stresses. I shoved food in to shut up its efforts to tell me about its pain. I couldn't hear and still it feels like too much to deal with. I was not invincible as I had thought. It was very sobering to realize that I could still manage my life if I chose, but had this happened before the discovery of insulin I would soon be dead.
>
> I was terrified. I looked around the ward full of older people with diabetes. Blindness, amputated feet, heart and kidney problems. I was more terrified of life with these various complications than of death.
>
> I didn't understand how this came about. I certainly had not intended to bring diabetes onto myself. I certainly did not understand that my compulsive eating from childhood could have this devastating effect. After all I had tried to be a good person. I had never intended to be self-destructive.
>
> At that time, my terror was my main motivation for taking responsibility for my body. I realized consciously how much I wanted to live. I wanted to contribute what I had to give. I never understood before how my food addiction dulled my capacity to give. I had to learn to love my body, how to use food to nourish it.
>
> I was forced to confront my addiction. I knew all that stuff about feeding my soul. Intellectually it all made sense. It was a different task to *use* the information. I had to learn about my soul and what my soul needed just as I was learning about my body and what my body needed.

Still in her thirties, Brigette is under the threat of severe illness, coma or death. In the absence of that primal bonding, she is trying to open to the receptive feminine. When she first realized her situation, her animus tyrannized her body more than ever. She was obsessive about exact weights of food, exact measures of exercise. Her body reacted with fluctuating symptoms: back tension, left hip in spasm, left side of her neck and shoulder wrenched. (Symptoms were all on the left side, symbolically associated with the feminine.) By trying to analyze everything, she was still victimizing her body. Her fear of uncertainty escalated as she watched her blood sugar once again in flux. Again she found herself in hospital.

I realized that no matter how hard I tried to control my body, my pancreas was decompensating.

I was a worse diabetic than I had realized because I could not control my illness through medication, diet and exercise. The more anxious I became, the more difficult the blood sugar became to control. I was doing everything. I was frantic. I had to deal with levels of terror in my body that I was afraid to go near. I had to accept that I had to take insulin every day.

I began to see how hard I had been on myself. A big step to admit that! I began to understand my basic insecurity. I had so little protection from my internalized mother, I felt I was being eaten up in the world. My parents were true orphans, dispossessed Germans, imprisoned as children in prison camps during the war. They married in Canada. My Germanic background made me feel guilty as a child. I had to be better than the terrible Nazis. I had to be the very best daughter, sister, wife, friend, patient. I always avoided situations where I knew I wasn't the best, or situations of unknowing where I didn't know how much I was liked. I performed. I tried to put my life together my way. That fed my obsession and the belief that I had to be the best. That produced paranoia. Now I have to put myself in a position of no control. I've finally realized I can't carry my parents' pain anymore.

My whole struggle with food is trying to connect with God, opening to that energy source within me. That can only come from the love of the receptive mother. That connects one to one's own soul. Then I can say, "Yes, it is thrilling to live." Where I functioned before I felt my soul needed pizza and coke. I was still connected to the adolescent thrill of seeing TV advertisements that I had lived outside of.

My back felt like broken concrete, or bits and pieces of a dried-out clay vessel. Then as I concentrated doing yoga, I could feel water in my body. I was a riverbed. I was flowing with all my little life forms. That made me feel that I had a place in this world, that maybe my life had meaning after all. Images previously had been like intuitive flashes, insights in my mind. They weren't able to filter down because there was nothing to go into, like a womb with no blood lining on the walls that the embryo could plant into. Nothing could take form.

Now I do yoga regularly, taking images into my body. I concentrate on a willow tree taking root. They say it takes three generations for transplanted people to feel rooted. I am trying. As I breathe into my spine I use the willow to breathe life in and I'm surprised and thrilled to feel my body take it in and melt. Then I feel connected to the earth and thankful to be alive. I don't know if I would have understood all this had I not crashed into the wall.

Brigette has had to face the question, "Do I want to live?" She has responded with a resounding, "Yes!" She who could never imagine herself free of her prison house of fat is now standing to her full beautiful stature. Increasingly, she is recognizing how she had avoided her real trauma—her separation from her own body. By treating it "like a donkey," she forced her body to carry her burden of guilt, alienation, and unacknowledged feeling.

She is still dealing with the problem of power. Tyrannical matter once rendered her powerless over food; tyrannical spirit now threatens to render her powerless over diabetes. Phrases in her description reveal the unconscious power drive that wipes out her personal soul-feeling.

As she was trying to hold herself together in the hospital ward, she saw the older people as a heap of broken images. She related to her soul as a stranger whom she "had to learn about," and her body as something she had to try hard "to control" with an undertone of punishment. Later she realized, "I performed. I tried to put my life together my way." Still the marching orders ironically creep in when she says, "I have to put myself in a position of no control." The shoulds and oughts still undermine her freedom and keep her distanced from herself. Nevertheless, the work she is doing with imagery is teaching her a new way of letting go. Her body relaxes, opens to light, and she feels God within. She loves and knows she is loved. "There's no way to understand that," she said. "You have to experience it."

Brigette's inner man was a real dragon slayer whose analytic attitude alienated her from her instincts. Now she is giving herself time to relate to him and he in turn is relating to her. Together they are learning to differentiate, and thus honor, the instinctual realm.

> My diabetic program is exact. Every morning I stick a lancet in my finger and take my blood sugar. If it is over six I can have two starch exchanges for breakfast; if under six, I can have three. If I am to have a physically active morning, I can have an extra fruit. Every morsel I eat and every walk I take I must be aware of. I am learning that by allowing my body to soften and take in, my body is fed. There are energies within that do feed me. Learning that takes all my strength because for me to soften feels like death itself. I keep working with the energy of the willow. Bringing that life-giving energy into my body, I am nourished. The receptivity melts the compulsion.

Her illness is evoking affirmation of self in Brigette. As she leaves behind the tyranny of the old father complex and the inertia of the old mother complex, she is finding the virgin within who decides what is sterling in her silver chalice and she also finds the masculinity strong enough to defend it.

Trust leads to surrender. If the surrender has been betrayed, then trust becomes almost impossible. The opposite to surrender is possession, being taken over by a driving energy that blindly clutches onto everything or throws it away. To melt into surrender requires a feminine container, a matrix strong enough to *choose* to give oneself over to the unknown. The world of metaphor is a world of surrender, of play, a willing suspension of disbelief. Those trapped in an addiction cannot play, cannot willingly suspend their disbelief because they cannot surrender. They cannot trust a world that allows for choice. For them, there can be no varying levels of participation. Life for them is either clutch or let go. Surrendering to metaphor—dance, music, art, imagery—is playing. It is a leap of faith. It is connecting to the creative matrix where all genuine transformation takes place.

Had she been able to stay with the magical world of illusion, Brigette would have made her life into a work of art. The violent upheavals in her body, however, reveal the ceaseless fight her unconscious is waging to shatter that illusion and prevent her from turning her life into a cold performance. The physical ravagement of matter works underground to release her from the psychic ravagement of spirit. The body that she has treated "like a donkey" holds the very energy that is struggling to release her from the compulsive drive for the perfection of spirit. Nature is trying to bring her into life.

The compensating dynamics between the conscious and unconscious are in this struggle: nature that seems to be waging a brutal struggle against the ego is, in fact, struggling to release her from the false magic of spirit. At the same time, disembodied spirit is increasingly recognized as the tyrant who, far from enhancing life, is destroying it. The energies of nature that Brigette so long despised are the very energies that contain her creative fire. Recognizing that, she can work consciously to redeem matter. What she thought was going on outwardly, abandonment by her mother, reverses itself in the unconscious to become the very ground of her creative strength. Relating to the images in her body, she pulls the energy out of the complex into her conscious ego. The dragon mother is sacrificed. No longer the enemy of the ego, it becomes Sophia, the wisdom and love that are the life force of Brigette's being. Sophia's loving, consistent discipline dispels magic and opens her to reality, physically and psychically. Abandonment by the physical mother left psychic space for the entry of the archetypal mother. Trusting her, the addict experiences Grace that heals the betrayal of trust.

In the slow process of surrender, Sophia's clown energy is important. As the ego goes through what feels like the tragedy of giving up its control, Sophia often comes in dreams with a practical, loving nudge that sets the dreamer's values straight. She sees the divine mess that human beings unconsciously live. But at the core, however rejected the dreamer feels, she focuses on the soul, the one thing needful. In juxtaposing the humdrum and the eternal, she laughs because she sees from a different perspective. Sometimes in dreams she turns somersaults or takes the dreamer on a midway ride that turns everything upside down. Her clown energy takes the dreamer outside collective attitudes because she speaks the forbidden truth that collides with the illusions we live. She IS in the immediate moment.

As Brigette is struggling to listen to her inner feminine and playing with the images that arise in her body, she is contacting her own inner healer. She is discovering in the consciousness of her own body what she had formerly conceptualized as her desire to connect with God. She is discovering that the service she always struggled to perform for others has been a displaced love of her own body which she had, in fact, rejected. She is now at last bonding with her body, thereby cleansing her own temple. As Brigette describes it, this bonding with her rejected body has been a very humbling and, at the same time, empowering experience. Sometimes her body seems to mock her; sometimes it is the very ground of her authenticity.

The relationship between rejected matter and spirit is nowhere more poignantly imaged than in the story of Christ's so-called triumphal entry into the holy city, Jerusalem. With full knowledge of the prophecies he would fulfill in the following week, he had instructed two of his disciples to go into the village and loose an ass and her colt and bring them to him. And all this was done, that it might be fulfilled which was spoken by the prophet, saying, "Tell ye the daughter of Sion [Jerusalem], Behold, thy King cometh unto thee, meek, and sitting upon an ass, and a colt the foal of an ass."[8]

The disciples, having carried out their instructions, put their clothes on the ass and set Christ thereon. With the colt, they proceeded into Jerusalem. The multitude, who would spit on him within five days, spread their garments in the way, cut down branches from the trees to wave, and shouted, "Hosanna to the son of David: Blessed *is* he that cometh in the name of the Lord."[9]

---

[8] Matt. 21:4-5.

[9] Matt. 21:9.

Had the mob seen what was in front of their eyes, would they have been so quick to wave their palms? This ridiculous clown seated on motley, riding an ass to what they hoped would be his coronation? Here was Christ scuttling the collective image of kingship. Here was consciousness borne by outcast nature, mother with child trudging beside him. Here was made visible the leap in consciousness which the world is still trying to make. Here is the bridegroom coming to the holy city with a released body now elevated to a blessed state—the light of consciousness harmonious with nature.

This concept of the way to the holy city cannot be "moulded into an intellectual ideal."[10] Kingship in this image "proceeds not from the traditional moral code but from the unconscious foundation of the personality."[11] This inner authority Jung calls conscience. "If one is sufficiently conscientious," he writes,

> the conflict is endured to the end, and a creative solution emerges which is produced by the constellated archetype and possesses that compelling authority not unjustly characterized as the voice of God. The nature of the solution is in accord with the deepest foundation of the personality as well as with its wholeness; it embraces conscious and unconscious and therefore transcends the ego.[12]

That "solution" is what Jung calls "the third," arrived at through the passion of crucifixion and resurrection.

Julia and Kate and Brigette are three among many who are learning by experience what Franny and Zooey Glass knew by intuition. Christ is the fat lady in the front seat.

*

Having put the final period on this chapter, I was thinking of the delightful animal trickster dreams I had not been able to include.

---

[10] Jung, "A Psychological View of Conscience," *Civilization in Transition,* CW 10, par. 831.

[11] Ibid., par. 856.

[12] Ibid.

Reluctantly, I was preparing to put my black marker through "tricksters" in the chapter title. Suddenly, out of the place of those dreams, a clear, light-hearted voice piped up from beneath my left arm.

"Here I am," she laughed, bouncing into my lap, like a little fox.

While I couldn't see her, I felt her sparkling presence filling the space between me and my black pen.

"I've been here all along," she almost sang. "I've been playing under, over and through the text of the whole chapter."

To my astonishment, I realized she had been this capricious voice of nature that speaks her truth, however top-heavy the head becomes.

"Let's dance," I said, laying aside my magic marker.

Kitchen Thoughts

Sometimes I feel frail. My psyche needs padding. Although I eat the same number of calories, I put on padding.

The virgin in me says, "Slow down. Listen. Decide what you're here for." The masculine voice says, "Discriminate. What is garbage? What has to be thrown out? You cannot go on accumulating. Think of new ways of relating to food." I wonder about some of my relationships too.

It's not a food issue now. My whole body is less willing to tolerate concretization. It's an issue of allowing light into my matter—breathing, meditation, journaling—healing the scar tissue of my soul.

There is an energy in me pulling me toward death. It is in my fat shadow. Right there is where the Self strikes.

Whenever I binge, my ex-husband goes off with a mistress in my dreams. Is it possible that food is so seductive an object of desire?

I don't want to fight with a fucking bowl of spaghetti for the rest of my life. I can eat half a cup instead of the whole pot.

When I dance, I am heavy in body, but light in soul.

When others are munching doughnuts and drinking coffee, it's hard for me to keep involved, if I'm not munching too. That situation forces consciousness. My financial nitty-gritties also force consciousness. In those situations, I now realize I often fall into my shadow. I don't want to suffer. I retreat and fall back into binging.

Is it not likely that men with eating and other obsessive-compulsive disorders like myself are revealing a more general problem facing *men* trying to "make it" within a patriarchal culture, men who feel they must suppress their positive "feminine," intuitive, receptive side? And is it not likely that, as more and more men gradually—consciously and unconsciously—rebel against the constraints of patriarchal culture, they will be beset with the kind of identity and spiritual crises that seem now to be plaguing many more women?

When you're up to your ass in muffins, it's hard to remember your original intention was to clean the fridge.

He sat with me while
I ate.
While I ate the hard
boiled fists of his
shadow
While I ate the marinated
curls of his arrogance
While I ate the
sweet-sour balls of
his anger
While I ate the
toasted crusts of
his innocence
While I ate the
stiff whipped foam
of his fame—
He sat with me while
I ate.
He left the table
when I asked for
something to drink,
and did not return.
      —Jaffa.

. . . for he *is* like a refiner's fire . . . . and he shall
purify . . . and purge them as gold and silver.
      —Malachi 3:2-3.

This condition of the crucifixion, then, is a symbolic expression for the state of extreme conflict, where one simply has to give up, where one no longer knows, where one almost loses one's mind. Out of that condition grows the thing which is really fought for. For Nietzsche, it would be the birth of the Superman. We would say it was the birth of the self.
      —C.G. Jung, *Nietzsche's Zarathustra.*

3
Mother As Patriarch

As an analyst I share the archetypal depths with my analysands. I feel their aloneness. I honor the courage with which they dare to face the unknown images that confound understanding. I talk to men and women who, for whatever reasons, are not in analysis but are nevertheless faithfully recording their dreams, trying to understand the internal process that is evolving according to what appears to be an organic unity. They too are being propelled beyond the consciousness they have known, beyond the rigid world that is stifling creativity. Similar patterns occur in different images in different dreamers.

Consciousness is slow to grasp the new images born of the unconscious. Sometimes the symbols are so bizarre we catch only fragments or nothing at all. Sometimes parts of ourselves that are too far from consciousness to manifest in our dreams as people come through as a voice on a telephone. Often the message is quite startling because it is foreign to our conscious adaptation. If we can dialogue with that voice, something very new may be integrated into our daily life. Eventually the voice may appear as an image.

In the chaos of the breakdown of patriarchy, these startling images can guide us in dealing with the outworn mother and father complexes that must be left behind if we are to find our own lives. This requires making a distinction between the actual parents and the complexes they become in our fantasy absorption of them.

Each of us has our own individual imagery, as we have our own individual appearance. Yet just as we share the physical characteristics of humankind, so we share archetypal motifs in the collective unconscious. As we begin to realize that others are dreaming similar dreams, we know we are not alone. Indeed, it seems that some pattern far beyond our comprehension is being woven in the profoundest depths of the collective unconscious.

With this in mind, I asked Jaffa, one of my analysands, if she would share the part of her journey having to do specifically with her parental complexes. Her friends do not call her Jaffa, but Jaffa was the name given to her in a dream. She accepted the name as a gift from the unconscious, and chose to acquaint herself with it while working on the part of her process that appears in this chapter. (Personal details and family names have been changed, as with others in this book, to protect her anonymity.)

Jaffa, like myself and others who have contributed dreams to this book, has done so in the hope that the dream motifs we are exploring will shed some light on the unconscious processes that are so bewildering and dangerous when they are acted out instead of integrated into the psyche. The danger in acting out a fantasy structure is that it is by its very nature a distortion of the real world. To perceive the personal mother, for example, through the eyes of the mother complex is to rob her of her own identity by imposing upon her an archetype that belongs to the realm of myth and fairy tale. While children inevitably impose archetypal figures and patterns upon their actual parents—and indeed, all children's literature teaches and encourages them to do this—the failure later in life to differentiate between the personal and the archetypal can have very serious consequences.

When Jaffa entered analysis, like most people she could not maintain a distinction between the actual and the archetypal. She was in the grip of her complex. To act upon it could lead to acts of violence or withdrawal so complete as virtually to extinguish her own identity. Psychosis resides in the identification with an archetype. So long as there is resistance, which is to say pain or illness, the individual is able to maintain a precarious differentiation. Pain protects us from psychosis.

For several months Jaffa and I have discussed new depths of understanding in the dreams, because images take on varied shades of meaning as the full tapestry of the unconscious is revealed, and as the analysand through differentiation is better able to perceive what at an earlier stage she was immersed in. Together we are committed to the dream process as it is guided by the Self quite independent of our personal hopes. Together we have been committed to the writing process: we dialogued, I wrote, Jaffa corrected what was not exact, I rewrote, she brought further insights. Her current process, which is not unveiled in this chapter, has leapt ahead. We have been careful not to attempt to verbalize her mystery. The holy of holies in any temple is not to be violated.

Jaffa was a triangulated child, the battlefield on which her parents fought their unconscious battles. Moving in like a pincer movement from two sides, their opposing attitudes met, collided, and fought to an impasse in the ravaged psyche of their daughter. They fought, not knowing what their battle was about, leaving it to Jaffa to bring to consciousness what they, for good reason, preferred to leave alone. When Jaffa first began to see who she was, who she was becoming, she did not like what she saw.

When we see ourselves becoming someone we do not want to be, we seldom ask who is seeing us in this way. To say it is the ego learning to resist the id, or the superego imposing its collective values, misses the point. The person being shaped by the pincer movement of her parents was not an authentic person. She was a radical distortion of her true self, a battle-weary, battle-scarred child, crippled before she had taken her first steps toward her own authentic life. But Jaffa was determined to live. To live meant two things: 1) to cast off the false self system unconsciously imposed upon her by the unnamed struggle of her parents, and 2) to identify with the true self that was prepared to embark on an almost impossible task, a task that was in essence a long, painful and at the same time exhilarating process.

While a false self system makes itself known through the pain and suffering it causes, the true self remains, at least in the beginning, almost completely unavailable, enmeshed as it is in the wiles of the false self. What Jaffa could not initially know was that the true self was her experience of her false self as pain. Her true self was struggling to break free of the false self. That struggle was causing the pain. In some women this is experienced as numb acceptance with the aid of compensating fantasies that can never be anything more than fantasies, like Laura's glass menagerie, for example, in Tennessee Williams' play.

Crucial to the success of analysis is the affirmation of pain as the voice of the authentic self. Suffering in analysis has nothing to do with masochism. The pleasure derived from pain is the recognition that within it is an authentic voice, like the cry of a child who has accidentally fallen into a well. All the villagers set to work around the clock to rescue her, encouraged and energized by the sound of her cry which can still be heard. If they can reach her before the cry stops, they know she can be saved. Her cry is their guide and their hope. In the early stages of analysis there is not much more than that cry to work with. We must follow the path of the pain. Knowing that rescue is at hand makes the cry all the more intense. It is less a cry of fear than a cry of hope. It declares, "I am here, I am alive."

Jaffa need not have cried. She need not have been in pain. There was an adjustment that could have been made, an adjustment not unlike that of her parents which, had she accepted it, would have postponed to another generation the suffering she chose to endure as the voice of her authentic self. How easily, given the parental dynamics working upon her, Jaffa could have settled for a false self system. That system had constructed a perfect trap, and that perfect trap, given sufficient numbness, sufficient unconsciousness, could have become a comfortable, complacent, certainly refined, bourgeois home. "The child is the secret of its sire," declares a Muslim proverb. Her authentic self rejected that offered home by making it a place of pain so relentless that it was not endurable. Jaffa had to get out because she knew that to stay there was death. In the unconscious battle between her parents, she had been taken captive and, as far as they were concerned, she would remain captive, a trophy of their divorce.

The providence present in calamity is a mystery not accessible to everyone. When calamity calls us—and eventually it does—few are able to answer creatively, to choose the calamity in order to mine its providence.

The story that follows, Jaffa's story, is about mining calamity for its providence. The presiding deity in this process Jung called the Self, which he defined as essentially similar to the traditional God-image—a divine providence at work within the soul. While God is in essence unknowable, what we can know are the creative workings in us and upon us, workings that are at the same time operative, in their own way, throughout creation. That is, there is a synchronistic relationship between the inner and the outer. Because it is acausal, it is unknowable, though quantum physics and the principle of indeterminacy may be bringing us closer to an understanding of how it works.

Jaffa, however, is not waiting for explanations, scientific or otherwise. She has proceeded all along on faith, which, I believe, is a gift not granted to everyone. Those who do not have it cannot attempt what Jaffa set out to do. In my experience, there are some people who cannot accept life as a gift. Jaffa has treasured her life and gone with her own impressive energies, and although they have, particularly in dreams, placed her repeatedly in positions of incredible terror, she has found these places exhilarating because she recognized in them her own authentic voice and spirit. She knew she was being rescued into her authentic self.

*

"Daddy's little princess" is the chosen child of her father. Blessed by his love, she may also be cursed by his love. Her special place in his dynasty sets her on a throne too remote for most princes to reach. Her throne is carved in ice, far from the nourishing warmth of Mother Earth.

A father's daughter whose lifeline is to her dad may try to dismiss what is not there for her in her mother. Dad has always been her cherishing mother and father. Why bother with what never was? If she decides to go into analysis, she will almost surely seek a male analyst because she respects men more than women and her energy is more vibrant with men. She may occasionally dream of her mother hidden in a mysterious room, but her own earth energy is so far from consciousness that it rarely manifests even in dreams.

Moreover, her attempts to free herself from her father's castle are so demanding and so intriguing that all her energy is focused on the prince who will release her. Too often the analyst becomes the prince whose castle is no less foreboding than the king's—and sometimes, if great care is not taken, the analyst may exploit his foreboding precincts for reasons he does not claim as his own. Sporadic dreams may tell her there is real trouble in her basement, that she must go down there and clean out the swamp.

If she follows that direction, she may be obliged to go to a female analyst who will constellate the mother. Then she faces the deeper problem: the bedrock of her feminine being is not present, except as an inchoate flow of lava. The loving mother who carries her unborn child in her warm, dark womb for nine months was not there to reassure her, nor was she there to welcome her into life. Instead, her months in utero were charged with Vesuvius-like fear or anger; her birth was a battle, her presence on earth a dubious gift.

A mother who cannot welcome her baby girl into the world leaves her daughter groundless. Similarly, the mother's mother and grandmother were probably without the deep roots that connect a woman's body to earth. Whatever the cause, her own instinctual life is unavailable to her and, disempowered as a woman, she runs her household as she runs herself—with shoulds, oughts and have tos that add up to power. Life is not fed from the waters of love, but from will power that demands perfection, *frozen* perfection. Meanwhile, dad may in fact not be king but prince consort, so that father and daughter are unconsciously bonded against a tyrant queen—the mother as patriarch.

Jaffa was born into such a family. In her mid-twenties she realized she was in deep trouble. Unlike many fathers' daughters who choose to go to a male analyst because, they say, "I know I will fall in love with him," she chose a female analyst because she knew she needed a woman. She has been in analysis and body work for over five years. Together we have chosen a few dreams out of hundreds that pinpoint her path from victimization to approaching freedom, dreams that illustrate transformation that is always in process at the archetypal level. Only at that depth does real healing take place. There the Self in its infinite wisdom protects the ego, tearing away the veils of illusion as gradually as the ego can assimilate the truth. It daily balances and rebalances the maturing masculine and feminine energies so that the inner partnership is constantly in flux. While the images may at first seem extreme, these images are the language of the unconscious, the language of fairy tales and myth.

Jaffa's mother, in the village in which she lived, was respected as a very civilized, cultured woman, a responsible and good mother. To her young daughter she was an evil witch. Jaffa's father was an artist whose "exquisite hands had never held a hammer." His gentleness created a loving, sensitive space to which his daughter attuned herself. She basked in the cultural heritage he brought to her. Jaffa's mother was also an artist, without incorporating into daily living any of the refinement that the love of beauty may bring, if that beauty does not mask a tyrant.

"I see my mother wearing ugly clothes," says Jaffa. "She is leaning over the kitchen table, her huge breasts hanging down. She has brought home excellent food. She is gobbling it down, shoveling it in. Her cheeks are full like a hamster's. She is talking, always talking—or whistling. She eats two-thirds of what she has brought and leaves one-third for my sister and me. She seems to be eating me.

"At sixteen I couldn't stand it anymore. I couldn't eat. There was no space in me for anything. I was closed with no opening. I was ready to explode. For days I ate only dry bread. I began smoking and went out after school for martinis. I just wanted to die. I needed to be as unconscious as possible in order to survive. I collapsed one day. I couldn't understand why the doctor said there was nothing wrong with me. I found out afterward that my mother told him I was only simulating sickness, that I had eaten chalk. That compulsion to chew and drink comes over me even now when I am anxious."

Jaffa's mother lived in Europe during the Second World War. Like many people who have lived through war, she was quite silent about her experience. She wanted to forget. While Jaffa rarely heard a war story, her unconscious picked up the brutality and deprivation that her mother had experienced. Deprivation is brutality in perhaps its subtlest form. Both manifest in her dreams.

Two years before she began analysis, Jaffa had nightmares of wild dogs ripping off her limbs. The following is a major dream in a series of dreams about not having her own body.

> "Arm or leg?" bodiless voices are calling out.
>
> My limbs are being roasted on my live body. Someone wants a piece of thigh and cuts it off with a knife. I myself have to eat a piece. Roasted flesh hangs off my bones but I feel no physical pain.
>
> I am to hook a rug (a wall hanging), but I can't do it since I don't have arms or legs. Someone is starting it for me. Part of the left side is finished in a pattern of daisies in white, silver and pastel blue. I hope to finish it myself one day and be able to use it. Right now I can't because my arms and legs are "out of order."

Jaffa's father left his wife and two daughters when Jaffa was fifteen months old. Because she was her father's favorite, her mother was vicious with Jaffa and fervent in her attention to Lara, Jaffa's sister. Her cannibalistic attitude toward her older daughter is clear in this dream. The arms Jaffa needs to grasp reality, and the legs on which she should take her standpoint, are being roasted, perhaps in the rage that exists between mother and child.

Even in this nightmare, however, the possibility of healing is suggested. She must eat a piece of her own flesh, must incorporate (literally, take into her own body) her own power. She must, that is, give birth to herself, which is what the analytic process is all about. Moreover, she is to hook a rug, which on a symbolic level means her task is to assimilate the pattern of her life. The rug in the dream is a wall hanging—not yet a place on which to stand—but already it incorporates an image of hope, her favorite wildflowers. "I had no standpoint then," says Jaffa, "but lots of float points—like the rug on the wall."

Part of the left side, which is related to the unconscious, is finished, suggesting that while the ego cannot consciously do anything to establish a standpoint, the unconscious is hooking whatever bits of life it finds into a recognizable pattern. All is not chaos.

Seven years later, in a contrasting dream, Jaffa was walking through a meadow and found plenty of long threads in glorious earth colors with gold and silver spun threads that could be woven. Now instead of having her life hooked with little bits of thread, she could take responsibility and weave the long threads herself.

It was extremely important that she found these threads because given her artistic environment, in which dismemberment masqueraded as nourishment, she was tempted to turn her own fragmented existence into a work of art to be hung on a wall. A hooked rug offered itself in her earlier dream as an obvious hook for her projections. What might at first appear as a healing image could easily become, and indeed at the time was in danger of becoming, a reification of her illness. Between the hooking with bits and the weaving with long threads, the journey has been long and fearsome, particularly since at every stage the temptation to reify life into art has had to be dealt with, without at the same time interfering with the process.

One year after she entered analysis, Jaffa dreamed she was delivering her own body to a gas chamber. She was holding it under her left arm and hoping at least to possess the ashes. Her mother's cannibalistic "eating her up" was repeating itself in her husband's behavior in their marriage, and, unable to find enough ego to stand up for herself, she was unconsciously delivering her body for burning.

The positive side of this devastating image lies in the dream ego's recognition that her body has to undergo the fire. Fire is the heat of emotion that will reduce the overburdened shell to ashes. Without that fire, the analysis would be merely an intellectual exercise. While the dreamer will undergo fire hot enough to destroy life as she has known it, she will perhaps retain the ashes. Although there is no mention of a phoenix in the dream, Jaffa knew about the fabulous bird that periodically regenerated itself.

According to legend, the phoenix lived in Arabia. When it reached the end of its life (500 years), it burned itself on a pyre of flames,

and from its ashes a new phoenix arose. . . . According to
Herodotus, the bird was "red and golden and resembled an eagle."[1]

Much later, in drumming sessions, the phoenix became her power
bird, in close relationship with a tiger.

Jaffa began very gentle body work, gradually reconnecting with
the buried emotions in her body. She sensed that what lay buried
was volcanic, too dangerous to uncover quickly. Until recently,
whenever she talked about her early childhood, her energy con-
gealed. She was freezing, shivering with cold. In her youth she was
operated on for intestinal problems. Gradually, with the body work
the pain manifested in heart palpitations, rib, chest and back spasms,
and a constant possibility of tears.

Jaffa and her sister Lara are like two sides of the one coin that is
their mother. Jaffa describes Lara as a woman with two faces: the
one she turns out is hard, judgmental, seductive; the one she turns in
is withdrawn, dark, lifeless, so veiled it is albino in quality. Her
sexuality, says Jaffa, has a nymphomaniac at its core—gulping, devouring, putting claws into a man's shoulder. At the same time it has
no feeling value, and therefore is always on the prowl, never satisfied, always searching for another kinky toy.

Lara too is an artist, living on the edge of society. Conversely,
Jaffa, bound to her father, is aloof in her sexuality, often closed.

"If my body were just going for sex, it would be devouring,"
Jaffa says. "If I attached no feeling value to my body, my sexuality
would be wild like my sister's. But when my love and my body are
connected, my sexuality can become transcendent. Violence for me is
unthinkable. Yet I married a man in whom violence and sexuality are
connected. My mother not only raped us psychically, she repeatedly
beat us even after puberty.

"I began playing truant from school at sixteen, began dating secretly. Hell opened at seventeen when I decided I would betray myself no longer. In the filthiest language my mother had accused me of
perverted sex, using words I had never heard. I looked straight into

---

[1] Columbia Encyclopedia, 3rd edition.

her cold, killing eyes and said, 'This is betrayal. I will not allow it.' She became a dragon and chased me out of the house. For two days I ran and ran. When she caught me she drove me to a nunnery, jabbering all the time that she was taking me to a juvenile jail. She was the Gestapo personified.

"There was nothing I could do to please her. When she went into the hospital to have a hysterectomy I went to her hospital room to give her a big kiss, and when I turned around she said to the woman in the next bed, 'This is all a performance for you. She is pretending to be a good daughter just to show off to you.' A sword through my heart was the outcome of my genuine gesture of love."

Early in life, another sword struck Jaffa's attempts to perfect herself. Her homework was checked every night with such vehemence that the young girl was terrified of tests and examinations. The fears manifested in different styles of handwriting. On one occasion when her mother was checking an essay, she accused Jaffa of not doing all the writing herself. Jaffa insisted the essay was her own. Her mother's eyes became deadly cold, like Medusa eyes that turn their victim to stone. "You're lying," she said and struck Jaffa across the face so hard that her nose flooded with blood.

The mother's projections are clear in her responses to her daughter. Her own frustrated raw lust is projected onto a pubescent schoolgirl who is as yet unawakened. Her repeated dissimulation of acts of love, her pretending to feel kindness in the hollow shell of her being, her dishonest acts in hope of being recognized as outstanding in the community, are all mirrored in what she projects onto her child —deceit, guile, lying, ostentation.

Jaffa's great-grandparents were famous for their perfectionist standards. Their daughter was outwardly submissive but in fact she lived as passionately as she pleased. She raised a daughter, Jaffa's mother, whose basic *raison d'être* was to hate men. Carrying the shadow of those stern grandparents, Jaffa's mother existed in an internal wasteland. She lived the only life a hollow reed can live— counterfeit and cowardly. Her daughters were to fulfill what she could not fulfill; thus "responsibility first" was her motto. No child had any rights until responsibilities were fulfilled. Punishment and avoiding punishment became the dominating motivation for every act. The daughters saw their father emotionally blackmailed even after he left, and also experienced themselves blackmailed because they saw the dishonesty in everything their mother did. Her right hand never knew what her left hand was doing.

A woman who renounces her own truth will renounce the truth of her children, forcing them, if they have any spirit left, to lie. Jaffa held onto her own sense of justice by becoming secretive. Whoever she was, whatever she really felt, she never showed because there was no outer safety. Mechanically she fulfilled her duties. Outwardly she lived her shadow; inwardly she clung to whatever she knew of her own soul values.

Jaffa's inner world was reinforced by contact with her father. He became her savior, and, ironically, her jailer. In her aloneness and longing for companionship, she found in him the man to whom she could entrust her soul. This was gratifying, but his walls were covered with photographs of herself. She was encapsulated in his image of her. Physically ravaged by her mother, she was psychically ravaged by her adoring father. Her mother, of course, hated everything in Jaffa that resembled her father and systematically set out to kill him in her.

Jaffa's mother exemplifies the patriarchal woman who has lost touch with her own soul. While she appears extreme in her cruelty, her very extremities highlight what happens to a woman who loses touch with her femininity. Who she in her beingness is, what her values and feelings are, her emotions and genuine needs, are long since buried. Without contact with either her eternal or instinctual world, she is without love. Bitter, disillusioned, she lives out her emptiness and insecurity, trying to be part of the status quo that has destroyed her. The power drives that have wrung life out of her, she turns on other people, poisoning her innocent children with the hatred, revenge and perverted sexuality that she denies. She is victim and Hitler in one person and that unconscious collusion she attempts to set up in every relationship.

Unless such a person becomes conscious, the abused child within becomes the abuser. Like grandmother, like mother, like daughter. Only years of intense inner work can break that cycle. To walk out of that prison a free soul demands years of fingernail-filing on the prison chain until there comes a moment when the prisoner breaks the chain and leaps toward the light at the end of the tunnel, never turning back. That leap into freedom is the leap out of a power-driven existence into a life lived in love. That is the leap from powerlessness into empowerment.

Jaffa's fingernail-filing on the chain involves meticulous body/soul work and dream work with her mother, her shadow sister and her spirit father. And so she dreams:

> I am sitting on a bench with my sister. In front of us a body is roasting in an outdoor oven. Macabre!
> Then I am with my father on a country estate. I had prepared a fish which we were eating together. My father urges me to take some sauce, I stay with only fish.

As Jaffa's body/soul work intensifies, the alchemical fire is no longer a gas oven but a prepared retort out-of-doors which she watches with her sister. From her somewhat detached position, she is beginning to watch and understand her body symptoms as manifestations of unconscious psychic conflict. Part of that conflict is in eating the fish she has prepared with her father. Jaffa associated her father's "sauce" with sentimentality. In the dream she chooses the naked truth, "only fish."

Eating is very important in dreams. The mouth and teeth are like the kitchen in fairy tales; the kitchen work has to be done before the princess can go to the ball. The raw energy of nature (raw meat, raw vegetables—the dream is exact in which energy is required) is brought into the kitchen. There it is cleaned, gutted and chopped until it is transformed and ready for the fire which must be kept at exactly the right heat to cook the meal without leaving raw or burnt bits. (As one impatient woman was informed in a dream, "There are no microwave ovens in the royal kitchens.") The teeth that bite, tear and chew are the transformers of the energy; thus rotten or missing teeth are very significant in dreams.

After the meal is cooked in the transformative fire, it is taken to the dining-room table (often symbolizing a domestic altar where one form of energy is sacrificed for another) and eaten. If it is not bitten into, chewed, swallowed, digested and assimilated by the body, with the waste evacuated, the process is incomplete.

Jaffa then is eating fish with her father. Jaffa's problem with her father lay in the fact that her love for him was idealized beyond its human bounds, encapsulated, outside of life. She was trapped with a disembodied spirit who lured her away from her own body/soul. Thus any man she believed she truly loved beguiled her away from her own reality.

Disembodied spirit is just as tyrannical toward the soul as is unintegrated instinct. Such a spirit is Lucifer, the Morning Star, so bright, so proud, that it challenges the true God, sets up its parody of harmony and creates Hell. This is precisely what Jaffa's mother had done—set herself up as an all-powerful Lucifer in her own hell. Her father withdrew from that pandemonium and set up his own world of art outside of life. Thus there is a double danger for a woman like Jaffa. Not only is she being driven out of her body by the witch mother who is determined to possess her (as happened with Lara), she is also being lured into disembodiment by her father with whom she dare not express her love sexually.

Eating fish has to do with assimilating the suffering of being an eternal soul in a human body. That is what incarnation is about. Many people, bent on perfection, deny their yearning for death and escape from life through unconsciousness. The spirit that longs for the perfection of art, music, science, truth is trapped in a non-perfect world in a body the ego usually condemns. To eat fish is to recognize the perfection and at the same time to filter the yearning for it through the limitations of the body. Soul living in body yearns for spirit; spirit living in fantasy is nothingness until it unites with soul. Each yearns for the other—soul for the illumination of spirit, spirit for the vitality of substance. Eating fish then brings the treasure of the water of life (the unconscious) into actual living. The wisdom born of the suffering of the body, of being human in an imperfect world, is incorporated. To put it another way, eating fish is turning a page of a book and seeing a Rafael Madonna tenderly touching the face of her baby when you have just had an abortion, or just learned you will never have a child.

Metaphorically, Jaffa was eating fish in actual life. She was accepting the reality that her mother's deadening letters totally denied who Jaffa was, barely acknowledged her daughter's suffering. In fact, Jaffa had separated from her husband, was working on custody arrangements and studying to make herself self-supporting. She was also experiencing the pain of not being able to paint. Hands and voice are for her the essence of life. Having had her mother's index finger driven into her shoulder for years, the pain of actually using her hands and voice to express her own being was excruciating. The loss of her self-expression was the sacrifice.

The following dream illustrates a decided shift in Jaffa's attitude toward authority.

Preparations are being made for a funeral service. People have already gathered; they are in no way sad or mourning.

Meanwhile the dead and still stinking body of a man is being carried to the front. He reminds me of the slimy Daryl, the patriarch in the film *The Witches of Eastwick*. A woman sits with the body. She is apparently used to the stinking smell at such rituals. She seems to be the mistress of ceremonies. Some women have pearls they move like rosaries in their hands. My sister is there. She reminds me of myself in her looks and way of laughing. The dead man was her first husband. She says that his seed is inside her.

"How paradoxical!" I think. "She is already married to a generous, warm-hearted teddy bear."

The dead man had been just newly married and impregnated his eighteen-year-old wife. My sister shows me a photograph of him and his wife. In the picture he is a "superman," over-big, holding himself and his wife—maybe my sister. He used to smoke cigars and stinks still after his death.

Afterward, I am in an apartment opposite the funeral home in a gathering of women (maybe including my sister).

In this dream the patriarchal energies personified in "the slimy Daryl" are dead but still stinking. In the movie, Daryl, played by Jack Nicholson, is the archetypal, arrogant, manipulating patriarch with whom his three women at first collude. In the end they tar and feather him.

In her associations Jaffa said she hated cigars—the demon's weed, phallic image of the stinking patriarch. But as she reflected longer, she remembered her uncle Edward, her father's older brother, whose home had been a refuge throughout her childhood. "He was not a demonstrative man, but he lived what he preached," she said. "He was the personification of love and justice. He was truly the shepherd of his sheep. Each day after dinner, he read his paper and smoked one cigar. It was a ritual never to be interrupted."

The stinking corpse then is not entirely negative. The father image has within it the security, love and justice which were islands of sanity in her childhood. The stink of the dead patriarchy does not bother the "mistress of ceremonies" (perhaps an image of her mother). Because she is so used to it, she does not notice the stench. The juxtaposition of "pearls" and "rosaries" in the hands of the women suggests that while they have lost connection with the traditional Christian beads, they have not lost connection with the essence of their own soul symbolized by the pearls. They are praying their way through the funeral of the stinking patriarch, holding in their own hands the soul substance distilled through suffering.

Facts from Jaffa's actual life are important in order to understand the dream. Both sisters married what was unattainable to them as children. Lara yearned for a father, Jaffa yearned for a mother. Lara, her mother's favorite, married an artist like her father whose shadow side was a patriarchal dictator. Jaffa, her father's princess, married a pacifist who refused to join the army. He himself had been an abused child and in the marriage physically and psychically raped Jaffa repeatedly. Lara married her father. Jaffa married her mother.

In the dream, the shadow sister is attending the funeral of her first husband, the patriarchal dictator, but his seed is within her, although she has married his opposite, a warm-hearted teddy bear. In the transition period, the shadow has within her both the seed of the patriarchy she deplores and the beginnings of union with a masculinity to which she can relate. The shadow sister is in a double-bind because although she has divorced the patriarch and remarried, she carries a photograph of the patriarch and his eighteen-year-old bride who is now pregnant by him. In short, both the shadow and the maturing eighteen-year-old feminine are carrying the seeds that could repeat the cycle.

What that could lead to is clearly defined in the photograph—a superman dictator, protective tyrant over his wife. The photograph epitomizes the world Jaffa has lived in, and the world she will live in, unless she brings to consciousness the seed that is in her developing feminine and in her shadow. The seed itself carries new creative energy and the stench of the cigar is not without positive though seductive associations of a just and loving man. If she can recognize the dangers, recognize how she collaborates with the dead attitudes, and take what was good in the patriarchy, then she can take her own stand with the feminine energies across the street. The final image of a dream points the direction in which the energy wants to go, not where it now is. If it is not attentively followed, it may fall back into unconsciousness.

In life, Jaffa had repeated her marriage to her mother in a second marriage, less violent but no less oppressive. At the time of the following dream she was in deep depression, recognizing the chasm that was developing between her husband and herself. She could no longer endure his sexual demands, nor could she make him understand what relationship in life and sexuality could be. Her body work in coordination with her dreams was bringing her soul into her body and she could not endure what she experienced as the nightly rape of her sacred matter. The repeated betrayal of herself was over.

This dream occurred a few days after the preceding one:

> My sister and I are walking on a muddy path through a forest. Walking is extremely difficult. Suddenly the trees look more luxuriant. We are approaching a very different part of the forest. I am relieved and breathe deeply.

Suddenly the path becomes a wild, dangerous river. We turn around immediately to survive. On the way back, there is a hospital in front of which a man moves. My sister notices that his index finger is missing. Farther down we pass a hospital or apartment building. Behind one of the windows a woman (East Indian?) is pointing a gun. Quickly I run out of sight.

Again the sisters—the two sides of the one mother—are together, walking now in a forest that Jaffa associated with her own life. "Not my mother's or my father's—my own." No sooner are they in the welcoming world of their own instinctual energy than their lives are threatened by a raging torrent. Jaffa was beginning to touch into her repressed instincts, and ego and shadow sister are in danger of being consumed by their ferocity.

As they travel back they see a male patient in front of a hospital. In real life, Jaffa was attempting to stand firm to her own truth and put her own masculinity into action in organizing a study course for herself. While her masculine energy is still in a hospital, at least that index finger that has tyrannized her life is gone. It reappears, however, as a pointing gun held in the hand of a dark woman (an unknown part of herself). The evil energy—that is, energy destructive to life— once personified in her personal mother is now beginning to manifest as impersonal, unknown energy closer to the archetypal level.

As the struggle for soul survival intensifies, the ego becomes stronger, but so do the forces ranged against it. Archetypal energy, whether positive or negative, carries awesome magnetic power. It is possible that the unknown woman in the dream represents a hitherto unacknowledged feminine energy in Jaffa, an energy that will at first manifest with considerable rage (e.g., the gun).

Seven years after the dream of her roasting body without arms or legs, she hears a powerful voice in a dream saying, "Arms for all-embracing, legs for all-moving." It was as if her soul had taken up residence in her body and she was incorporating her standpoint and her hold on reality. Now it was as if the Self were giving her new strength to counteract the negative forces. Her arms are ready for "all-embracing" and her legs are strong enough for "all-moving."

This voice affirmed Jaffa's dedication to her inner work and opened her to a new level of trust in the healing process taking place. Such a strong voice from the Self often opens the way into the deeper secrets of the psyche. Once the ego is strong enough to endure the naked truth, the dreams move into the heart of darkness. Within the darkness lies the light that can set the soul free.

> I "escape" into a bed with a woman whom I am attracted to and want to be loved by. I ask her whether that is okay with her. She says, "Actually I am only comfortable with my friend, Jeffrey." I accept it. Now we are friends with more distance.
>
> I am sitting beside my mother now. She offers me some underpants that I try on, and then take off again. There is a feeling of shame because I am wearing only underpants.
>
> My mother points to a crow which seems to be tame and calls the bird toward her. There is a cat there, and I shudder, thinking it might catch the crow. The crow comes forward and the cat lovingly licks the bird's wing feathers.

This dream further clarifies Jaffa's problem with her mother. In the first section, when she yearns to make love to the woman, the woman replies that she is only comfortable with her friend Jeffrey. Jeffrey was her mother's maiden name. In associating with the dream, Jaffa said that her mother was never really married, never bonded to her father. Her idea of relating was to make Jaffa, Lara and their father responsible for her misery.

As a child, Jaffa's chief goal in life was to be loved and accepted by her mother. The love/hate bond that existed between them was incestuous. Thus both of Jaffa's husbands were very much like her mother's power-driven animus. When Jaffa recognized how narcissistic her mother was, she also recognized that she and her sister were used merely to mirror their mother and fulfill, however inadequately, the mother's needs; hence began their profound lack of self-esteem. Because the child was expected to mirror the parent, instead of the parent mirroring the child, the young potential was stifled.

The "intimacy" with her mother is broken in the second section of the dream. Associating with the underpants, Jaffa remembered the horrid, long woolen underwear her mother bought for her daughters. Jaffa used to stop in a woods on her way to school, step out of the long brown pants, leave the small white ones on, stuff the big ones in her briefcase and proceed to school. As an adult, she could never allow herself the luxury of delicate lingerie until she broke the power of her mother complex. In the dream, the transition begins when the mother offers her white underpants (which she never did in real life) but Jaffa cannot receive them from her. All she can feel is the shame of being partially naked. This echoes her early childhood fears of being naked in front of her mother. Even then she sensed the violence in her mother's sexuality and knew that her nakedness and Lara's excited her mother.

The last section of a dream, the lysis, points the direction in which the energy wants to move. Here, Jaffa's strong Celtic roots are echoed in Odin's bird, the crow. The spiritual energy symbolized in the crow is balanced by the instinctual energy symbolized in the cat. Jaffa expects them to be natural enemies. But the cat lovingly licks the crow. Transformation of the incest bond that links sexuality and violence between mother and daughter has begun in this dream. When that shift reaches consciousness a new relationship is possible between spirit and instinct. The two energies, instead of being enemies, can find a natural harmony; far from destroying each other they can relate.

Spirituality and instinct are like the two snakes in the caduceus of Asclepius, separating and uniting, each with its own strength, one harmoniously balancing the other.

As she became more conscious, both through her dreams and her body work, Jaffa's ego strength was tested inside, outside, by her husband, by her children, by her new teachers and by her own memories. The child in her that was all too willing to be taken care of was increasingly being duped; the mother in her that found her impossibly stupid harangued incessantly. "Am I taking care of my children? Will they be alright? Am I giving them enough?"

She dreamed of a circle of fire; her whole body became fire. Reflecting on the circle of fire she remembered that Wagner's *Ring*

The Reunion of the Soul and the Body, by William Blake.
(Etching by Schiavonetti, for Blair's *The Grave,* 1808)

cycle had always fascinated her. In the opera, Siegfried kept his vulnerable spot in the center of his back covered by a leaf. The evil one, Hagen, tricked him, and when Siegfried lost his gentle green armor, he was vulnerable. Jaffa was suffering intense pain caused by a vertebra behind her heart. So long as she didn't breathe too deeply, didn't take in too much life, it didn't hurt too much. She was beginning to realize through her body pain the depth of the cutting that was going on.

"I can't carry the weight of my head anymore," she said. "It's too heavy. For so long I have intellectualized my suffering. I see intellectualizing now as an excuse. I was so stuck in my head and spirit that I smiled a smooth, secret smile and said, 'I'm grateful for my suffering. This is how I've learned. This is my maturing.' Head stuff! Totally ignoring my body! This is such a grand stand I've taken. Quite arrogant really! Let her suffer! Let her burn in the fire! I didn't know what real suffering was. I had gone through everything with my body closed down. I didn't want to look at anything, didn't want to suffer. Now I see what it really was. My life before was just headlines, no substance. All I wanted was coziness for everybody. I accommodated to everything for peace. Now I want freedom to live my life."

The transformative fire brought up associations with Wagner's Brunnhilde. Brunnhilde, favorite daughter of Wotan, saw what human love could be and turned against the perfectionist values of her father god, Wotan, in favor of the human hero. Her enraged father put her on a rock forever. But Brunnhilde persuaded him to encircle her with a ring of fire (passion), a ring which only a hero could break through to release her.

Wotan agreed, but with a price: if a man dared to come through the fire to awaken her, she would no longer be a goddess. She would become a human being.

The Brunnhilde image is evoking not only Jaffa's mature feminine consciousness but her focused, assertive masculinity as well. Having achieved a temporary plateau in the development of her feminine side, the Self now guides her to growth in her masculinity.

I walk through my home town on a badly lit road. I could have reached my goal on a different road with more traffic but I chose a back alley. I sense danger. A man follows me, becoming even more creepy when he calls out my name. He must know me and have observed me for a long time! He must have planned his attack cleverly!

An accomplice of his is now approaching me from the front. I remain conscious of the danger, but don't panic. The first man now grabs me around my ribs in a sweet-sour way. I don't fight, don't run, but know I must protect myself. I see a car parked with three women inside, and slowly walk toward it. The men allow me to go to the women. I guess they must after all be harmless. I ask the women whisperingly to secure my protection. All three agree silently.

Later, at the three women's house, two of their fathers are visiting. Against one wall the first of the two attackers sits and paints! I am astounded, for I thought he was a criminal! The other father is sitting at the table gobbling down food like a madman. I think it is a pity to gobble and not enjoy. Hot hunger! The women now tell me that the first father is quite harmless, and known for that.

I think I should look him in his face and de-harm him for myself, best upside down. I imagine how either I myself, or he, would hang on the balcony railing, and how we would, in this way, look into each other's eyes and recognize one another. SHOCKED!

Slowly, inevitably, this dream drives the sword home. Having chosen to leave the collective road, the dreamer is moving through the back alley where she meets her assailant and his accomplice who know her well. When she is grabbed in a "sweet-sour way" she experiences the attack exactly as she experienced the hands of her husband—cold, intrusive, violent in the sexual act. The assailants either hold the power or she projects her own power onto them. As the violence closes in, there is danger of violence meeting violence, but she does not fight or panic. Instead she slowly moves toward the protection of women in the nearby car. The assailants allow this.

This moment of transformed action—where the ego stands firm, doesn't panic, faces the rapists head-on and realizes they are now "harmless"—can only come after months or years of hard work. In the early months of analysis the weak container would try to run from the danger or fight it, thus setting up the very dynamic that would end in violence. When soul and body are in harmony, the body supports the ego, the ego can face the assailant. The face we turn to the unconscious is the face that is reflected back to us. So long as we keep running, it chases us and sometimes trips us. When we turn around and face it, its monumental terrors can be dealt with detail by small detail.

In the protective presence of her feminine energies, Jaffa faces the power drives she has been running away from all her life. While she does not have a chronic eating disorder, she does under stress gobble food, smoke cigarettes and rush from one thing into another and then fly out for more books. The "other father," gobbling his food like a madman, personifies the unconscious wolf energy that does not know what it wants but consumes everything in a crazed desire to be filled with something. Undermined by powerlessness and emptiness, it blindly lashes out, gobbling, not digesting anything. This father resonates with Jaffa's early memories of her mother gobbling at the kitchen table, eating her up. In this situation, the negative animus is the addict that consumes the feminine.

The other father is painting. The dreamer is astounded that he is not a criminal as she had imagined. Here is the core of what Jaffa will deal with. Both her father and mother were artists when they married. Her mother's creative powers, without a strong ego to pro-tect them, were swallowed by the madman gobbler whose negative energy, fired by the misappropriated creativity, became totally de-structive. The two sides of that creative fire are also juxtaposed in the criminal artist. Now Jaffa has to face the fact that her beloved father may not be blameless. His perfectionist standards in his own work and his support of everything she does rob her of her own creative fire. She is paralyzed when she begins to paint. In the last section of the dream, the dream ego realizes she must look this squarely in the eye but upside down.

This image is related to The Hanged Man in the Tarot pack, who

augurs the need for a voluntary sacrifice for the purpose of acquiring something of greater value. This might be the sacrifice of an external thing which has previously provided security, in the hope that some potential can be given room to develop. Or it can be the sacrifice of a cherished attitude, such as intellectual superiority, or unforgiving hatred, or a stubborn pursuit of some unobtainable fantasy.[2]

Jaffa is now faced with an image that suggests that her idealized father was neither the god she imagined nor the criminal. She imagines either him or herself suspended, as indeed her life is now suspended without the perfection of her father at the center. Looking into each other's eyes, she will see her own masculinity, her own creativity, her own capacity for action—hung, feet in the air, upside down. The situation cannot be faced directly yet, for that would be to short-circuit the soul process and to short-circuit the soul process is to be electrocuted. This is a soul problem, not a behavioral one.

One of the tragedies of human relationships is that very often one partner cannot respect the soul process of the other. What is rape for Jaffa is not rape for her husband because he does not have her trauma. Ripping aside the veils is rape when one partner is not ready. Jaffa is being called to make a sacrifice, having to do with what was most sacred to her. It has to do with making herself vulnerable to the new possibilities life may bring.

Two months later, after immense efforts to change her standpoint, Jaffa dreams that her suitcases are packed but still in her father's apartment, exactly as the apartment was twenty-five years ago. As the dream develops, the reason for no immediate, radical change becomes clear; chaos threatens:

> My sister, as a baby, chatters uninterruptedly. My mother talks of "putting the kleenex away" after having made love to me in order to keep it secret from my little sister. I am strangely aware of her assumption of intimacy between us.
> Then one word—AGAMEMNON.

Again the collusion of mother and father complexes is apparent. Obviously, father is happy to have Jaffa stay in his house (power) forever. "The suitcases are my soul that I put down in my father's apartment and left there," Jaffa said.

---

[2] Juliet Sharman-Burke and Liz Greene, *The Mythic Tarot*, p. 59.

The second part of the dream stunned Jaffa. Whether physical incest actually took place or not, she does not know. The dream at least suggests that as a child Jaffa's psyche experienced her mother's attitude toward her as an intrusion, a deviation from a healthy mother-daughter relationship. The baby sister who "chatters uninterruptedly" is that unconscious, innocent part of the child that cannot believe the violation is happening. Denial is the only defence a child has against the impossible truth.

Jaffa's strongest reaction to the dream was an all-consuming resentment at her mother's assumption that her daughter would make love to her. Her "absolutely not" in response to the dream contained all the energy that blocked out the act.

When one being is invaded by another, whether it is body or soul that is raped, or both, the symbolic language of the dream is the same. The inner world is so devastated that the trauma may be split off, isolated in the unconscious, while another part of the psyche chatters incessantly, camouflaging the truth.

As Jaffa worked on this dream over the next few months, she realized that there had indeed been an incestuous overtone to the beatings. The mother would become so excited and strike so hard on the child's buttocks that the imprint of the hot hand remained on her, in her, all day.

Then the one word, AGAMEMNON, delivered a blow even deeper than the incest section of the dream. When she looked up the story in Edith Hamilton's *Mythology*, she found that Agamemnon sacrificed his daughter, Iphigenia, and years later was killed himself by his wife and her lover. The words that Jaffa underlined were "a mother's love for a daughter killed by her own father."[3] She took AGAMEMNON as a command, as if her psyche were to say, "Look at me. There's more here than spirit. Demystify spirit."

Jaffa realized that by making her his queen, her father had not allowed her to live. In fact, he had talked Jaffa into giving up the man she loved and staying with the man she first married. "If I had gone

---

3 Edith Hamilton, *Mythology*, p. 240.

off with my lover," she said, "Father would have been threatened. 'Come to me,' he says, 'Come to me.' He sacrifices the woman I am to his image of the perfect woman for *his* salvation. I became a willing victim to the extent that I sacrificed my body. What Father did to me, I did to my body."

There is one other factor that must be kept in mind in working with this dream. So long as Jaffa needed to abreact her anger, I did not suggest a deeper meaning. The fact is, however, Jaffa is an artist and her creativity is grounded in the matrix of her being. If that matrix is seeking union with her, some new development may be happening. Jaffa is the product of her life circumstances, as are we all. There is some danger that she could be trapped in the chattering child who can only deny the experience instead of moving into the adult who seeks the meaning and gives it form in her art.

When Jaffa began to take full responsibility for her own life, she worked patiently at finding a new home for herself and making time for her studies. She relied on her own sense of discipline and will power. Something, however, was missing, as is clear in the following dream.

> The Queen Mother is in a wheelchair.
>
> At a castle ruin: I am walking toward a kind of jacuzzi (old bathtub, round, made of wood.) I hesitate when I see my father in the tub with a woman. Then I feel an urge to find out more about the woman. I had somehow been aware of her having a son about fifteen years old. Now she seems to totally ignore the fact that she is apparently sitting on top of her son in the water. I cannot do anything, but am alarmed and extremely concerned. Finally she stands up, completely unconscious, feelingless. Now I can see that indeed she had been holding her son under water all that time. He has shrunk to the size of a fifteen-year-old baby. He seems without any life, even though soft (not dead, but stiff). It is a horrible sight. I cannot help. I walk away slowly. Should I call for help?

The mother complex is now crippled. As the old queen crumbles, it is natural that the outworn, patriarchal world (the castle) would be in ruins. In that ruin is an old alchemical tub, a feminine container, wooden and round. In what could be a creative place are the father and an unknown woman who sits feelingless on top of her fifteen-year-old son who has shrunk to the size of a baby. He is not dead although he seems to be.

Fifteen years earlier, Jaffa, at her father's request, said goodbye to a man she loved, a man whom she associated with her creativity. "It was a time of death," she said. "Everything around me died. I could concentrate on nothing." Her father's anima, his soul, who loved painting, has been sitting on top of Jaffa's creativity for fifteen years. Everything about the tub—old, wood, round, water—suggests the creative matrix, but Jaffa is not in the tub and her creative masculine is being held in the unconscious by an unknown woman. Here is a very different kind of patriarchal woman—more subtle but no less destructive. "I love you so much, I know what is best for you," is her message and it has nearly drowned Jaffa's creative spirit. In this dream, the dream ego is so shocked it does not ask for help.

The following dream suggests that Jaffa is seeking help in the wrong place.

> My son is sitting on the couch of my father's living room. In front of him, on the floor, a white (!) Negro doll (size of a two-year-old child) is standing. She can talk. My son says to her, "I am not your grandmother!"

Her young masculine energy is now in her father's living room. Her young femininity (deficient in instinct—Negro doll, but white), which was crippled into a doll-like puppet by the age of two, is able to talk but the boy rebukes her. Perhaps she was looking to him for understanding, for nourishment, for all that she needs to look for in the Great Mother. This would be the old pattern repeating itself, the starved, ungrounded, feminine projecting strength and caring onto the masculine. Then the masculine grows fat while the feminine remains anorexic (which was precisely what was happening between two of Jaffa's children). The dream seems to be warning Jaffa not to make her son into her loving mother in real life, and not to indulge herself in a doll-like femininity that would feed on her creative masculinity. It needs all its own strength to mature.

In the next dream a vibrant, creative energy is beginning to manifest.

My husband has taken his car apart.
At a lake: I see some people on a strange kind of lift, just jumping off onto a platform and from there onto land. They are older people. Then I find myself high above the lake lying flat on my stomach on a small flat lift. I am lying quite still, and do not get dizzy. I am spiraling downward and land safely.
Unexpectedly I walk through a village in which all the inhabitants are participating in a funeral or memorial ceremony. Everyone is dressed in black. People have camels and cows with them; I am trying to squeeze through. Egypt seems to have a deep importance.
I am conscious of the presence of magic: first in the form of a man and/or his voice which enables me to figure skate, even though normally only my sister can do that. Then the magic seems to come from a cat.
I return from a hike with my father to the center of town. He steps into an empty bus. I want to follow him. As quick as a wink the doors shut, the bus takes off and I am furious!

A car is a metaphor for the way our energy moves through life. Our body is our most immediate means of locomotion. As patriarchal rigidity is dismantled in the musculature of Jaffa's body, the shifting of the energy patterns is at times excruciating.

In the second part of the dream the lift is like a crane holding a platform that comes spiraling safely down, first over the lake, then over the land. It reminds Jaffa of joining hands with her sister and swirling like two dervishes until they found the still point at the center and spiraled around the outside without becoming dizzy. As T.S. Eliot puts it,

> Except for the point, the still
> point,
> There would be no dance, and there is only the dance.[4]

At the still point, spirit embraces soul. Soul is in time, in matter. Spirit penetrates soul, bringing meaning to what might otherwise be

---

4 "Burnt Norton," *Four Quartets*, lines 66-67.

endless, meaningless time. Their union creates the dance that is a celebration of all that lives.

That celebration is further developed in the third part of the dream. Something has died but something new is being born—and the dream ego is "trying to squeeze through." Egypt is very important to Jaffa because as a child she escaped from her depressed world and went to the museum where Egypt lived in her imagination. She loved the ancient beauty, the power of the pyramids, the regal faces, the majestic forms. She loved the jewelry, the whole milieu of sun energy that brought her close to the divine.

As she reconnected with that world of her childhood, she developed a love for belly-dance music, which evoked a sensuous, sacred energy that brought her into touch with the feminine power in her body. Isis, the Black Madonna, is in that energy.[5]

The powerful Black Madonna energy finds a partner in the next section of the dream. Masculine energy in the form of "a man and/or his voice" infiltrates the atmosphere with magic and Jaffa is able to figure skate. "I love to watch figure skating," she said. "It is embodied spirit moving." All the lightness, the magic, the grace she once projected onto her sister, she is now claiming in herself. And with that thought, the magic she associated with a man seems to come from the feminine energy associated with a cat. Light enters matter.

Where does the energy want to go? The lysis makes that clear. The energy that is personified in the father gets into a bus and the ego still wants to follow. "Quick as a wink," the unconscious shuts the door between them. The ego, furious at being left alone, has to accept the cut she has not the conscious strength to make. Father, of course, will sometimes return but right now, Jaffa has to allow her own masculinity to grow without projecting onto her father or modeling herself on him.

This episode is a splendid example of "the fullness of time" having arrived and the unconscious taking the action which the dream ego is not yet able to take.

---

[5] See Jung, *Mysterium Coniunctionis*, CW 14, par. 14.

In a later dream, Jaffa and a male friend are visiting a married couple who are preparing dinner for the four to share. The husband is mixing spaghetti with the chicken his wife is cutting up. Jaffa likes Italian men because, she says, "they are not threatened in their masculinity. They can do what they need to do and work with a woman doing what she needs to do." In the dream each is independent, sharing without burdening the other. The dinner the four will eat together has feminine and masculine components blended but each defined. This dream, simple as it is, points to uncontaminated masculine and feminine energies uniting while holding their uniqueness.

Life has moved in many directions since Jaffa had these dreams. Covering a span of seven years, they make clear the dark foundations that have to be renovated in order to create a secure base for the new structure. While that structure is taking shape, the dark incubation period of healing requires sacred inner space. The depth and breadth and height of the process can only be suggested. Each of us travels our own path, but recognizable patterns emerge. After Jaffa read an initial draft of this chapter she said, "I see a gaping wound with a thread of healing going right through."

Jaffa's "gaping wound" has the mother patriarch at its core. The mother's perfectionist ideals not only created a split in her daughter's femininity but also undermined her self-esteem and creativity. The healing thread is the unconscious process that is honored. Gradually it transforms destructive power into energy that allows Jaffa to move into life with her own integrated sexuality and her own creative fire.

The destruction by the father's anima who sits on the woman's son in the bathtub is more subtle. The anima too is a product of the patriarchy, as is the puer father who married the devouring mother. Her clinging devotion colludes with mother's animus to drown the daughter's creative masculine in the unconscious. Any picture the girl creates will be colored by her love for her father.

The danger for such a woman in analysis is that she will turn the analysis into a work of art. Jaffa realized this.

"I was always aware of the possibility of addiction to analysis," she says. "The irony is that after all these years I am only now beginning to incorporate my analysis into my life. I used to leave this office thinking I would phone to ask you how to deal with what I had just learned. How was I going to go out and live what the dreams were telling me? It all felt like theater, a fun hour, a photograph. Symbolism means a lot to me but what do I do with it? The hooked rug is off the wall now. I'm treading it. Now I dream of real meadows, real daisies. Where there was an avalanche, the ice is now melting into a waterfall. I don't need a wall hanging any more. In my mother's house and my husband's I needed images to survive."

Similarly, the danger of analysis, particularly for an artist, is that life will be turned into art, that the analysand will create an artificial life. If you don't feel you have parents who created you, if you've never been born, if there was no life there, analysis could give you a hooked rug on the wall, beautiful to look at, but always once removed from life. If you are an artist who puts everything into the analysis, and makes the analysis your art (music, dancing, acting, writing) you are in danger of sacrificing your art to analysis.

Many artists fear analysis because they believe that if they work out their pain in the analytic process, they will no longer create. Anything that is too painful to be dealt with finds a less painful way to express itself. For an artist the less painful way may be in music, painting, acting, whatever the creative outlet is. So long as the process is moving, the art is alive; if the process ceases to move, the artist creates the same conflict again and again but the life force has gone out of the creation. The sense of loss may be so painful that it is avoided through an addiction.

Analysis, if it is working, takes a person through an embedded conflict. It is like a superstructure. Eventually it comes down. There is a life process going on which analysis can support but not replace. Artists whose life blood is imagery may confuse the analytic process with life itself and, in an effort to find the life they never had, sacrifice their art and create an artificial life in analysis.

To prevent this, it is crucial to keep a creative outlet open during the analysis. If the analyst can encourage the artist to play with the imagery, allowing it to take whatever form it happens to come up with, the energy locked in the shadow will emerge, bringing with it the buried creative fire. In that new integration the Self brings healing for the soul and energy for the art. The soul blossoms in the mystery connecting it to the Self. This is the mystery analysis dare not touch.

Jaffa's commitment to her body/soul work is the best protection against her analysis becoming a substitute for art or life. The continual shifting of the pain in her body keeps her in touch with her own Black Madonna wisdom—wisdom that keeps her grounded not only in her matter, but in the consciousness in matter. When pain or grief or anger are recognized and given space to express themselves, raw instincts transform. Like animals who are loved, they bring their wisdom into our lives and guide us where we would not dare to go alone. They know what we do not know.

And as her femininity takes up residence in her body, Jaffa's masculinity struggles to connect with it. She is well aware of the light that would sweep her off the earth. She is not fooled by images of the demon lover as a dark, ugly, malicious murderer. She knows Satan is too clever to clothe himself in that disguise. Handsome, intelligent, in love with beauty and truth, he comes in radiant light. He charms with music, poetry, gracious manners and sparkling wit. He charms but he has no feeling. Once he has conquered, lured a victim into stony perfection or death, he carelessly moves on.

Jaffa, like so many other women reared in a patriarchal home, is trying to bring to full consciousness the heart of incest that pulses at the center of Luciferean Light. The bond may be with the father or the mother's animus, or both. If the Luciferean energy sacrifices its power and forgives itself and others for being imperfectly human, then it must connect to the feminine that can contain the suffering. If that surrender takes place, Lucifer transforms into Christ. The creative masculine becomes the true bridegroom.

Jaffa's initial dream when she came into analysis tells her story. Here it is in part:

> Many people are gathered in a small space, my sister and husband too. They are occupied with things that seem unimportant to me. Nobody helps me birthing my baby, which I am sad about. But I am

doing it alone. Immediately after the birth I take the "creation" (the new-born) with me into the bathtub. There we are having a glad and relaxed time. "It" smiles at me. Until now I have only seen the head: black hair, Indonesian facial features. Only now I look for its sex. It is a girl, and I am ecstatic, so happy . . . .

It will take many years of work until we can see each other as friends, which is more difficult than a depth-psychological relationship. Do we want this?

The *coniunctio,* union of opposites, as harmonious
interplay between male water and female fire.

Mother's Patriarch in Me

My animus is antiseptic, like my mother's. He likes cleanliness, order, clarity. I can't stand the muddle my husband likes to live in. Sometimes I sneak one of his dozens of boxes into the garbage and he goes out and says, "Oh, what's this?" and brings it back in. My animus likes to make a clean sweep of everything. He would have thrown our messy marriage out. Thank God, my husband is a bit bumbling. It never occurs to him that we can't work things out together.

Love is where the power is so I better start to love.

I get up in the morning to write in my journal. I think I'll just wash a sweater while I wait for my coffee. Then I have such a good suds I think I might as well wash another, and while I'm trying to find that one, I find several smelly scarves and by heaven, there's the letter I couldn't find six months ago. So I put the scarves to soak in Woolite and water my plants while I try to think where my good stationery is and then I find some bills I forgot to pay. I see the mess I'm creating, just like my mother. I decide to dance. Distractions! Distractions! So much to do. I do anything to avoid focusing in my journal.

I inflict pain on myself in order to bear the soul pain. Otherwise my soul would explode. I have to feel the physical pain in order to recognize the soul pain. My soul has no way out. My mother secretly punished her body.

My killer animus lets me see no alternatives, no wit, no fun. He keeps me heavy, exhausted, obsessed with my own fatigue. My daughter is my "tough love." She hears me. She doesn't say this is terrible. She says this is what you can do. She's breaking the cycle.

I'm splayed. One part is the powerless victim of the man I adore; the other is the powerful professional who is outraged that she can't get what she wants on the job. The whole administration operates on who is sleeping with whom. The Old Boys' Club has got it tied up.

My mother is a quiet ball-crusher. She's always telling me what my father ought to do. Now I say, "What about you? What do you want? Say it. Don't blame him. Stand up for yourself."

let it go - the
smashed word broken
open vow or
the oath cracked length
wise - let it go it
was sworn to

go

let them go - the
truthful liars and
the false fair friends
and the boths and
neithers - you must let them go they
were born

to go

let all go - the
big small middling
tall bigger really
the biggest and all
things - let all go
dear

so comes love

—e.e. cummings.

"Apparently, she felt she had handed herself—not her body, but her soul, her essence—over to Frank Holt. . . . [She] seems to think of Frank Holt in religious terms. He . . . would redeem her and . . . remove all imperfections from her. When he told her he no longer wanted her, she felt as if he were betraying her soul. I asked her if, when she thought of shooting herself, she realized she would be ending her own life. And she said no, she hadn't thought so. Her life had ended when Frank Holt told her he was through with her. He had killed her soul. After that, she said, she was not really alive."

"Did she believe that Frank Holt's soul had been entrusted to her?" asked Mr. Kingsley. "Oh, yes," said the doctor; "she said that without her, he would be lost. He would never carve the statues he was meant to carve. . . . She said that although they had not been married, theirs was a marriage of souls."

—Susan Fromberg Schaeffer, *The Madness of a Seduced Woman.*

4
Lover, Can You Spare a Dime?

*[Some of the material in this chapter was delivered as a lecture in
St. Paul's Centre at Trinity, Toronto, April 21, 1989]*

The wheel is come full circle! I am here.
—*King Lear.*

We are all unconsciously bound to the wheel of fortune. It goes
round and round and we go blindly around on it until one day something happens that wakes us up, face to face with ourselves. What
for years we could not or would not see is made visible. The unconscious is made answerable to consciousness. The Self demands a
reckoning: the ego must recognize what it has so long feared and rejected. Whether we grow or wither in that encounter depends on
whether we cling to our ego's rigid standpoint or whether we choose
to trust the Self and leap into the unknown.

Tonight my wheel is come full circle. I am here. In preparing this
talk, I have had to bow to the Self. How it has craftily maneuvered to
force me to look at what I tried to leave behind is awesome. However, destiny has brought us together here tonight. What is present
for me I will tell you in a story.

One morning last June I was walking through the park thinking of
a title to submit for this evening's talk. "Lover, can you spare a
dime?" flashed into my head.

"Hmm, interesting!" I thought, and all summer brooded on possibilities.

In October, I learned that I would speak in St. Paul's Centre at
Trinity. Because I like to know the feeling of places before I talk, I
took a subway ride to the Spadina station. As I walked west it
dawned on me that St. Paul's Centre at Trinity might be what I had

always known as Trinity Church. Sure enough. I checked the sign outside and my blood ran cold. I knew the place well. I climbed the steps. The organist was practicing. I sat in the pew where I used to sit every Sunday as a student at the Ontario College of Education. All the mutterings of forty years ago churned through my belly. Once again I was a young woman asking God to give me voice enough to teach my class tomorrow.

Again I felt the volcanic tremors as I stood in front of forty huge young men at Harbord Collegiate. Again I lived through that January morning, when, as a student teacher, I was trying to put into practice in the classroom the theory I had learned in the college. I was to spend three weeks with Dr. Johnson, who was reputedly one of the best English teachers in the province.

I was to teach Wordsworth's *Michael*. Because the story of the poem is important to this discussion, let me give you a brief summary. Michael in the poem is a simple shepherd of immense integrity. He loves the hills with "The pleasure which there is in life itself."[1] In his late years, he and his younger wife, Isabel, have a son, Luke, who is beloved, because

> A child, more than all other gifts
> That earth can offer to declining man,
> Brings hope with it, and forward-looking thoughts.[2]

The three live in a Garden of Eden in the English hills. Luke brings "Light to the sun and music to the wind."[3] Then Michael receives word that his land is forfeit for a bond he once made with his brother's son. In an effort to keep the land as a legacy for their own son, Michael and Isabel decide to send Luke to the city to work for a kinsman. As a covenant between them, Michael asks Luke to lay the cornerstone for a sheepfold which he will work on while Luke is gone. Luke goes to the "dissolute" city. He never comes home.

---

[1] Line 77.
[2] Lines 146-148.
[3] Line 202.

Many and many a day, Michael went to the field to work on the fold,
"And never lifted up a single stone."[4]

Well, Tuesday morning my lesson plan was as perfect as I could
make it. I stood in front of the class elucidating the theme:

> There is a comfort in the strength of love;
> 'Twill make a thing endurable, which else
> Would overset the brain, or break the heart;[5]

After two minutes my lips moved; there was no sound. Eyebrows
raised, noses snorted, shoulders shrugged. Dr. Johnson took over.

This scene was repeated on Wednesday and Thursday. Furious,
Dr. Johnson phoned the Teachers' College. Dr. Katz came at once. I
sat where I was told to sit, at the back of the room. I had not done
well before Christmas and I knew this was my last chance.

"What did you send her to me for?" demanded Dr. Johnson, virtually ignoring my presence. "She can't teach, she can't even speak!"

"That's why I sent her, " said Dr. Katz. "Look at her notes. Make
a teacher of her, Johnson." And he strode out, leaving Johnson and
me writhing in each other's presence.

Dr. Johnson read my notes. He changed color. He looked at me
as if I might be somebody. He went to the window and stared out.

"You see that fellow over there shoveling coal down the shute?"
he said. "That's what you've got to learn to do—shovel coal into
your cellar. Go home. Don't open a book. Lie on the floor. Breathe.
Don't come back until you can shovel coal."

I hadn't the slightest idea what he was talking about, but I was
grateful for the dime of kindness I heard in his voice, and grateful for
any reprieve.

On Sunday I sat in that very pew, fuming at the minister who
thought he knew so much about wise and foolish virgins. I finally
turned him off and implored God to help me shovel coal. He and She
did—though I didn't know it at the time.

---

4 Line 466.
5 Lines 447-450.

What I did know was that something crucial had gone out of my life. It was personified in the poem I was trying to teach—Luke going away to the city and never coming back. My inner Luke had disappeared and with him went my creative imagination, that spirit that brings "Light to the sun and music to the wind." While I was conscious enough to know that life could not be Paradise, I also knew it was never meant to be an endless load of duty and responsibility.

Looking at those forty young scholars, I was face to face with the achiever I had become at university. I too had wanted A's. I knew the sacrifice I had made to get them; the poem brought me face to face with my betrayal of my intrinsic energies—love of nature, love of poetry, love of life for the sheer joy of living.

Luke in the poem and Luke in me had been seduced by the false standards that were turning my life into a nightmare I did not wish to live. To speak was to tap into the rage and grief in my cellar. Luke would appear in that classroom in my tears. I dared not cry, therefore I could not speak.

But I had no future without teaching. I was too traumatized to let out the cry of my soul. I left her silent as a stone. I had to learn to be soul deaf in order to function at all. I learned to speak with a thin little voice that had no connection to who I was, no resonance that would betray my authentic feelings and sensitivity. I did teach composition on Monday. I did become a teacher. And I am grateful to Dr. Johnson and Dr. Katz, without whose awareness of that profound disconnection I would never have been granted the teaching certificate that allowed me to deal with the problem in my own classroom.

Tonight the wheel has come full circle. I am very conscious of the irony of this situation. Here I am, standing in what in my childhood was the stronghold of the patriarchy—the pulpit. It was the place of God, of my father—the enthroned father. Because my father was a minister and I identified him with the Word spoken from his lips, I equated my heavenly father with my earthly father—my childish version of incarnation. Here was the heavenly father in the flesh of my earthly father. Not only preachers' kids unconsciously make that equation.

For me to break out of patriarchy, therefore, is an act of betrayal of my personal father. Because I loved my father and he loved me, and because I was his handmaiden in religious rites—baptisms, weddings, funerals—the whole of my sacred life was locked into patriarchy. So far as I was concerned, patriarchy was heaven on earth. That's what it's like for a child who is the beloved of the father, be he minister or carpenter.

Here I am, then, standing in a pulpit, giving a talk on the theme, "Lover, can you spare a dime?"—a title that mockingly denounces patriarchy. In the imaginal world of my childhood such an act is an act of Satan. *"Non serviam,"* I will not serve, was his declaration to God. I had to come to grips with that Satanic metaphor in order to understand at a conscious level what in heaven's name, what the hell, and what on earth I am doing here. It is my answer to those questions that is the subject of what follows.

So what am I here for? To say what I have to say. The tragedy of the pulpit as a symbol of patriarchy is that it has become a sacrificial altar for both masculinity and femininity. Neither masculine nor feminine identity is possible in the pulpit configuration. This is not a sexist issue. It is not even a gender issue. It is a human issue. I am coming out from under patriarchy to speak not as a woman but as a human being, even as men must come out from under patriarchy to speak not as men but as human beings.

Since my experience in Teachers' College, it has taken me forty years to come to this, to understand what it was all about and to find a human voice, one not tied to gender or sex. Without a human voice, I wouldn't give a dime to be a woman or for that matter a man. "Lover, can you spare a dime?" For what? So I can be that fantasy called a woman and you can be that fantasy called a man and we can play that game together? A killing game, that! Not worth a nickel, let alone a dime. It's selling the soul for a mess of potage.

I did not choose to be lecturing here tonight, but it happens to be the same church I attended at Teachers' College. I could dismiss this as a simple coincidence, but my soul would give me short shrift for that. No, I must see this occasion as a clever connivance of the Self;

I must ask myself why I am required to speak now when I would not, could not, speak then.

At that time, at a completely unconscious level, I had already rejected patriarchy in the form in which it had always dominated my life. The feminine in me realized I could not spend the rest of my days being a handmaiden of patriarchy. Yet, there I was with two patriarchs who were trying to make a teacher worthy of their system. I was to teach a poem about a sheepfold passing from father to son. That is a patriarchal covenant, an inestimable gift which demands the son's loyalties to his father's values—a male mystery rite from which the female is excluded, even if she has inherited her father's birthright. I identified with Luke, the son who in breaking the covenant went underground. I grieved for the heartbroken father and mother. I knew the feelings I brought to the poem had no place in that classroom. Fortunately, I had a cohort in Emily Dickinson whose rebellion against Jehovah was as virulent as my own.

> Of Course—I prayed—
> And did God Care?
> He cared as much as on the Air
> A Bird—had stamped her foot—
> And cried "Give Me"—
> My reason—Life—
> I had not had—but for Yourself—
> 'Twere better Charity
> To leave me in the Atom's Tomb—
> Merry, and Nought, and gay, and numb—
> Than this smart Misery.[6]

I rejoiced in the bitterness of this poem. I roared it out to my bedroom walls when I was studying alone. I understood Emily's silence while she lived. I applauded her for refusing to change one line of her poetry in order to please the patriarchal judges who rejected her innovative style.

Conscious femininity and conscious masculinity will never be acceptable to patriarchy. If we become sufficiently conscious, how-

---

[6] *The Complete Poems,* no. 376.

ever, we do not have to be Tess on the altar at Stonehenge, nor Hamlet murdered by the intrigues of his stepfather. We do not have to be sacrificed. We can reject the knife. We do not have to be Portia masquerading as a male lawyer, speaking with a woman's voice, "The quality of mercy is not strained." There is a time coming when a woman's voice won't have to be disguised in a man's garment. Nor will men ever disguise themselves in women's garments. There is such a thing as a *human* garment. That garment is the inner marriage. The unlived life of men and women will become the source of life when consciousness liberates us from patriarchal power.

In preparing for this talk, I experienced terror and rage at a deeper level than ever before. In attempting to give voice to those parts of me that went into seclusion for safekeeping some forty years ago, I have emerged profoundly connected to the men and women who are recognizing the origins of oppression in themselves and are determined to free themselves from bondage to an obsolete patriarchy. My talk, therefore, has both a personal and a collective meaning. While focusing initially on the personal meaning of my present initiation, I am at the same time focusing on the meaning of the initiation that men and women everywhere are undergoing.

As I see it, this moment in history is demanding not a slow transition but a mutation, a leap in consciousness. Our task—men's and women's both—is to release ourselves from the power of patriarchal oppression into the love that radiates at the core of our own authentic lives. Intellectually, you may say, "So what else is new?" Feelingly, strip yourself naked and you will understand.

For the purpose of this discussion, we need first to separate women and men and later bring them together. Since a father's daughter is a prime victim of patriarchy, let us begin there. Having been immersed in patriarchal standards, she values logic, order, mind, spirit, goals. She expects nothing less than heaven on earth, a heaven that circles around the all-loving, all-powerful God-father-lover, an ideal that shatters in the fist of brutal reality. Having expected all, she loses all, and so long as she strangles in that complex she survives on whatever dimes the male world throws her way.

While "Lover, can you spare a dime?" has a sardonic twist, it carries a horrendous truth. A woman who has mirrored her father since infancy takes on his anima projection. Hence she has little, if any, feminine identity grounded in her own female body. Her concept of femininity is a man's notion of what is feminine, and her self-esteem is dependent on men's smiles of approval. She performs, whether from the soles of her delicate Guccis or her sturdy Oxfords. Professionally and socially, she automatically becomes the mirror in which men see their inner woman. In intimate relationship, she sculpts herself to manifest her lover's image.

Such a woman's dependence puts her into a love-hate relationship because the very intensity of her conscious devotion is compensated by an unconscious terror of loss. Whatever real feeling she has is undermined by self-loathing because, however self-reliant she appears, she knows her very lifeline is connected to a man who may cut the umbilical cord whenever he chooses. "Lover, don't take it all," is the terrible fear she rarely faces. Her survival game drives her to rely on charm, charm that attracts an equally charming man. Both are trapped. Neither is in touch with real feeling and the performance is ultimately doomed. In such a situation, however, one dime—one phone call, one pathetic gift, any token gesture—can keep her in thrall and paralyze any attempt she might make to escape.

A father's daughter is often a woman whose father lived in the shadow of his wife's dad. In other words, the daughter's mother was also a father's daughter, disillusioned by the man she married, bitter that he was not the shining knight or the loving savior she once projected onto him.

Stepping into that gap between fantasy and reality, the daughter may identify with the fantasy and try to be for her father what her mother failed to be. The configuration varies. The father may indeed be a beloved judge, respected doctor or lawyer in his community. He may truly be a great man. Conversely, he may be absent through alcoholism, divorce or death, in which case his young daughter may fantasize about how perfect life would be if only Daddy would come home.

As a grown woman she looks for a daddy-lover who will cherish and nurture her, a daddy to whom she can be everything. Because she is not in her body, she craves intellectual or spiritual Light. What she often finds is a Luciferian Light-bringer, drunk on his vision or his whiskey or his drugs, a man who constellates in her the unconscious mother who may try to save him but will end up pandering to a narcissistic little boy.

At an even deeper level, she may find that the men who magnetize her are not, in fact, like her father, but like the idealized masculine in her mother. Then she has to swallow a bitter truth: the unconscious image that snared her mother is the very image that is snaring her. Ironically, she is living out the unconscious of the very woman she has spent her life determined not to emulate.

Where incest—psychic or physical or both—has been the reality she grew up with, unconsciously she will find a lover who will exploit or abuse her. A father's daughter grows up blind to the shadow side of her father, indeed to the shadow side of any man; therefore, men for her are of a different species, more than human, closer to the gods—spiritual or animal. Confronting a man's shadow constellates her unconscious devils and her mother's rage against men. Immediately she feels betrayed.

Depending on her psychology, she will aim her loaded gun either out or in, murder or suicide. When it goes off, it explodes in both directions. Killer rage—whether rampant or repressed—is loosed and every soul in the environment is in danger of being raped or murdered. Without her doing anything, her children, her husband, her students, are being poisoned by her attitude.

The dark side of the masculine that manifests as magician or demon lover can be almost indistinguishable in dreams. Often they turn into each other or dissolve into a figure that transcends both. In discussing the Trinity in *The Grail Legend,* the authors make distinctions which differentiate Father, Son and Holy Ghost. I find this clarification valuable in understanding a progression from magician to demon lover to Perceval.

The figure of the Father, which is manifested in the Old Testament, is that of a creator and originator of all things, who turns a benevolent as well as a destructive aspect towards men. Men stand to him in a childlike relation that does not ponder the nature of this undivided, dark and light father God and is unable to exercise any criticism concerning him. . . . In an age, however, in which the figure of a Son of God appears, the condition of human consciousness is also different; from the original unity of the *one* a part is split off which becomes its opposite or *other,* which is why, in most religions, the archetypal form of the Son of God is a figure of suffering. For instance, it falls victim to the powers of darkness and must be freed again for the salvation of the world. . . . While on the human side the image of the Father corresponds to a childlike state of consciousness, where a ready-made way of life that has the characteristics of law is uncritically accepted, in the next stage, the Age of the Son, a conscious consideration of previously accepted things begins and with it criticism, judgment and moral differentiation. The condition of the Son is, accordingly, one of conflict. . . . [As Jung writes] "The exemplary life of Christ is in itself a 'transitus' and therefore amounts to a bridge leading over to the third stage, where the initial stage of the Father is, as it were, recovered."[7] This third phase, the Age of the Holy Spirit, corresponds on the human level to an attitude that, through recognition of the guiding and enlightening function of the unconscious, strives to move beyond the state of being suspended in conflict. This does not mean a step back into the first phase, although a wrong turning of this kind naturally always threatens, but the submission of individual independence to the spirit . . . . Together with this goes the release from a faith resting merely on authority, whether such authority is psychological or that of a collective organization.

Perceval is indeed the *tierz hom,* clearly destined to play the part of the man who, growing beyond the state of conflict characterized by the condition of the Son, should become conscious of the guiding, inspiring principle in the unconscious and thus realize and recognize the inner wholeness.[8]

---

[7] "A Psychological Approach to the Trinity," *Psychology and Religion,* CW 12, par. 272.
[8] Emma Jung and Marie-Louise von Franz, *The Grail Legend,* pp. 321-322.

Joan's development illustrates the shadow side of this progression. Identified with her father-husband, she trusted his authority implicitly. Suddenly she was faced with the terrible truth that he no longer loved her. They separated. Months later, she dreamed that they lived in a foreboding, cold castle like the one in *Wuthering Heights,* and her shining husband had turned into a mad Heathcliff who beat their dog, raped their daughter and screamed her name as he pounded through the corridors looking for her. In actual fact, Joan had neither daughter nor dog and she was living in a safe apartment. However, with an inner demon lover totally devoid of femininity, she was incapacitated by "criticism, judgment and moral differentiation."

The dream suggests that the real problem was rage, rampaging to reduce everything to victim. She summoned up enough assertiveness to do body work and, after months of intense physical pain, holding in herself the tension between victim and tyrant, she discharged the rage. Then the transcendent function brought forth a healing image of the transformative feminine. A Black Madonna, a radiant ten-foot woman, took the dreamer on her lap, nestled her curly head beside her great beating heart and rocked her. When Joan was able to mother her own ego (herself in the dream), her soul (her child) and her instincts (her dog), victims and tyrant were reconciled. While the dream ego relates as a child to the Madonna in this dream, it was the beginning of trust in "the guiding, inspiring principle in the unconscious."

While all women are not fathers' daughters, we are all daughters of the patriarchy, and although we are becoming more aware of oppression, we need to open our eyes to the projection of our intelligence, strength and feelings onto men. We need also to take responsibility for our own unconscious collusion with tyranny. Fighting for our liberation in the business world, in court, in university and in politics is important, but public victories are merely band-aids so long as the private world is in chains. That fact manifests in countless dreams of raped and murdered little girls. Because dreams are photographs of our reality taken from the perspective of the unconscious, we have to keep asking, "What are we unconsciously doing to ourselves that our inner feminine is so often left starving and bleeding?"

And gentlemen, you sons of the patriarchy, is the feminine flourishing in your dreams? Men talk about feeling guilty when they realize what the patriarchy has done to women. They are the would-be rescuers in the victim-tyrant-rescuer triumvirate. That response is itself patriarchal, for the patriarchy can no longer be identified with men. Women can be equally patriarchal. Men have no monopoly on the power complex. I assure you, actual men are no worse than the male figures in women's dreams. And no better. They too dream of their little daughter being dead.

In 1988 at the Great Mother Conference with Robert Bly, I saw in a flash one of the fundamental problems between men and women. I asked the audience what they associated with "mother." The women instantly responded with such words as "nurturing, cherishing, enfolding, giving, caring." Not a man spoke.

"Come on, men," I said. There was a roar—"devouring, demanding, manipulative, suffocating, castrating."

We stared at each other, shocked. Women who thought of themselves as selfless and loving suddenly saw themselves in a very different mirror. Their one-sided attitude had constellated the negative mother in the men. And the dragon slayers were unsheathing their swords. That apparently simple word, "mother," had polarized the sexes.

Then I asked for their associations to the word "virgin." The women called out "self-confident, knows her values, lives her truth, strong, grounded." The men responded with "ineffectual, naive, pure, uninitiated, unravished."

Granted there is a problem in the connotations surrounding the word "virgin," but whether we use that word or "mature feminine" we need to look at the problem she, or what she symbolizes, poses in relationships.

To illustrate, let us look at the Greek myth of Demeter and Kore. As a little girl, Kore (which means simply maiden), lives in a symbi-

otic dyad with her mother. Not until she is snatched out of that unconscious bonding and initiated into womanhood by Hades, does
she take her own name, Persephone. Psychologically, she has been
ravished by the creative masculine. She becomes a virgin, embodied
feminine energy separated from the maternal unconscious. That energy is strong enough to receive the penetration of the god and bear
the divine child.

No longer maiden, Persephone returns to the sunlit world for
eight months of the year. As virgin, she *relates* to Demeter without
identifying with her. The unconscious dyad is broken. For four
months she is queen with Hades in the underworld. Her transformation was celebrated every year in the Eleusinian Mysteries. Men as
well as women were participants, hence this myth has profound importance for both sexes. Then as now, both men and women were
attempting to break the symbiotic bond between mother and maiden
in order to release the virgin who could bear the divine son.

The Greek myth prefigures the Christian myth of mother, virgin,
child. While the Greek myth focuses primarily on the soul process in
the feminine, the Christian myth focuses on the product, the divine
child. The apocryphal story tells of the young Mary predestined for
the temple by her mother, Anne, taken out of collective society at the
age of three. At puberty she is betrothed to Joseph, but in her empowered aloneness she is visited by a god. In the fullness of time she
brings forth a divine child. "Empowered aloneness" is the important
phrase here. Unless their femininity is strong enough to stand alone
in their own authentic truth, without the support of mother or the
collective, men just as much as women are locked in the status quo.
Then there can be no new consciousness, the divine child, springing
from the depths of the psyche, the womb of the virgin.

The virgin is involved in relationship problems in that many
women are struggling to break their identification with the mother-
maiden dyad and are finding their own virginal standpoint, while
their men, whose femininity may be still locked in the mother-
maiden, continue to project a split feminine. It takes a strong creative
masculine spirit to break that unconscious feminine dyad. The nega-

tive forces that protect it are formidable. Women have to use every tactic and every strength they have to bring that dyad to consciousness, in order to avoid identification with the unconscious mother.

Perhaps it is even more terrorizing for a man, especially if he had an overbearing mother. When he experiences his partner standing up for herself, his devouring mother complex is constellated. But if he retreats from what he fears, he becomes the very thing he is running away from. Failure to connect with his own masculine spirit leaves his anima vulnerable to falling into one side of the dyad or the other: mother or little girl. Either way he sabotages his own and his partner's attempts to grow up. His sentimentality does not encourage the affirmative action necessary to a mature consciousness. Little girls can be sweet and compliant but they cannot demand or receive mature masculinity. Liberated femininity is satisfied with nothing less.

It is also worth noting here that the "truth" a woman stands to is not truly her own until she can tell the difference between what her complexes blurt out and what comes from her essential integrity. Until then, one moment she may scream if her husband tries to coddle her, and the next smother him with sex or sherbet.

Men have not escaped the massacre of the feminine any more than women have. The Nazi officer in the unconscious of a patriarchal mother stamps down the little boy's soul and a macho father will not tolerate a "sissy." A sensitive boy raised by such parents is victimized twice over—by them and by a culture that mocks his tears, scorns his sensitivity and labels his gentleness "effeminate." His mind/body split is even deeper than his sister's, resulting in a tragic loss of connection to his authentic feelings. His anima may fly to the ideal rather than walk with the real, in which case he may become an addict attempting to escape the brutality of life. Or he may fall in love with words or dance, science or philosophy, and devote himself to a world of perfection, quite divorced from troublesome human involvement. He then becomes the perfect hook for the demon lover projection. Worshiping ideals, however, is no less dangerous for men than for women. Sooner or later the body vetoes the search for perfection.

We are all aware of the very real victimization of women by male overlords, but we must be equally aware that these overlords are rampant in the unconscious of both men and women. Judging and blaming the other is destroying relationships.

Take, for example, the man who projects Great Mother onto his wife. He tends to take her unconditional love and service for granted, because on some level he is a child and mother is always there. Mother in that situation has no personal identity. She is merely an archetypal caretaker. Like the daughter unconsciously bound to her father, he is tied to his mother-mate by an umbilical lifeline that he trusts she will not cut. At the same time his childishness blinds him to his own shadow who fears, perhaps even hates, the woman he is bound to.

It is not uncommon for such a man to have an ongoing affair with another woman and yet to be genuinely shocked when his wife says, "Choose between us." He may claim his love for one enhances his love for the other. He loves them in different ways. He may blame his wife for not activating his sexuality. If he looks at his dreams, however, he may realize that part of him craves the protection and comfort of the mother, and another part lusts for the mistress with whom he has contacted the life force. If he and his wife are committed to consciousness, both may become aware of the overbearing mother in themselves; then, through their relationship, they may find the liberated virgin who brings lust and love together.

Or take the man who one day says to his aging wife who has served him all her life, "My dear, I am making my will. I am giving everything to my children." Or equally cruel, the man who leaves everything to his sons, trusting they will take care of his widow and daughters. Like produces like. The women are lucky if they receive a penny. Their efforts to get their share are viewed as harassment of their brothers who are involved in important work. Money is energy, and how people handle their money reveals only too clearly what they value. Unfair financial deals often appear in dreams as rape. The sons and daughters of parents who hold the feminine in such contempt do not find the depotentiation of their inner tyrant an easy task.

Paradoxically, the feminine soul in our culture subsists on dimes, while millions are spent to dramatize her victimized condition. Imagine what would happen if images of the victimized feminine were banned in our culture. We would lose many of our classical dramas—*Tamberlaine, Othello, St Joan*. Opera houses would not resonate with the anguish of *La Traviata, Lucia di Lammermoor, Madam Butterfly, Anne Boleyn*. Theaters would not play Tennessee Williams, Eugene O'Neill, Samuel Beckett. Bookshelves would be depleted without *Anna Karenina, The Idiot*, the poetry of Robert Browning, Sylvia Plath, Anne Sexton. The list is endless. The cruelty of the victimization is veiled by the beauty of the art form in which the images are enshrined. Without those diaphanous veils, we have something quite different—*Dallas, Dynasty, Miami Vice* and ubiquitous examples of advertising where the feminine is raped by male and female alike. At the bottom of this barrel is pornography.

Jungians are often accused of being idealists, muddle-headed mystics who cannot be taken seriously when it comes to real living. Critics question the validity of Jungian psychology because it focuses on the inner world instead of the outer. They call it a cop-out because it turns the problems of individuals back on themselves instead of addressing actual persecution in the world. But I believe the real cop-out is ignoring the Nazi killer in our dreams. Those of us who dare to look at our own shadow know that Nazis do exist, do pitch innocents into concentration camps in our own homes, and do bleed trying to keep the barbed wire on our own bay windows. To take responsibility for such images in our own dreams sensitizes us to take responsibility in our culture. We cannot be indifferent to the bureaucracy whose precious policies resulted in the massacre of the innocents in Prince William Sound. We are the system and we are the dead sea otter.

So long as we are blind to our inner tyrant, we blame an outer tyrant, some person or some system, for victimizing us. That maintains the split because victim and tyrant are dependent on each other, and together they must be healed. Either/or thinking is symptomatic of this split. It is patriarchal thinking and maintains the destructive status quo. It allows people to smile benignly and say, "I don't know what you're going on about," when they themselves have had a medically inexplicable heart attack or their own cedars are dying of acid rain. Broken hearted or terrified, they smile, unaware.

Take a walk down any street. Look at the faces in a bank line-up. Look into the eyes that look back at you in a store and you will see T.S. Eliot's "Burial of the Dead" everywhere.

> Only
> There is shadow under this red rock,
> (Come in under the shadow of this red rock),
> And I will show you something different from either
> Your shadow at morning striding behind you
> Or your shadow at evening rising to meet you;
> I will show you fear in a handful of dust.[9]

Fearing the shadow that strides behind us before the noon of life is as natural as fearing the shadow rising to meet us in the evening. What is different in the fear that Eliot is describing is the pervading sense of loss in so many people in our twentieth-century waste-land—loss so deep that the vital spark goes out, leaving a hollow shell. Patriarchy is crumbling. The values that were taken for granted for centuries are being questioned as we watch our raped planet wither under the pressures of acid rain, toxic waste, overpopulation. We can choose to tyrannize our inner victims and deny our fear, as millions of addicts are doing, or we can try to connect to the soul energy in our own handful of dust. Oppressed peoples around the globe are hearing their inner victims and fighting for their freedom in whatever way they can.

In any revolution the greatest danger is that the oppressed become carbon copies of their oppressors. They fail to see that fighting back with the same tactics, same values, same psychic weapons, can change nothing. Sudden decisions to draw the line and shout "enough" won't work. Men and women who have worked diligently to liberate their femininity from internal Nazi prison camps dare not

---

[9] *The Waste Land,* lines 24-30.

rest on what they have accomplished. Too soon they may unwittingly find themselves once again collaborating with the very energies that imprisoned them in the first place. Since these regressive complexes resist giving up control, they become more subtle and more dangerous. Hope withers into despair, unless creative masculinity protects the feminine values.

Tom is a prosperous businessman who has been in analysis for five years. He was beginning to despair of ever being able to solve the conflict between his soul values and the magnetic pull of his expanding business and the stock market. One night he was stunned by a long series of dreams, part of which follows:

> I was making a journey across the country, possibly carrying an item of value. I had traveled far and I was descending through a mountain range. As I looked up there appeared a small army of Vikings on horseback. They were warriors apparently bent on stopping me from reaching my destination. I sensed a battle was going to take place. I proceeded down the mountain to a wooden bridge that crossed a creek filled with rushing water.
>
> As I began to cross the bridge, I got into a battle with Jesus or Christ. We fought with our hands and bodies and while doing so I realized I had this enormous penis. It was one of the biggest in the world. As we fought, my great erection was sticking out through my clothes. On the opposite bank, some of the Vikings were watching us. Finally I was able to subdue Christ and I pushed him through the spaces of the wooden bridge into the creek below.
>
> Crossing the bridge and reaching the other side, I was greeted with a flash of light and the appearance of God. The air was still filled with battle and as we turned to face each other for the fight, he just grabbed my hands in an iron grip and looked me straight in the eye. I realized at once that there was no way I could challenge his strength. His power was absolute. So there was no battle and he allowed me to live.
>
> Then I was watching a cow give birth to a calf in a straw-filled stall in a barn. She was in a lot of pain because the birth was a difficult one. A little boy was trying to help me by pulling on a calf's leg. It wasn't responding well. I couldn't tell whether it was a stillborn calf or the one trying to come out.

Now the cow turned into a beautiful black woman who was bearing down, giving birth. I could see the new being arriving. All was well. It was a marvelous birth, leaving the woman tired and triumphant.

Tom was so moved by the dream that he could hardly voice the final scene. Tears welled in his eyes. "I could see the new being arriving," he said. "It was such a joyous birth—spiritual, beautiful. I have to listen to my soul. It is hard to believe it's my dream."

The archetype of the long and arduous journey on which the dreamer carries "an item of value" is reminiscent of fairy tales and myths. Among the obstacles Tom met this night were the Vikings, the strong, primitive warriors who personify his virile strength in a powerful male body whose physicality sometimes causes him considerable conflict.

These are the wild men, still in touch with nature, who, in fact, do not attack him. Indeed, they constellate a bridge—a transition from one side to another—over a dangerous current.

Tom is not a churchgoer and therefore associates Christ with a collective value. Interestingly, he was fighting with "Jesus *or* Christ," as if his unconscious were separating the historical Jesus, the more collective figure, from the Christ, the divine essence within. In writing down the dream Tom did not make this differentiation and so in his mind it is the collective god with whom he wrestles. Throughout the action he is aware of his own huge phallus—the immense creative and intuitive energy he puts into trying to figure out his own values in relation to the traditional moral values that constantly irritate and threaten him. The Viking energy may, in fact, be his best friend, closer than he realizes to the Christ energy he forces through the spaces of the wooden bridge.

Then he does cross the bridge—a crucial detail in dreams as in life. Having had the stamina and courage to reach the other side, he is met with "a flash of light" and God facing him for a fight. That "bolt out of the blue" is never negotiable. It is our encounter with the Self. This dreamer is wise enough to know that he has to surrender to a strength greater than his own. "I could have been destroyed," said Tom. "I have to listen." And what he has to listen to is in the lysis of the dream with its overtones of the Christmas story.

The emphasis which initially was on masculine energy turns to the feminine. The dreamer finds himself in a stable as a cow labors painfully to bring new life into the world. His own young masculine is trying to assist him. There is a possibility that a twin calf is already dead. This could be an image of new life that died before it came to birth; it could suggest that all the energy is in the calf determined to be born. Five years of concentrated work in analysis make possible the almost instantaneous shift from instinctual to spiritual energy: the cow transforms into a beautiful black woman in labor.

Energy cannot be killed. It can be repressed, but it will return later either as a destructive force or transformed into creative power. The Christ energy that was pushed into the water of the creek is now struggling to be born anew. This creative energy, symbolized earlier in the dream by the Vikings and the immense phallus, is now pushing its way through the Black Madonna energy, incarnating itself in the new-born child.

Tom was so awestruck when he awoke that he wasn't sure whether he actually held the baby or not. He wasn't sure if it was a boy or a girl, and it didn't matter. He only knew he was determined to commit himself to new interests that would nourish the new life. Faithful to his commitment, he now makes time to become acquainted with animals and to pursue his interest in the sacred rituals of the Native American people.

Dreams can be interpreted in many ways. The important thing is to experience the essence of the images so that the ego opens to new possibilities. The Black Madonna repeatedly appears in modern dreams, and her presence suggests the possibility of a feminine consciousness as yet unknown to us. Her coming presages a new understanding of light in matter, light in nature, light in our own bodies. As for what her child symbolizes, most of us can only imagine. Our dreams try to guide us with images we do not yet comprehend. They urge us to cross bridges, leap over dangerous chasms, out of the world as we have known it.

As consciousness changes, new images appear. The adolescent rebels that are being let out of jail in our dreams were put behind bars because they refused to bend the knee to a corrupt tyranny. They and the wild men who fled to the woods refused to twist themselves into a rigid status quo that kills life. While rebels and wild men are not the grooms for the emerging brides, they are certainly the groomsmen. They are still in touch with the instinctual energies that give them the courage to defy the collective chains that would maim their imaginations. If we lose touch with those rebels and wild men in our dreams we are lost because the old models are dead. We must learn the discipline of the Olympic high jumper who stands concentrated until he can see himself going over the bar at a height he never jumped before. If he can imagine that jump, his physical body will follow his subtle body. Soul and body will go over the bar together. If, however, he cannot concentrate intensely enough to imagine it, he knows before he runs that he will fail. When our imagination fails, we stand traumatized, unable to step back, unable to step ahead. We feel our terror silent as a stone.

Or we may be too afraid to feel the stone. We may have spasms in our back instead, or kidney failure, a stroke or heart attack. We may dream we are our present age huddled in a baby stroller, bent double, head down, eyes staring into the ground, incarcerated in a buggy too small for us and a heavy bar of pain across our shoulders. We may awake in a flood of tears, having dreamt our daughter is dead or dying, and as we hold the little body in our arms we know we cannot go on without her.

These are soul images. They tell us as no words can where we are. If we see ourselves rigid as stone, imprisoned in a baby buggy with a bar of responsibility breaking our backs and bending our heads to the ground, we dare not be sentimental about ourselves. We dare not fall into "Poor me." And if our soul child lies dead, we cannot get up the next morning and go on as if nothing had happened. Attention must be paid.

Breakthroughs occur—if they do—from impasse. This is true in our solitary journey and in our relationships. Moreover, and here is the divine fatality operative as human destiny—or to use our original metaphor, the wheel that comes full circle—the impasse is the constellated Self. When we find ourselves shaking uncontrollably from head to foot, we may be in the presence of the living God.

The Self confronts us in the impasse. In our utter powerlessness, and in the face of utter impossibility, god and goddess confront us as frozen divinities that contain our paralyzing horror. We see the frozen gods we can no longer worship. We thaw those frozen images with our tears, restore the stone gods to life by enacting them in our own flesh. We endow them with the blood of our own suffering. So long as we are trapped in the frozen dead gods of the past, we are abandoned. We fall into the supreme abandonment: "My God, my God, why hast thou forsaken me?"

If in that utter darkness we can give blood to the stone, tears to our grief, voice to our rage, truth to our deceit, then "the darkness shall be the light, and the stillness the dancing."[10] Detached from the dead gods of the past, we lose all and find all, for in the moment of surrender the living god and goddess enter. We move from a place of total abandonment to a place where we can never be abandoned. In that moment of knowing, soul and Self are one. No longer dependent, no longer afraid or needy, we are given the gift of love. With open heart we surrender our souls to the Beloved.

Jung calls this the path of individuation. This path strips away all facades, false expectations, dead gods. It ultimately leads into the heart of the impasse where genuine love abides. If we are ever to be free of patriarchal chains, free of the power drives that imprison us, free of our fears of abandonment, free of our rage, free of our addictions, free of our dependency on the dimes that others choose to bestow or withhold, we have to strip ourselves naked of these dead gods. Then love can come to us. The living god and goddess can enter. Then we are empowered.

*

---

10 T.S. Eliot, *Four Quartets*, "East Coker."

June 4, 1989

As I rewrite the conclusion of this lecture, tanks are crushing university students in Tiananmen Square in Beijing. Stunned, sobbing, the survivors still cry out for freedom. Soldiers are shooting blood-soaked doctors and patients in hospitals or rebelling and burning their own vehicles. Barbarism has broken loose. Students around the world are rising in outraged protest. Tom Brokaw on NBC is saying that the world at this time today is a very different world from the world as we knew it yesterday. And now he announces that Ruhollah Khomeini, the religious tyrant who ruled with his own acknowledged hate and revenge, is dead. Impassioned crowds mourn his death as he lies in an elevated glass coffin in the center of Teheran. Even now the rebel faction is making ready its revolt. Now we hear that the first vote in Poland in forty-five years has given Solidarity unprecedented strength in the Polish government. Now the worst train wreck in Russian history has claimed eight hundred lives and Mikhail Gorbachev, whose vision is so unlike the dictators before him, is at the site to bring his personal compassion.

The world as it has been is crumbling. We in our comfortable nests are too often deaf to our own soul and do not realize that the dictators out there are being mirrored by the dictators in our own dreams. And so we sleep in feathery chains. We have the freedom to be free, but, cowards that we are, we are afraid to fly. Instead of soaring out of our prisons, we gobble alcohol or drugs or whatever poison suits our particular paralysis. We rape our souls. We kill our imaginations. Then we opt out, "There's nothing I can do about it." But if we trust our frail masculine rebel energy to stand up for our soul values, we *can* do something about it. We can contact the inner images that will show us what to do and where the future lies.

Patriarchy is self-destructing. Events of the past few days make it clear that the old dictators are being seen for what they are. Surely our responsibility living in a "free" country is to focus on the new life that is being born. NEW LIFE—not the old life of abused becoming abusers, tyrannized becoming tyrants. If power replaces power, our planet cannot survive.

What is our new global village going to look like? Each of us is responsible to the new images being born in our own unconscious, images that will give us the courage to leap into the darkness of the unknown. To dare that leap, we must be empowered by love rather than driven by power.

I know now what "Lover, can you spare a dime?" was about. No more dimes! No more weeping for old Michael or yearning for young Luke. Luke, the son, broke the covenant he once made with his father over the cornerstone of the sheepfold. I, my father's daughter, broke the covenant I unconsciously made with him over the pulpit (though I still acknowledge the gifts he gave me for my ongoing life). Each of us has an outworn father and an outworn mother. Each of us has our own covenant made, consciously or unconsciously, over our own cornerstone. Our task is to release the new spirit from the old stone, however painful that may be. Then and only then can we say, "I am alive. I will be free."

Bedroom Thoughts

He wants to make love, then talk. I want to talk, then make love.

I make sex carry everything. I keep thinking, "If only I had a sexual partner, all would be well." That's the wrong attitude. I know that projecting everything onto the sexual act brought on hysterical outbursts in the past.

When you take the penis, you take the man who comes with it.

I don't want to live with a brother or a son. I get furious. I think, "Take me as I am." But then I look at my body and think, "Maternal, plump body." I suppose his body thinks so too. It does not desire me.

I think he feels undermined when his words don't give me support, courage, insight. He feels powerless. He becomes impotent. He thinks I am putting him down when I'm just telling him my truth.

During intercourse I make up my shopping list. In my sexual life, I have rarely had the experience of turning off my head. I wish I could install a switch.

I am very good in the role of victim. Instinctively, I have known all along that my husband was unfaithful. I have been sleeping the deep sleep of denial and avoidance. I choose to be a depressed, non-coping, sick person in a death marriage of my own creation.

Why can't I tell him straight? Why can't I be honest in the most intimate issues? Why do I have orgasm with another man and never with my husband?

I think I've accepted the necessity of being tamed, which for me is giving wildness form.

The fire in my solar plexus! Excruciating! It's a monument to the past that I pray beside every night. The last bastion of Christian morality—that's me—beauty, truth, light.

Just when the sun came to noon, total eclipse. Words must be spoken, but there is nobody to speak. NO BODY. Where will I go? Down what street that does not smell of dead lilacs? He is gone. Three words only. I open my mouth and out comes an animal howl.

Unrealized consciousness becomes a burning fire.
—Marie-Louise von Franz, *Shadow and Evil in Fairytales.*

Learning must break the patterns of stonelike repeatability. This pattern can only be broken if it is originated through the complementarity principle of choice. Our brains are split into complementarity boxes so that evolution has a chance to succeed in its plan to make all matter conscious.

—Fred Alan Wolf, *Star Wave.*

How is woman to rediscover her Femininity?
How is man to realize the values of the heart
without losing the bright sword of his spirit?
Only the images by which we live can bring
transformation. The future hangs on this
quest for the heart of love by both sexes.

—Helen Luke.

For groups as well as for individuals, life itself means to separate and to be reunited, to change form and condition, to die and to be reborn. It is to act and to cease, to wait and rest, and then to begin acting again but in a different way. And there are always new thresholds to cross: the thresholds of summer and winter, of a season or a year, of a month or a night; the thresholds of birth, adolescence, maturity and old age; the thresholds of death and that of the afterlife—for those who believe in it. Therefore to cross the threshold is to unite self with a new world.

—Arnold van Gennep, *The Rites of Passage.*

5

Cripples, Rebels and Criminals

Few of us can envision a genuine androgyne and few of us want to be androgynous. Like many potent words, androgyne has lost its true meaning. Nowadays, it suggests unisex, a mushing together of undifferentiated masculine and feminine energies so weak in themselves that they cling together to survive.

A genuine androgyne, psychologically speaking, is an archetypal image in which the conscious differentiation of masculine and feminine energies is always being finely tuned. It is like a Stradivarius violin or cello, wrought to reverberate with the strength and delicacy of both energies in exquisite balance.

Ann, an analysand of mine, is an accomplished cellist. She arrived one day looking haggard and distraught.

"Too much spirit," she said with a grin.

I didn't quite understand what she meant. Impatient with my musing silence, she suddenly sat forward in her chair, opened her legs and began playing an imaginary cello. Her long, powerful fingers vibrated on the imaginary finger-board and her fine-boned arm danced fiercely with the imaginary bow. She glanced up from her playing, fire radiating from her eyes.

"Can you imagine," she asked, "what it's like to have Wagner coming through your vagina, up through your body, into your heart, into your head and into your very soul, night after night?"

Of course, I'd never thought about Wagner with those progressions. Nor had I seen Ann play. But looking at her transformed instrument—body and cello as one, enraptured delicacy and strength, right there in front of me—I had some idea.

"Can you imagine," she said, still playing, "how strong your body has to be to receive the archetypal power that pours through whether you're ready or not—wave after wave of sheer energy?"

131

I could imagine! I could imagine too why her dreams were telling her to open up the new rooms in her house, rooms with large windows to let in the light. She was intensifying her body/soul work in order to do that. The artistic balance which she had practiced with her cello since childhood was now being incorporated into her life in a new way. Ann realized that before that new balance could take place, she needed to relate to the handicapped male energies appearing in her dreams.

In this chapter, we will concentrate on a few images of ravaged masculinity as it appears in women's dreams—masculinity that has been so bludgeoned by patriarchy that we can only imagine what creative masculinity is. We are stumbling along with few role models. We are programmed with old questions, old answers. Like Perceval, the most naive and mother-bound knight of the Round Table, we do not know the right question to ask. Like Perceval too, we have to come back to the consciousness of our own suffering. To shut off the pain is to shut off the soul. Only when we can consciously articulate the question which the unconscious is forever formulating can the answer come. The answer is in asking the question. In these last three chapters, new questions will emerge and, with them, glimmerings of a new relationship between masculinity and femininity in the inner marriage and, therefore, in outer relationships.

In our power-oriented society, many women complain that they cannot find a man strong enough to support and enhance their femininity. Their courtly lover fluctuates between worship and rage, both archetypal, missing the personal target. He turns out to be homosexual, bisexual, alcoholic, a wife-beater or a mere infant still clinging to his mother's breast.

Whatever he turns out to be, of one thing we can be certain—the woman confronts her own ravaged masculinity personified in her partner. If she leaves him, as many women do, her own damaged masculinity will seek out and find his double. Unconscious women can repeat this pattern forever. The ravaged masculine belongs not only to the man but to the woman that seeks him out as her necessary and inevitable partner.

Equally the wounded feminine in the man will find, as if directed by destiny itself, the castrating woman who was his mother. If he decides to leave his witchy wife, as many men do, it will be to search for her again, because, until he works on his own inner femininity, for all his protests, he remains a boy, bound to, perhaps possessed by, the negative animus of his mother.

The terrible truth is that the sexes are bound less by biology than by neurosis. As within, so without. The ravaged groom is in the man and in the woman. Men as much as women have been the victims of a patriarchy in which the differences between the sexes have been exaggerated to the point of rendering them antithetical, one inferior or superior to the other. The result has been a shared tragedy in which it would be futile to decide which of the two has suffered the more.

Crucial to this discussion is clarification of the word *power.* So long as we are not in contact with our own potential, we are vulnerable to being controlled by others. If we do not know ourselves, we cannot stand to our own truth and are, therefore, in constant danger of invasion by others, male and female. Those who have been raised by parents whose only source of potency is power over their children will use that same power over their own children. Fearful of what the neighbors will think, fearful of failing to meet conventional standards, fearful of anything new, they are terrified of their child's creativity. They cannot love the child as it is. They cannot be the mirror in which the child sees itself. Their concern is simply to force the child, whether gently or cruelly, to do their will. As a result, the child's feminine beingness cannot trust. Without trust, the masculine thrust to go out into life, to move with the flow of new possibilities, to penetrate with love into new relationships, is thwarted. The child is trapped in fear and boredom, consciously or unconsciously hating the power that has taken away its potency, at the same time leaving it crippled, dependent on that power. For Jung, power was the opposite of love. "Where love reigns," he wrote, "there is no will to power; and where the will to power is paramount, love is lacking."[1]

---

[1] *Two Essays on Analytical Psychology,* CW 7, par. 78.

How does the lack of phallic penetration manifest in women's dreams? As the young feminine matures in the individuation process, a woman relates to her sexual shadow and soul essence. She gradually moves into consciousness, confident in her own matter and her own feeling values. Naturally she looks for a masculine partner. Suddenly, dreams may be irretrievable. "I try hard," women say, "but I am so far down I cannot bring the dreams up when I awake." This can happen when the unconscious introduces new imagery so foreign that consciousness cannot hold onto it. One captures only a few fragments each night, until the dream sequence begins again. The new sequence may make clear that the virgin has been brutally raped in the unconscious, that a miscarriage has taken place, that a whole country with a sick king has been laid waste, or that a beloved man has been killed by a demon.

In real life the blossoming feminine has not been protected by a loving masculinity. The pressure of work, the fear of not measuring up or the terror of leaping into the unknown has taken over; the sword of discretion, which insures time and energy every day for loving inner growth, is simply not there. Then the capacity to move out into the world, empowered with one's own inner reality, fails. Terror of life, terror of going beyond where the parents went, guilt and rage castrate what would be the natural phallic thrust.

Unknown male figures begin to appear in dreams. These are the masculine energies, the forgotten fugitives, so repressed and so damaged that they are incomprehensible to the consciousness of the dreamer. Here is the brutal ape-man or the hired killer or the suave mafia grandfather. Here is the quadriplegic, helpless young man. Here too the fierce, natural, wild man. A man dreams that his father killed an infant boy; thus he must find within himself his own masculinity without depending on the model of his father. A woman dreams that her grandmother killed her mother's twin brother. The mother in reality had no twin brother. Symbolically, then, the dream suggests that the grandmother destroyed her daughter's creative masculinity, leaving her granddaughter with no model of how masculinity manifests in a woman. The dreamer's adolescent son may appear as a robber holding hostages at gunpoint or a rock star in black leather wildly throwing knives into the air. The "light child," incapable of recognizing its mother, may appear filthy and abandoned in a hostel for delinquent children.

Among the many, the rebel appears in countless variations. Sometimes, he is a criminal. A man dreams, for example, of a handsome blond youth with ruthlessly cold eyes staring him down. A woman dreams of a young street urchin wielding a knife, killing without conscience. Another dreams of standing at the gate of a high-rise jail. An adolescent boy in coveralls, cigarette dangling from his lips, arrogantly shrugs his shoulders as he passes by. He has just been released from the top floor of the prison. Fierce, defiant, arrogant as that outlaw may be, his is the energy that will not bow down to outdated laws and outworn conventions. Ranging free and uncivilized beyond or on the fringe of society, he can manifest in the dreamer's life in the form of uncouth manners, rampant defiance, unquenchable energy. His energy, however, is not mature. One dreamer offered an unsolicited statement to a pair of punk rockers. "Adapters/pleasers and rebels are the same," she told them. "They are both dependent upon another person. You always have to have someone to react to or you are lost."

Not only in dreams is this young rebel present. Take a walk down any strip in any city, any night, and you will see bold young punkers, their hair plastered down or plastered up in a mohawk crown, being anything but what their parents want them to be. Think of the men you know whose shadow side delights in beating the bureaucracy or beating the wife, or stories of people who do. Think of the women you know who have fallen in love with a criminal or someone on the fringe of society.

So long as he remains outside consciousness the rebel is the natural partner of the feminine shadow. Where a woman has adapted in childhood to please her parents, her rebel may appear in female form. In life, her false ego has striven to attain a highly respected position in the community. Suddenly, her shadow rebel may do something outrageous that scuttles her chances to achieve what she believed was her coveted goal. We see the outcome of this kind of polarization in the television evangelists who are undermining their own power, or in the dramatic demise of Gary Hart.

Liza, whose dream follows, was living a very productive life. Nevertheless, her well-mannered upbringing would not allow her to speak and act out of her genuine energy.

> I am sitting near the front on the right hand side of a bus which is very crowded. There is a young, tough, punk teenage girl standing in the aisle near me. She asks about the diamond ring that I am wearing on the baby finger of my left hand. I am suspicious of her motives. As she leaves the bus, she calls out something about the ring. I look down at my hand and the ring is not there. I jump up trying to get off the bus to get the ring from her but before I can get off, I look again and the ring *is* on my finger. I look out the window and our eyes meet—her gaze is so direct, honest and straight!

If we think of the bus as the collective society which Liza is trying to please, we understand why this young punk is suddenly there. She is the "direct, honest and straight" truth in herself, which Liza has to face. Even the dream ego's attempt to get off the bus puts the ring back on her finger. Liza's active imagination clarifies the dynamics. It is given here just as she wrote it, lacking some capitals.

> *Liza:* ring, I value you and do not want to lose you. you are important to me.
> *Ring:* you cannot lose me for I belong to you. I represent your inner value and riches. I am intrinsically yours.

Liza then spoke with the punk girl.

> *Liza:* I do not trust you. I am suspicious of your desires toward my ring.
> *Punk:* I know that. I am admiring your ring, I am attracted to it and yes, I want it but I could not take your ring from you.
> *Liza:* your integrity is unexpected somehow. you do not appear as you really are.
> *Punk:* I know this too. my appearance can be misleading and deceiving. I am a test for you—to look deeper and see my essential nature.

Liza: your look, as I discover my ring on my finger, is so direct and straight.
Punk: another challenge to you!

Many people, like Liza, discover in analysis that their true ego was sucked into their shadow at a very early age. Their real energy, fun and creativity were buried in the unconscious.

The image of the masculine rebel is so prevalent, so potent and so totally repressed that we need to stop running and turn around to look him straight in the eye. Having taught adolescents for many years, I know only too well the brilliant youth, son of a brilliant father, who sits defiantly in his seat refusing to pass his examinations because he won't please his old man. Moreover, he despises his classmates, calling them phonies who sold out long ago to please parents and teachers, phonies who read Salinger's *Catcher in the Rye* like a Bible, adore Holden Caulfield, and yet are afraid to say, "Fuck off."

When this figure began to appear in dreams in my office, I asked myself, "Who put him in jail? Why? When?" Then several incidents happened. A young woman who had always been most cooperative brought in a picture of a child she had painted. She was hesitant, defensive, reluctant to look at me. When she finally pushed the picture forward, I was astonished at the six-year-old energy so vibrant on the page. I looked at it for some minutes.

The woman muttered, "She has blue hair."

"Yes," I said, "wild blue hair."

She eyed me, then in a child's voice she said, "My teacher told me, 'Children don't have blue hair.' I never painted again. Now I've decided I'll paint what I want."

She was reconnecting with the rebel energy that had been driven into her unconscious by a teacher who was clearly no admirer of Matisse. Silently but unmistakably, she was saying, "I don't care whether you like my picture or not. I'll paint what I like."

This resonated so poignantly with my own experience that I instantly knew when my own inner boy was put in jail. Grade One, to be exact. He could hardly wait to go to school, to play with other children, to read wonderful books. He loved to paint on newspaper because art paper was too small. His brilliant blues and reds and yellows faded into pale washes when I went to school because the teacher did not like my messy color schemes, and kept me in after four "to paint properly." When I asked her what color *she* liked, she said, "Green." I carefully ruled margins and with infinite care painted a variegated green scene for her—two green hills, a green sky, and a green sailboat on a green sea. At 5:30, exhausted by my effort, I proudly presented her with a picture I was sure would delight her. She screamed at me that the sky was not green, that I was a defiant, stubborn child and then she tore my picture in pieces.

That was one episode in a series that left me convinced, by the end of my sixth September, that school was not for me. Since I had to go, I decided to sleep there and go home well rested to read. I learned to keep my hands tucked under my head on the desk so the teacher could not strike them with her pointer. The expectant, jubilant energy with which I had gone out into the world was caged within one month. That teacher's castrated masculinity feared and hated my creative fire and determined to destroy it.

Alice Miller, author of *For Your Own Good,* has much to say about German children raised by power-driven, psychopathic adults who believe in iron-willed pedagogy. I suggest that the young man many of us are seeking in our dreams was driven into psychic prison by more subtle, but no less destructive, psychological torture. So long as parents and/or teachers are acting out of power, whether consciously or, more disastrously, unconsciously, the creative masculinity of the child is without the seed bed of love in which it can mature without fear.

The following dream illustrates the beauty and the tenacity of the abandoned masculine.

An unknown man tells me to go to the woodshed of my childhood home to find a black box. I find the box. It has a hole in one end. I cautiously put my hand in the hole and feel the quivering warm body of my pet bird. I begin to cry because I have forgotten him and left him alone to die. I am afraid of what I may see when I take him from the box but I cradle him in my hand and lift him out. As my tears fall over his little body, barely more than bones, he transforms into a tiny baby boy. "I only wanted to sing my song," he says. "It was the translation of every tune I ever knew."

I woke up sobbing, "Don't let him die. Dear God, don't let him die."

Without love, fear of life splits our throats. We cannot sing our own song. Some of us cannot even remember we ever had a song to sing. Without love for ourselves and for each other as we are, we are abandoned, left alone to die.

Eros is a masculine god that contains the receptive love of the true feminine. Love that emanates from the Self, from the Buddha or the Christ within, like the love that shines through Mother Teresa, has the potency to penetrate to the life that is yearning to be lived, transforming ugliness into beauty, illness into health, despair into hope.

Mother Teresa's uniqueness is rooted in the inner marriage of the receptive soul and the penetrating spirit. Anyone who has watched the documentary on her work can never forget the helpless, gyrating arms, legs and head of a sick child writhing in his bed. When one of her sisters took him in her arms and firmly rubbed his chest, never taking her eyes from his, the flailing body became quiet and like golden sunlight bursting through cloud, a radiant smile suffused his anguished face. He looked into her eyes. He was Home.

The little boy in the above dream is not Home and without him the dreamer is distraught. Often either soul or spirit appears metaphorically as a bird, especially a beloved pet the dreamer cherished as a child. Sometimes the bird is forsaken in the attic, sometimes, as in this dream, in a shed. Overcome with grief and guilt, this dreamer weeps bitterly. As her tears fall over the little living skeleton, the bird transforms into a tiny boy, lost long ago. Sentimental tears would not accomplish this transformation. These are tears of love that is willing to work to bring new life to the buried spirit.

The creative masculine that yearns to sing is a repetitive motif in contemporary dreams and the cause of his silence is a repetitive cause. Here the cause is a black box, a feminine image—the dark tomb in which the mother-bound masculine is incarcerated. The dark womb can also give birth to the triumphant young masculine whose song translates the transitory into the eternal, the eternal into the transitory.

The image of the black box is like an image used by William Blake in *The Marriage of Heaven and Hell.* He laments the loss of visionary power in the writing of Swedenborg whose vision was deadened by its subjugation to cold logic. Blake compares these writings to Christ's linen garments carefully folded up in the empty tomb. He then goes on to suggest that his own writing is the resurrected body that has no use for these outworn garments which are the dead letter of the law as contrasted to the living spirit. William Blake is indeed a master at translating the transitory into the eternal, the eternal into the transitory.

> A Robin Red breast in a cage
> Puts all Heaven in a rage.[2]

> A Skylark wounded in the wing,
> A Cherubim does cease to sing.[3]

Just how difficult it is for this crippled inner boy to mature is apparent in the lives of many people who are trying to befriend him. Typically, those with an immature masculine side are terrorized by anyone who has power over them. They are always on the alert for others acting out of power, and in fact see it where it doesn't exist. Whether the power coming at them is real or whether they project it, they will flee or fight or drug themselves into unconsciousness with alcohol or some other soporific. Love can crack this armor, leaving the immature masculine vulnerable. Love brings individuals into contact with their own human warmth, either overwhelming them with fear of being weakened, or stimulating transformation. Jimmy Boyle, once known as Scotland's most violent man, fought authority like a savage through years of solitary confinement in prison. When

---

2 "Auguries of Innocence," lines 5-6.
3 Ibid., lines 15-16.

his mother arrived with his children, "It opened up the parts I was trying to kill," he writes, "the cherished parts of me that made me feel human in an inhuman situation."[4]

A man with crippled masculinity remains tied to his mother. He may live his life trying to please his partner, but the price is the destruction of his own feelings and ultimately his own life. If he contacts his genuine responses and dares to act from them, violence often erupts in the relationship. Similarly, a woman's crippled masculinity may chain her to her father-husband. She may suddenly burst into rage when she realizes her own life has been a prison to which her partner (as she imagines him) holds the key. The man may be a good hook for her projection, but she needs to deal with the infantile tyrant in herself.

In a man, the infantile masculine may erupt when his partner begins to express her authentic truth. He feels attacked. He is so shocked he cannot hear her. He feels as if he is living with someone he never knew. He hopes she'll come back to herself, that she'll stop being so difficult. He may accuse her of duplicity, of having pretended to be someone she is not. And he is right if she has never attempted to integrate her shadow. If he is still projecting his idealized anima onto her, he will simply not believe his ears. *His* woman does not talk like that. And he is not being perverse; he is genuinely unconscious; his infant boy is losing mother.

In an effort to hold onto what he experiences as his ground of being, increasingly he may identify with the disappearing mother as his wife gains consciousness. He may begin to do the motherly tasks in the household, all the time burning with resentment that manifests in rage or impotence, or jibes and gestures designed to make his wife feel guilty for abandoning him and the children.

Likewise, when the woman does not have a strong Hades to ravish her maiden Kore out of Mother Demeter, her masculinity is mother-bound. She will fear the aggression in her own unconscious rebel and, therefore, aggression in others. Her creative masculinity is

---

[4] *A Sense of Freedom,* p. 180.

not strong enough to protect her young feminine and she will back away from defending her own truth. She hides what strength she has in order to make her threatened partner feel stronger. She is lying to herself and projecting weakness onto her man in order to keep things "running smoothly." Here's how one woman described it:

> Jeff serves me. I hate it, but I don't say anything. My sins are sins of omission. I thought that not lying was being honest. Not so! I know he will reject what I say so I don't say it. The silence is the lie. He can project whatever he wants. He still doesn't know who he's married to. I feel barbed wire around my heart. He brings me a coke. I don't want it. He brings himself a sandwich. I'm angry. He goes to bring me a sandwich. Thirty minutes later he brings me a salad. I don't want it but I don't say, "Jeff, I do not want you to serve me. I want to eat with you. I want to share." So I don't express either my anger or my truth.

Of this couple, we may well ask, "Who is the betrayer and who the betrayed?" Neither is facing the rage in the rebel, within or without. Both despise their complaisant masks and compliance with the collective. And so the caged rebel's rage fumes. If his aggression can be channeled in the right direction, he has the energy to pull the feminine out of the cave of the collective mother. The dark cave, however, is resistant to light, and without immense courage and cunning the rebel remains repressed.

In the failure to confront the rage, the archetypal energies unconsciously governing the relationship are not tapped. Because both partners can sense the dangerous depths of a bottomless abyss, they are determined at any cost to avoid them, although they may realize that avoidance is no solution. They are conscious of running on treadmills in opposite directions so that, for all their expenditure of energy, rather than moving toward or away from each other, they are not moving at all. They are paralyzed because consciousness is cut off from the numinous depths in the unconscious.

When Christianity became frozen in a series of dogmas that merely arrested the deeper dynamics of the soul, several heretical movements found their way into our culture despite the attempts of the church to eradicate them. The greatest of these, arising from the intercourse between Christianity and Islam during the Crusades (eleventh to thirteenth century), was the cult of courtly love in which the feminine, taking precedence over the masculine, became an object of devotion. The knight or courtly lover was in service to his lady. It was during this period that the Grail legend in its earliest form fired the imaginations of medieval poets. They saw in the Grail a feminine vessel that signified *"the whole psychic man* (not his ego) *as a realization of divinity reaching right down into matter."*[5] The shining vessel was an image of the soul in which life was lived in both its darkness and light. Thus the shadow side of Christianity resurfaced. Perceval, the knight most closely connected to the Earth Mother, was the one singled out to bring to consciousness the question: "Whom does the Grail serve?"

With the resurgence of the feminine in our culture, Perceval is the archetypal image of the young masculine who, however shadowy, slips into our dreams. The great danger, now as then, is that the young man who appears in our dreams with a bleeding penis or no penis at all, will become the dead son lying on the lap of his grieving, triumphant mother—the image of so many Pietas. The cult of the Virgin Mary which gained ascendancy in the later days of courtly love is still influencing contemporary men and women. They tend to idealize the perfect, pure mother on her pedestal and split her off from their Mary Magdalene sexuality. Thus they love one partner and lust after another. Where perfection is worshiped in consciousness, imperfection is magnetic in the unconscious. Splitting light from dark denies human wholeness, a denial that can lead to son sacrifices and dragon slaying.

We are no longer living in the Middle Ages (although many dreams are set in medieval castles). Our Perceval dare not regress into unconscious nature, dare not regress to archetypal images that, however obsolete, are yet capable of autonomous cruelty. If he goes

---

[5] Emma Jung and Marie-Louise von Franz, *The Grail Legend,* p. 159 (italics in original).

to sleep, or falls into addictions, he may live the dream and fail to wake up to what he is doing.

We need to move beyond the conflict inherent in the cult of the Virgin Mary. In worshiping idealized perfection, her devotees rejected their human limitations. Their shadows fell into the unconscious and subsequently these shadows were massacred as witches. This is essentially what is happening in many relationships today. The woman is trying to be her imperfect, honest self. The man is terrified, becomes the Spanish Inquisitor and sentences his imperfect beauty to the flames. His beauty may not be blameless. In spite of her developing consciousness, she may still play sweet Earth Mother to her big strong wild man. While she plays that coy role, he may see what he has lived with for years: her terror of criticism, lack of faith in her own decisions, the inability to take action. In a crisis, then, he does what he has always done—he protects and takes control.

He assumes that when she asks for his opinion, she is really asking him to tell her what to do. She listens; he believes he is in command. The old model! Then she goes away, makes her own decision and acts on it. He feels duped. The bumbling little girl/mother has transformed into what he sees as a defiant, mocking Medusa. Now he is complexed. He may hurl invective at her. He may be more shrewd and try to undermine what she is attempting to do for herself, labeling her initiative as desire for power. She turns the man into a sadist. In such a scenario, who is sadistic? Who is masochistic? Who is the betrayer? Who is the betrayed?

Such a situation once appeared in a dream where the dreamer, in a premature dash for freedom, ran into the street, straight into the arms of a demonic bully who, with the help of his henchmen, stuck a needle into her arm. With mad, mocking laughter, he snarled, "In six weeks you'll have rabies." During the six weeks that followed, she fought to maintain her new standpoint, but the negative animus voices within snuffed out her ego strength and she became ill.

As such a woman struggles to establish her own ground, she may make a decision, but without a model for decisive action she is apt to crumble into the little girl role. Her sadistic inner voices tell her she has a slave mentality. "You were born in a cage. You're afraid to fly out when the door is open. You will die in a cage. You're not strong enough to leap into liberty." The solo voice she hears from her mate is fully orchestrated in the chorus of criminal voices that brutalize her from her own unconscious.

Falling into this depth of unconsciousness can lead to the panic which results in the archaic behavior of dragon slaying. It allows the shining Grail to pass by unnoticed. Perceval does not know there is a question, let alone have the courage to ask it. What has passed like a dream before him is the world of the collective unconscious in which he is so immersed he does not know he is there. He lacks the consciousness to interrogate what he is in, an interrogation essential to the healing process the dreamlike procession potentially contains. Perceval in the castle of the wounded Fisher King is in thrall to the mother, whose presence we must keep in mind as we turn to the exploration of another dream.

Kate is a woman struggling to break free of the negative father, whose rage is closely identified with the archetypal figure of Kali, the dark, destructive mother whose place of worship is quite often the kitchen, where mysterious ritual acts are sometimes performed. The real action between the inner masculine in women and the masculinity of men takes place at the archetypal level. In order to understand this, we need to examine how the dream reflects what is going on in the actual relationship. Since a woman's masculinity is shaped by her early bonding or lack of bonding with her father, let us begin there.

Kate's father loved poetry, but was unable to channel or discipline his own creative potential. He squandered it in alcohol, experiencing at the onset of drunkenness an explosion of power that soon dissipated into incoherence, leaving behind the ruins of a pleasure dome vibrating with the sound of shattering glass against a kitchen wall, and his own voice raging. The spectacle of ruin that confronted him, not only with the wanton dissipation of his powers but with the fragments of an ideal world which his soul longed to inhabit, filled him with even greater rage. This he directed against his wife and children as if they were the destroyers of the paradise for which he yearned. The devastation of his drunkenness was projected onto his family; the punishing discipline which his conscience created in himself was displaced onto them. When he wasn't drinking he was silent, and when he drank his bouts of rage became worse. Finally Kate herself, as a young teenager, initiated the court action that forced him from the house forever. The determined will, or ego strength, that Kate required to do this she learned from her mother. This same willfulness contributed to her professional success, despite the conditions to which she was initially subjected.

Along with her mother's single-mindedness and determination, Kate inherited her father's creative drive. While she did not consciously think of her own development as an attempt to redeem her father, that need was a genuine catalyst in propelling her toward integration. Crucial to the acceptance of herself—the ability to embrace and rejoice in her own abilities so that she could put them to use in her own life and in the lives of others—was her release from the shadow of her father, the undisciplined alcoholic who had deserted his family long before he was forced out of it. As long as her own responsible life was haunted by this dark figure, all her efforts were continually undermined despite her will and determination.

One of Kate's greatest fears, however, was that in exorcising her father's shadow as it lived in her, she might lose the creativity which she so much loved and admired in him. This unconscious fear of losing her creativity revealed itself in Kate's inability to claim it as her own. Where the expression of one's parents' creativity is associated with painful conditions, to embrace a creative life oneself is simultaneously to reexperience punishing pain. She therefore had to keep her distance from her own creative energies. Thus she could not fully live the destiny that was hers as her father's daughter, both in terms of her creativity and in the kind of man with whom she could be involved.

Kate's highly ambivalent attitude toward her father, which became an equally ambivalent attitude toward her own inner masculine, defined her relationship to men. Afraid to relate at all to highly creative men, she found herself involved with less creative ones who felt safe to her, but who never managed to hold her interest for long. She found a temporary resolution to this impasse in working with young people whose creativity was unfolding. She could nurture them in a way that would avoid the kind of collapse she witnessed in her father. In working with these young people her own immense energies were shaping the father she longed for and never had.

With adult men, however, it was a different matter. The damage, as it were, was already done. Relationships for her were haunted by overpowering obstacles; somehow, the men to whom she was attracted always turned out to be weaker than she was. As much out of pity as out of love, she entered relationships with them—relationships which were doomed from the start because she recognized that her pity was no more than a holding action, temporarily delaying an inevitable split. What she had not worked through with her father she could not work through with men to whom she was erotically attracted. Her wounded inner masculine had imposed intolerable restrictions on her development, restrictions she was determined to overcome through personal analysis. She trusted that in bringing the light of consciousness to the faulty dynamics revealed in her dreams, she would be able to change those dynamics in her daily relationships.

In the following dream, the shadow father kills yet another of her lovers in a theatrical performance—a pantomime—that shows the degree to which the drama is enacting a struggle she is still unable to fully accept as her own. Kate was in a relationship she wanted to continue. At the time of the dream, she and her lover (James) had broken up, but had decided to try once more. The dream makes clear the inner dynamics in Kate that were undermining the relationship. Unques-tionably, her lover's difficulties dovetailed with hers, but Kate's immediate task was to take responsibility for herself.

In my house, suddenly the front door opens and in walk three men and two dogs. My father opens the way, then a stranger and a shadowy man. My mother leaves. I am scared and try to get out of the way, but one man keeps making sexual lurches at me. He lays out beautiful linens for sale.

I am getting ready to leave when I see James trapped into looking at some linens and making arrangements to buy me a chartreuse and brown blouse and camisole. James pays the man. This man frightens me. He says to me, "What about getting him a beautiful shaman lamb?" I look at these lambs—great big stuffed theater toys. James is going upstairs and this man starts approaching me again and James comes down and puts himself between the man and me, shielding me. The man and James start fighting—holds and kneeing each other. James seems to be getting the better of him and bends his hand back. The man goes limp and looks as if he's finished. I nod to James, "Enough," so he won't go too far.

Then I see the man's hands are at James' eyes and he is holding a piece of broken glass in his hand. I am scared he'll gouge out James' eyes. I take the glass away and go to the kitchen to bury it in the garbage.

I hear something at the stairs and come back. The man is standing there passive and James is looking dead, sprawled on the stairs. His body is painted with white theater paint, his hair dyed red. His head is blood soaked, his body stained with blood. I scream, "O my God, O my God!" and wake up horrified.

I would like to work with this dream in some depth because it carries so many overtones for so many contemporary men and women. For the sake of clarity, let us look at it in terms of a classical dramatic structure, through the four parts of a Greek drama: 1) the introduction establishes the plot, setting, characters; 2) the rising action sets up the conflicting energy patterns; 3) the climax brings about the confrontation and turns the action; 4) the lysis, the finale, points the direction in which the energy wants to go.

The setting is Kate's home. The setting of a dream is always important because it clarifies the point in the dreamer's earlier life with which the recent situation is resonating. If, for example, this dream were set in her adolescent home, then we would try to discover whether the present difficulties were echoing difficulties in her teens. In other words, is the energy blocked in the complexes in the same way as it was then? Is there a repetitive pattern operating? Since this

dream takes place in her present home, it suggests that this is a picture of the here and how, undoubtedly influenced by the past, but
dealing with dynamics at a depth unplumbed before.

Suddenly the front door opens and the characters arrive: three men
and two dogs. The number three often suggests that something having to do with masculinity is about to move into consciousness.
Since it is coming through the front door, the dreamer is going to
face it directly. Her alcoholic father, whose anger in herself she constantly tries to discipline and civilize, is opening the way. He is followed by his shadow, whom she does not know, and another unknown masculine part of herself. The three are accompanied by their
instincts. Dogs had scarcely appeared in Kate's dreams before, but in
subsequent dreams they appeared often as carriers of physical energy. When the psyche was unable to tolerate the suffering of unlived
sexuality, for example, wounded and badly crippled dogs appeared.
Through them, a gradual integration of psyche and body took place.
Over time the dogs healed, and eventually they became psychopomps
guiding her in her spiritual task.

One character, the mother, instantly leaves. This is a crucial detail
because so long as the negative mother complex is present, the
young feminine, whose standpoint in real life Kate is trying to establish, is not free to act from her own being in relation to the new, unknown masculine. In particular, the mother's departure reflects a
shift in Kate away from will power as her *modus operandi*. Although
it was useful in evicting her father from the family house, it now
serves as a block between her and the masculine, both inner and
outer. At the same time, however, the positive side of the mother
complex also leaves, taking with it whatever grounding in her feminine body the dreamer has. Thus she is bereft of the instinctual an-
tennae which would warn her of the real danger she is in.

Moreover, without the mother complex (which Kate had been
working on for four years) the energy in the father complex will
move in a different way. In Kate's psychology, her father was a
mother-bound man, paralyzed by the presence of that complex.
Although he was in the service of the mother, he would not be en-

slaved by her. His shadow hated women although it clung to them. Thus his feeling values could not be trusted; they were inconsistent, especially with women. Without the omnipresent mother complex, very new dynamics will develop.

The father complex creates further problems for the feminine by splitting the masculine: James, her lover, and the shadow-killer are in a love/hate relationship. James has impaired feelings, the killer has none. In spite of the shadow-killer making sexual lurches at Kate, James is seduced by the magician merchant's beautiful linens and gives him money (energy) for an earthy, springlike blouse and an even more intimate next-to-the-skin camisole for Kate. Her sensitivities are alert to her intuitive fear but she weakens; her curiosity lures her into looking at the "shaman lamb," however big, stuffed and theatrical it may be.

The magician is an ambiguous figure. He is the darkness that could go into even deeper darkness; he is also the part that is trying to connect to Kate and James and he does have the "shaman's lamb." Associating with the lamb, Kate said the big stuffed toy was "the cuddliness" she wanted in a relationship. It was a substitute for the early cuddling she never had as a child. But why is it a "shaman's" lamb?

With her dream lover hooked on the beautiful linens, and herself hooked on sentimentality, the wedge moves deeper into the split that will end in unconsciousness. James starts upstairs (into the head). Immediately the instinctual, uncivilized masculine lurches again. James is still strong enough to stand between the feminine and the untrustworthy masculine. The fight between the lover-father and lover-father-killer begins like a wrestling match, with overtones of homosexuality in the holding and kneeing. James takes control by bending back the shadow's hold on reality, his hand. The naive feminine, blind to her own terror, imagines she is taking control by protecting the killer from the anger she feels in her lover-father.

Anger quickly moves into rage—cold, broken-glass rage—the rage of her father smashing empty bottles, rage that can gouge the eyes out of the lover-father and leave the whole situation in total unconsciousness. Unable to deal with the blinding rage, unable to endure the confrontation, the dream ego leaves. Momentarily the dreamer is annihilated.

Kate associated this moment with the time when she used will power to remove her drunk and raging father from the house, opting for the single-minded determination of her mother. Now, in the dream, that determination is no longer operative. Will power was merely camouflaging underlying unconsciousness. Without the ego strength to replace will power, the dream ego drops into unconsciousness, and the climax must take place off stage.

To bury the repressed rage-ridden masculine energy by putting it in the kitchen garbage is to ask for trouble. The return of the repressed, its resurrection from the garbage, only reinforces the energy of what is denied.

When the dream ego returns, the scene is distanced—a theatrical tableau. Dissociated from her feeling, she sees the lover-father-killer unmoved by what he has done, unable to tell the difference between theater and life. She sees James "looking dead," sprawled on the stairs, his humanity painted out.

"He looked like Marcel Marceau," Kate said, "a mime artist. He's an artifact, covered with blood. Even the death isn't real. It is as if a fantasy Merlin stepped in, waved his magic wand and turned everything into unreality."

But the last image of the blood-soaked head and body of her lover does pierce the dreamer's feeling. She recognizes the horror of what is happening. Her energy leaps into consciousness—she wakes up.

This dream indicates that an impasse has been reached, in that the unconscious appears unable to go beyond waking up the dreamer. In such a situation, the lysis of the dream comes in the form of a tableau or frieze. The dream separates itself from its own reality to becomes the observer of itself, suggestive of ritual, which is the solution to the impasse and the next direction indicated for Kate. Ritual is the fashioning of a container out of the very energy it transforms. Ritual holds the raw energy with discipline, but the form of the ritual can only be determined by the quality of the energy it has to work with.

The separation of the dream from its own reality is evident in the figure of Kate's lover who is "looking dead" rather than actually dead, and the killer's passive pose. His face is completely impassive, as if waiting to be brought to life. But what kind of life? If both the lover and the killer are taken out of their still-life frame to continue the action that froze while Kate was in the kitchen burying the broken glass in the garbage, what will be the form of the action? It is as if the unconscious were asking Kate this very question as she wakes up.

The answer to this question also points toward the form that the ritual action will take if it is to transform the dream energy. The ritual has to be accompanied by a depth experience of the dream material. Otherwise ritual becomes merely another holding action against the inner masculine, not a redemption of it.

Kate needs to see what would happen if the interrupted action of the dream were to move from a pantomime killing to an actual killing. What might this look like and what would be the consequences? If instead of Kate repressing the father's rage in herself (by burying the broken glass in the kitchen), the killer were to use it (in the dream) to murder her lover, then Kate's dream-ego would have sunk to the psychopathic condition of her father in his drunken rages. In beating his wife and children, he was ritually slaying them. His brutal behavior when drunk repeats itself in the pantomime murder in Kate's dream. The energy in Kate represented by the lover-father-killer in the dream is in the same psychological state as her father when drunk.

More than that, the decision of her lover to leave the relationship because he was unable to confront the difficulties, repeated for Kate the action of her father. While she found his departure initially devastating, she also recognized it was increasingly impossible for them to remain together. Just as she and her father could not confront each other, so she and her lover could not, although she felt prepared to do so. The impasse in the dream, then, mirrors the impasse in Kate's relationship. Either they face each other and work it through or they kill the relationship. In fact, the relationship ended three weeks later.

"Why do I always have to pay and pay and pay?" she cried. "I'm just lost. I feel dead when I lose my lover."

In spite of her depression, she realized she was left with the possibility of redeeming the unresolved rage.

"I see now that there is a difference between paying for and redeeming," she said.

Determined to get to the core of the problem—and following the direction pointed out in the lysis of the dream—Kate intensified her body work and reviewed her dreams. She found a progression in the degree of rage expressed in the images of Luciferean rebels or criminals. A fierce man, for example, had stood on a balcony hurling silver candlesticks onto a table of food prepared by a sisterhood of women. Later, that same figure appeared as a Satanic dark man, dressed in a white suit sitting in a jeep, while his rebel boys blew up everything around them. The energy in that figure can move from rebel to criminal very fast. The dream is telling Kate to wake up because she could become possessed by the killer rage and move into its pathology.

"That evil was always floating around," she said, "always influencing my ego. The rage just 'glommed on' to my natural energy."

The dream prefigured the therapeutic work of the next two years. Kate realized intuitively that the situation could get out of hand. She also realized that while she lamented what had been lost with her father, she also had some sympathy for what had happened to him. She knew the immense energy in that killer figure could be transformed. Instead of thinking in terms of slaying the tyrant, she concentrated on the "shaman lamb," a transcendent symbol representing the possibility of healing power that would bring soul and spirit together in her heart. Gradually her feeling was able to go into that cold, unfeeling place in her matter, express it and thus transform it. In her dreams, a wild sailor danced and as he danced, he pulled down a shaman's mask. Weeks later, the sailor changed into a magnificent pirate, "shining with Christ energy." During this transformation she was consciously working on bringing feeling, rather than distrust, to the lover in her own psyche.

At the same time, the problem in the kitchen had to be faced. As in fairy tales, energy that suddenly disappears has to be watched for. Its very absence may make it omnipresent. In this dream, for example, the shadow mother energy that suddenly leaves may turn up off stage in the kitchen where the dreamer is burying the broken glass. The worse the confrontation between the masculine components becomes, the more the feminine loses her ground in her feminine matter (mother). She is experiencing the sense of betrayal that took place in infancy when she and her mother failed to bond. Without that trust in her own body, she is terrified of being too vulnerable. Thus, faced with the collusion of the betrayal by the shadow mother and the rage of the shadow father, the overwhelmed ego sinks into unconsciousness. The hope for Kate lies in the "wake-up" call, the death and resurrection of her lover being understood as the death and resurrection of her negative father and the freedom to embrace her own creativity.

This is not to say that Kate has a weak ego. In the healing process, the ego is not presented with this degree of danger until it is strong enough to deal with it. Dreams of pantomimes, theatrical tableaus, painted geishas and so on are not uncommon when the time comes to deal with the cold psychotic corner. "What is real and what is unreal?" is the question. "What is play and what is play acting? What is creativity and what is performance?"

Until real feeling penetrates that cold corner, the frightened soul cannot deal with the Luciferean (Light-bringing) spirit, and therefore there is always something imperative to wholeness left disconnected, unreal and floating nearby. Sentimentality not only keeps the anger at a distance, it also betrays genuine feeling. "Have a drink, girl—can't you have a good time?" That is one seductive voice that offers yet another emotional panacea. It does nothing to build the spiritual bridge to the Self. Love that says, "This is of value to me and I will go for it," may be strong enough to break the impasse.

After a year of confrontation, Kate began to embody the energy in a conscious way. Among other methods, she participated in a mask workshop over a period of eight weeks. In creating her own mask and performing in it, she was able to abreact some of the rage in ritual. She brought herself to move into the rage, experienced its shattering effect and came out on the other side. By pinpointing the situation in which the rage appeared, she realized its core was in her response to early false mirroring.

"What I put out," she said, "was not what came back. My parents manipulated me for their own narcissistic purposes. Very early on, I moved out of the center in myself and came from whatever point on the periphery suited the situation. Because I could not express my own aggression, I was terrified of other people's."[6]

In order to allow her young masculinity to grow, she needed to express her aggression naturally.

"Desire moves with aggression," said Kate. "I want to live my own life energy. I want to write. I want to make love."

Without that grounded, forthright outlet, masculine strength is not easily available.

This kind of repression is typical of what happens with abused children; the childhood trauma is driven into the unconscious and, therefore, disconnected from feeling. The person may cry hysterically for hours but because the crying is not connected to the cause of the crying, the trauma in the body is not released. There is always the uncanny feeling that the body is experiencing one thing while something quite different is coming out of the mouth. Extreme care must be taken to respect the body's resistance. If the ego container is not strong enough, a psychotic episode could result from touching into the trauma too soon. In women where the primary betrayal was in the relationship with the mother, the loss may be so deep that it does not even appear in dreams until the dreamer has worked on the father complex for years. Body/soul work is like dream work. The psyche understands its own timing. The work must never be intrusive. Until trust is restored through gradual, cherishing work, the resistance is self-protective and must be respected.

The lack of trust in her own body manifests in a woman's life in her inability to be vulnerable with a man. Being vulnerable, with

---

6 See above, pp. 48-49.

mature femininity relating to mature masculinity, does not mean regressing into little girl—"I love you, my wonderful Daddy. I will do all in my sweet power to please you." Nor does it mean camouflaging her lack of vulnerability by choosing a man who is incapable of being receptive. Sooner or later, if the woman matures, they will lock horns. He will become frightened and enraged and call her a presumptuous bitch. Without flexibility, his shadow will not endure what feels to him like overbearing aggression.

If, on the other hand, the woman works on her own fear of vulnerability by going back to the absence of primal bonding and the betrayal she feels in her relationship to her mother, then she has access to the vulnerability problem in her partner. Through the therapeutic process, she (and perhaps her lover, too) can learn to tolerate the pain resulting from that early denial and thus be able to risk opening to another human being who can respond with feeling and consistency. Both can then become capable of receiving love. If they are able to open to the lover within, then they can also open to the lover without.

As the lover within and without connects to his own feeling, he in turn relates to the shadow woman. Instead of fighting her, criticizing her for her lack of perfection, withdrawing from her sexuality, he cherishes and values her humanness. The transformation of the lover usually moves in direct ratio to the humanizing of the rejected shadow. As the split in the masculine and feminine heals, the polarization of good and evil, feeling and no feeling, also heals. The healing transcends the opposites. Then the way is open for the creative masculine to develop and shine through the ego of a woman who loves it, has intercourse with it and lives constantly in relationship to it, bringing forth the spiritual and creative children of the union. For many women, of course, the grand prize would be a relationship with a mature and loving man, but that relationship is the by-product of work that has gone on inside. If the product becomes the goal, then the inner lover will take second place to the outer relationship and once again betrayal will have taken place; the inner marriage has been desecrated, and the outer will not flourish.

Many women dealing with autonomous rage have dreams of the martial arts, involving both traditional Japanese Samurai and contemporary judo, karate or kung fu fighters. The martial arts enact ritual killing not as murder but as sacrifice, a sacrifice that releases participants from the chthonic fears that stand between them and the achievement of their full stature as human beings. Because ritual comes from the archetypal depths, as rage does, it is able to contain the rage while at the same time releasing it. Through contact with the creativity buried within them, the participants can embrace their own masculinity, relatively free of the negative complexes.

Whether a particular martial art is practiced as a daily ritual or not, the same rigorous discipline needs to be brought to the inner masculine if it is to be transformed.

Many men, ravaged by the negative masculinity of an abusive father or parent figure, find in the martial arts a similar outlet for their buried creativity, which they are initially unable to differentiate from parental abuse. From studying dreams containing knights and references to the medieval world, I would suggest that the chivalric code which initiated men into knighthood ritually enacted the inner transformation of the brutalizing influences of a barbaric society into a partnership with the feminine, often symbolized by the Virgin Mary or some other idealized female figure.

The medieval knights were prefiguring what is once again coming into consciousness—the possibility of the marriage within leading to a new world order without. While most of the masculine figures dealt with here have not the sturdy arms and legs, stout hearts and potent genitals that we associate with noble manhood, they can be healed. Taking hold of reality can heal their hands, holding a standpoint helps their legs. Subtle awareness is imperative in attempting to integrate feeling into heart and genitals. Patience and diligence do bring healing.

There may be a wounded figure, however, whose wound is his redemption. He suffers loneliness, alienation and crucifixion, sometimes physically, always psychically. The archetypal image that has stood at the center of Western civilization for 2000 years is that of a god who impregnated with his spirit a human virgin, was born in a cowshed, fled Herod, lived his own truth, loved the outcasts, collided with the collective, and was crucified as a criminal. Out of his wounding and physical death came spiritual life. His was a true search for consciousness. The divine masculine within us is still being wounded by the handicapped Caesars within and without. On some level the wounders and the wounded are one. In forgiving the handicapped, we release the spiritual power inherent in our wound. The god comes through the wound.

So long as consciousness is enslaved by the darkness of unconsciousness, we blindly live out these handicaps in our lives, projecting them onto our men or choosing defeated men as an image of our own defeat. The flames of our fear, grief and rage burn without light. Without realizing what we are doing, we can allow consciousness to fall into the service of darkness. If, on the other hand, we are conscious of the darkness, that very consciousness is the light that illumines the darkness. This is the journey into mature consciousness with arms and legs, heart and genitals, strong enough to bear the light.

Painted on an ancient Chinese screen two birds sit on a tree branch. One eats the fruit, the other lovingly watches.

Rebel Thoughts

I don't know what I'm doing anymore. I don't know what I'm going to say next. Nick got so angry with me, he pushed me. I screamed at him never to touch me again. I'm mad at everybody at work. They're mad at me. I've never felt such rage and I've never been so terrified of men.

I'm a linear, objective thinker. Show me, or it isn't true. I am a grab-your-dick-and-go-for-it man. That session I got inside my skin. I wanted to get out and avoid the feelings. A voice told me to stay and take it.

I have no real animus. I'm an animus hound. My animus becomes so driven it kills the feminine. A real animus—a creative animus—helps a woman to mature, cherishes her.

Anger isn't going to kill anybody. My volcanic, infantile rage may.

My father was a puer who never found a place in the patriarchy. Atonement for my rebel means redeeming my father's homosexual shadow—giving up all models and not being satisfied with a plaster image.

It's not sentimental if you've paid for it in blood. Fantasy is unearned suffering.

Are my rebels mother-bound? My punk girl is fat, but she doesn't want to be thin like everybody else. My young gangster hasn't got the strength to say NO to the chocolates that keep her locked in a mother's body, but he wants her to be thin like other sexy girls.

Why do I have to go on repeating the pattern? This one isn't quite the same because this man is really appropriate. I want this man. I'm afraid to lose him. I know what a loss it would be in my life. How empty! But right now I need time to figure out who I am. I know if we are together my animus will strike a death blow at the relationship. Consciously I don't want to get rid of him; unconsciously my animus is trying to put him out.

He notices my big stomach and says, "It's all right. I have a volcano of my own to live with."

This feels like deep sea diving. Still at the bottom, but the real danger is getting the bends.

Until you learn to name your ghosts and to baptize your hopes, you have not yet been born; you are still the creation of others.

—Maria Cardinal, *The Words To Say It.*

Listen to her silent tears . . .
Her eyes hear, her ears see.
Beauty has made her ugly.
Sentiment has turned her cruel.

Stashed away in a manger
Amid the death of birth,
She dare not wait much longer
To deliver Reality.

—June Reynolds, *Woman.*

Sophia is God's sharing of Himself with creatures. His outpouring, and the Love by which He is given, and known, held and loved.

She is in all things like the air receiving the sunlight. In her they prosper. In her they glorify God. In her they rejoice to reflect Him. In her they are united with Him. She is the union between them. She is the Love that united them. She is life as communion, life as thanksgiving, life as praise, life as festival, life as glory.

Because she receives perfectly there is in her no stain. She is love without blemish, and gratitude without self-complacency. All things praise her by being themselves and by sharing in the Wedding Feast. She is the Bride and the Feast and the Wedding.

—"Hagia Sophia," *A Thomas Merton Reader.*

6

The Bride

Sitting here on our island in Georgian Bay with my brain saying, "Let's go," and my pen saying, "Whither?" I've been watching the sun dancing on the waves. And as I've moved farther and further out, I've been remembering all the brides in my life, each with her unique aura of hope and fear, fullness and aloneness, as she moved, veiled or unveiled, to meet her bridegroom.

I've been remembering too how it felt to be the bride, standing alone at the back of the church, seeing the candles and the Christmas trees so lovingly decorated by my students, seeing our friends and families gathered to witness the vows that would forever change our lives. And seeing far in the distance my father in his ministerial robes, the groomsman, and the stranger who was to be my husband, I was shaken by the finality of what I was about to say. I knew I would never make it to the altar in my high heels. I kicked them off and walked, one solid foot ahead of the other solid foot, through shimmering candlelight.

It's good to remember these rites of passage that mark the end of who we were and the beginning of who we will become, and the images that supported us in our crossing. Weddings are a fundamental archetypal image in the unconscious. How do masculine and feminine relate in this particular couple? Is this a fairy tale wedding? Will they live consciously ever after?

An interesting wedding motif is manifesting in dreams of contemporary men and women, a motif I would like to weave into a story about a princess. While I write from a woman's point of view, let me remind male readers that fairy tales focused on a princess reveal much about the feminine side of a man, especially his struggle to release the young feminine from the mother. A man who is identified with the maternal unconscious is usually in a state of paralysis or

161

drivenness. He cannot act for himself because he has not developed his own feeling values. A man who lives his life serving and pleasing mother, albeit a metaphorical mother like some utopian cause which has nothing to do with his own feelings, is not living his own life. His search may take him into the known world for a known reason; nevertheless he lives within a collective container that supports the principles by which he lives. A principle, however, has nothing to do with individual feeling unless it has been brought to consciousness as one's own value. That value is often personified in men's dreams as a young woman. The degree of maturity in that young feminine is intimately connected to the shaping of a supportive and mature masculinity, a prince strong enough to embrace the liberated princess without becoming dependent upon her in an infantile manner. (A mature prince, for instance, would never address his wife as "mother.")

Once upon a time in the kingdom of Suburbia there was born an exquisite little princess and her twin sister who was not so exquisite. The royal parents, humiliated by their ugly creation, sent her off with an ancient gypsy and concentrated on their beautiful Ariadne. As her blond curls grew longer and her blue eyes searched deeper, the little princess performed on her parents' stage, making her entrances and her exits at their command.

Of course, no one ever mentioned nasty words like command and expectation, standards and laws. There was no need to. Ariadne's father was the King who carried the scepter. Her mother was the Queen who had once trippingly promised to "love, honor, and obey." Things simply were as they were in Suburbia. Everyone nodded and smiled in the complete certainty that in the fullness of time the Prince of Superbia would ask her father, the King, for Ariadne's hand.

The King believed in books and in training a young girl's mind. One day, as Ariadne was reading something called *Myths of the Greeks,* she discovered to her dismay that she was not the only Ariadne who had ever lived. What was worse, the Greek Ariadne had a half-brother who was not quite right. From that moment she refused to answer to the name Ariadne. She wanted no truck with half-man, half-bull brothers. She felt herself more air than earth, more music than plodding prose, and so she called herself Aria—Ari, for short.

Now having discovered her own name, Ari suddenly began to discover all kinds of things. She discovered her mother's vanity table and cut off her hair with her mother's fingernail scissors. She discovered secrets in her mother's drawers—crystal bottles full of royal jellies made for the queen larva in Cleopatra's beehive.

"I wonder if Daddy knows about Mommy's tricks," she thought somewhat anxiously. And Daddy slipped from King to man in her imagination.

Soon Daddy was shocked when Ari refused to obey him. Of course, "obey" was a taboo word. Everyone had simply taken for granted that when Daddy said, "The phone is ringing," Ari would instantly jump to answer. Now, when Daddy said, "The phone is ringing," Ari replied, "Yes it is, Daddy," and went on reading.

And when the Queen said, "Wouldn't you like some tea, Aria?" she boldly replied, "No thank you, Mommy," pretending she had not understood her mother's command for afternoon tea. She discovered jeans, tough pants that were not as pretty as her little pink frocks, but pants that molded themselves to her round little buttocks and allowed her to run and play in the forest as she had never done before.

One day as she was running in the rain she felt like a goddess, her skin alive and open to the sharp thrusts of the raindrops. She tore off her clothes and ran naked, her arms open, her head thrown back, until she tripped and rolled over and over in the mud. Not sure whether the water on her face was rain or tears, not sure whether the burbling from her belly was laughter or crying, she knew only that she was free. Her body was her own body, and not only her own, but part of the great earth body. She and the earth, the trees and the birds, the clouds and the sky—all were beating with one heart beat, one slow, nonnegotiable beat, the rhythm that from that moment would be her truth.

"I am," she cried aloud.

"And so am I," a voice answered.

Ari opened her eyes and looked into the fiery black eyes of a gypsy maid.

"I am your sister," the girl said.

Ari felt like a frog petrified by the eyes of a snake. Grasping for what she thought was her life, she bolted. She returned to the palace. She tried to tune her heart to that inner beat, but try as she would she could not remember its rhythm.

Then one day, the shining prince came from Superbia to ask for Ariadne's hand. The King was not at all happy to hand his daughter over to another man. However difficult she had become, she was still his music. Life with the Queen was like living with a wasp. Buzz or no buzz, however, life had to go on and Ariadne's wedding day was announced.

The bride-to-be was not radiant. Something was amiss. Between fittings for her bridal trousseau she attempted to master her new computer. Somehow being able to order that great giant in her bedroom to boot the system, to bring up the main menu, to enter, to save, to escape, made her feel like a powerful queen in spite of inner rumblings to the contrary. Much as she thought she loved the Prince, she felt herself diminished by his ever-ready smiles.

On her wedding day, Ari adorned herself in her white silk gown and placed her headdress on her cropped curls as she had been instructed in a dream. "Wear a Mary Queen of Scots cap," her wise old woman had said. "Wear the peak well over your forehead. Protect your third eye. You are not ready to be unveiled."

The wedding bells rang. Ari walked behind her bridesmaid to the altar. She awaited her groom. No groom appeared. She sat down on the steps of the chancel and fingered the daisies in her bridal bouquet. "You are not ready for marriage," her Sophie said. "Your groom is not ready. You have not dealt with your gypsy sister."

Ari left the court of her father and mother. She put on her jeans and her fur coat and went into the woods, fearful that she might not find her sister, more fearful that she would. After many days, she fell asleep and as she awoke she felt the slow beat close to her ear, beating through her whole body.

"I found you," the gypsy said. "I love you. Come with me."

Together they walked to a small cottage by a lake and there Ari met her sister's groom—a powerful man, his naked torso scarred, his head proud and erect with eyes that pierced her darkness with their light.

Now, I could go on and tell you how Ari learned to love the gypsy in herself, how she listened to the wisdom of the man in the woods, and how one day she found her own bridegroom and they lived together ever after. That is essentially the theme of this book. So also is the length and difficulty of the process—the keeping going with some kind of faith until "the question" is distilled from the very depths of our suffering.

As I have described her, Ari is the personification of the feminine attempting to find union with the masculine. Likewise, a man's soul is feminine, and his evolutionary process, like the woman's, leads to opening his soul to the infiltration of masculine spirit. Ari, like Perceval, moves through one situation after another, with no idea what question to ask. She is not, however, hopelessly meandering toward some unknown future. She allows herself to be guided by her old wise woman, her connecting link to Sophia, the feminine aspect of the Self, the feminine godhead. Our task, like Ari's, is to work toward the integration of the conscious and unconscious masculine and feminine elements in the psyche that function like a quartet. Speaking of the quaternity, Jung writes:

> Four as the minimal number by which order can be created represents the pluralistic state of [one] who has not yet attained inner unity, hence the state of bondage and disunion, of disintegration, and of being torn in different directions—an agonizing, unredeemed state which longs for union, reconciliation, redemption, healing, and wholeness.[1]

---

[1] "The Psychology of the Transference," *The Practice of Psychotherapy,* CW 16, par. 405.

Within ourselves and in relationships, the foursome works in many combinations, now one pair, then another, dancing in every situation. Diagrammatically, the foursome in our story can be pictured like this:

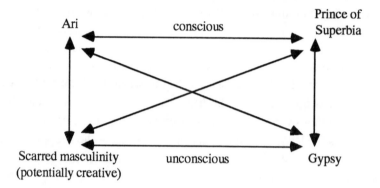

In earlier chapters, we have looked at several possible dynamics in this diagram: the failure of the persona relationship between Ari and the Prince of Superbia; the dangers of excess in the shadow relationship of gypsy and rejected masculinity; the collusion and deception in the relationship of gypsy and persona Prince; the anguish of relationship between Ari and the rejected masculine, with our eye on the magnificent potential.

While we have touched on the relationship between Ari and her gypsy, we need now to move to another level of the spiral, always remembering that the deeper the roots of the tree push into the earth, the higher the branches of the tree reach toward heaven. Without some image of that balance, the pain of descent—whether through physical illness, the loss of a partner or the loss of whatever else we considered essential to our lives—can blind us to the positive side of the darkness.

The positive side is the day-by-day building of a container strong enough and flexible enough to receive the ravishing presence of the unknown Light—a soul that can magnify the spirit. Far from cutting off relationship to another person, the soul, released from the old parental complexes, is free to open to Love that is not crippled by neurosis—a Love burning with an illuminating flame.

In moving to deeper levels of the spiral, we are moving to the basement (often below the known basement) in dreams. Ari realizes she must free herself of the parental complexes that have banished her so-called ugly instinctual side from the conventional standards of the court. She senses that she has been robbed of her birthright to life in her body, but she wants nothing to do with "half-bull brothers." Her own crippled instinct cannot tolerate fantasies of the bull instinct in the masculine. Although her love of nature briefly reconnects her with her gypsy, she is frightened to death of her sister and therefore initially lacks the feminine consciousness to reject a marriage modeled on the old stereotype, a marriage that can only duplicate the power dynamics of the household in which she was raised. The archetypal depths are not constellated.

Wisely, in her struggle to find her own nature and her own values, she has the adolescent courage to rebel and the intuition that listens to her inner voice. However, in the intimate dynamics of masculine/feminine relationship, she is faced with her deepest agony: she cannot stand to her own instinctual truth and, therefore, has no adequate groom.

Disconnected from the instinctual level of her femininity, she is disconnected from the passion of her soul in her own matter. In other words, she is disconnected from the life force in the lowest chakra, *muladhara,* and since that chakra is related to the crown chakra, she is unable to endure the potential energy of spiritual light. In archetypal language, she is disconnected from the Earth Mother and at the same time disconnected from the virile masculinity that would be her natural bridegroom. Temporarily, she must keep her spiritual eye covered with a Mary Queen of Scots cap, because she is too weak to receive the shimmering intensity, the potency of fertile masculinity. Her task is twofold: to love her gypsy sister, that is, her own rejected self, and to love the powerful masculine figure who, with the gypsy, lives outside the limits of the establishment in order to protect himself from the bludgeonings of patriarchal power.

Ari's receptive feminine energy is not strong enough or flexible enough to open herself to the powerful penetration of masculine otherness. In everyday life such a situation manifests in sexual intercourse. At a basic, biological level, it is reflected in the failure of the feminine to trust, to allow the body to let go into full orgasm. It is also the inability to allow the soul in matter to surrender to spirit, so that every cell of the body is filled with light and the soul is open to spiritual visions and full union with the Divine.

The fear of being receptive also manifests in emotional blocks that restrict dialogue in daily encounters. The feminine side in both men and women is so frail that anything radical coming in from outside has to be censored in order to protect the container against the possibility of shattering. On the other hand, the masculine side often lacks the strength to penetrate; terror of losing oneself in another overwhelms the initial thrust that could lead to deeper intercourse. This biological imagery clarifies the ways in which we all move between our masculinity and our femininity in daily conversation. But how many of us are flexible enough to fully receive another without critical judgment? How many of us are able to trust that we will be received unconditionally? How many of us are able to stand to our own phallic truth when we see our relationships endangered?

In dreams, when the starved little soul is finally released from the pile of garbage and shit in which she has been buried for years, the dreamer often asks, "Why are you there?" Her huge, frightened eyes look straight into the dreamer's and she says, "You would have killed me." I often see this terror in workshops when one person tells a story of her own soul's betrayal to two listeners, who are receiving with unconditional love. The floods of tears that are released make only too clear how rarely our soul is truly received and how dwarfed it is as a result.

On yet another level, the blocking can take place in the creative process: the conscious container is not strong enough to endure the penetration of the unknown phallos that thrusts through from the unconscious. The creative process, when it is fully functioning, is a surrender of the known ego boundaries to the unknown potential in the unconscious. Newton, for example, recognized in a flash the force of gravity in the fall of an apple. He built a container for that force capable of explaining (until this century) the motions of the universe. The materials of his container were already present to him through his long mathematical training. He received the fall of an apple as the disciplined mystic receives grace. The surrender of personal to transpersonal creates new life and takes living into a different dimension of reality. Unless there is sufficient love and integrity between the container and the penetrator, fear will hold the container rigid and render the phallos impotent. The greater the integrity, the stronger the container, the more powerful the penetration.

How then do we make our bride-to-be strong enough to receive the groom? In my story I incorporated an actual dream in which the dreamer was told by Sophia to wear a Mary Queen of Scots cap because she was not ready for her groom until she had dealt with her shadow sister. It is the actual dream, rather than the story woven around it, that I wish now to explore.

Awakening from the dream, the dreamer recognized that she was moving too fast spiritually. Metaphorically she veiled her spiritual eye, and turned her concentration to body/soul work. She, in fact, knew her "gypsy sister," a woman who had defied her rigid father by running away to marry a man to whom she was sexually devoted, but had suffered a nervous breakdown as a result. She attempted a leap she was not strong enough to take. The dreamer had no idea what was going to be demanded of her, but she foresaw that, if she became trapped by her shadow, she would not be equal to standing to her own truth.

These three themes—the veil, the shadow sister still in bondage to the old father or mother, and the opening of the spiritual eye—are common motifs in modern dreams (as they are in fairy tales). Therefore, we can assume they carry transpersonal as well as personal meaning. Moreover, since dreams indicate what is going on in the unconscious, which tends to move ahead of consciousness, such dreams suggest an unconscious thrust toward a new way of seeing, but a way that must be integrated at every step into a well-grounded

Grail. Such dreams are not about the feminine going to a union of male and female in one flesh. Repeatedly, the dreamer is warned that her spiritual eye is not yet strong enough to see what it will see when the veil is removed. Her spirituality is still too vulnerable to the old criticisms and the stones that will be aimed at her when she dares to speak what she knows to be her own truth.

Where a woman has not integrated her own femininity, has not sufficiently grounded herself in the Divine Mother or fully understood her Magdalene shadow, who might suddenly value herself according the laws of the old patriarch (the old king in fairy tales), she puts herself in a very dangerous position if she takes off her veil too soon. The resultant tragedy is clear in the lives of many nuns who have removed their veil, lost the security of the nunnery walls and found themselves unable to cope with a sexual, materialistic, brutal world they do not understand. They fluctuate between their freedom in the eyes of God and their slavery to their guilt and fear.

This tragedy is equally clear in the lives of countless women who yearn to throw off the veil of their imprisoning marriage to a father-husband whom they once promised to love, honor and obey. Gradually they realize they cannot live a free life because they have neither the inner strength nor the fundamental knowledge of the marketplace to survive. They are more afraid of freedom than prison because, although they are seeing with new eyes, they have not the inner marriage which would give them the strength to stand to their own virgin truth, strength that would allow them to say, "This is who I am."

In my earlier books, I have dealt with the integration of the feminine shadow in detail. I have further dealt with it at the level of abandonment by the parents in chapter two of this book. It bears repeating here from another perspective. As the veils of illusion are removed, and as the inner marriage becomes a possibility, the tension between masculinity and femininity intensifies, as it often does before an actual marriage. The problem is usually a discrepancy between masculine and feminine feeling. What is of value to one is either not valued or not perceived by the other.

Feeling is a major problem in our culture. Women are continually disappointed by men because, as one said, "He can't understand why I'm so upset. He hasn't got the eyes to see as I see." Men, confounded by the reactions of women, say, "I gave her everything she wanted and she left me. Why?" Feeling is not valued by the industrial and post-industrial macho machine that drives Western civilization. Women as often as men hand over to their inner or outer patriarchal judge the power of evaluating their own feminine worth, and end up dismissing their authentic feelings as "naive, illogical, stupid." This is profound self-betrayal.

Not only are women's values different from men's on specific female issues, but men in our patriarchal culture are trained to ignore or suppress their feeling values. Little boys who may be genuine feeling types are labeled "effeminate" by parents and peers. Their tears of outrage when their soul is betrayed are called sissy's tears. As adolescents and men, they have limited access to their true feeling. Instead of maturing with the rest of the personality, their feeling side remains at an infantile level; thus it may appear in dreams as a baby girl, or even a starved kitten. In the goal-oriented race to the top, men even more than women are side-tracked from what is of value to their essence.

Feeling without value, however, degenerates into emotion charged by a complex. Value then is in jeopardy. Actions become fired by emotionally charged complexes that dwarf the ego and live out their own inconsistent, often ruthless, behavior. That is to say, men and women who are "upset" by the attitude of their partner must learn to differentiate their genuine feeling—what something or someone is worth to them—from an emotional (complex-based) reaction. A woman angry with her husband, for instance, becomes sarcastic, repressing her rage between clenched teeth. "The darling boy goes right over me like a steam roller," she says. "He's in his cold, unfeeling side." That may be true, but she too is complexed.

Many women who like to think of themselves as conscious, helplessly hand over their feeling function to intelligent but feelingless (not emotionless) men. Their own father complex colludes with their partner and rapes the very feelings they have worked so hard to experience. Life again becomes an empty "so what?" Unless we have the feminine consciousness that values our feeling, we wallow in emotions that can run rampant, dragging us with them. If we can teach our inner masculinity to value our feminine feeling, then our partners may one day understand what the agony was all about.

Jane had worked for ten years to establish her own values through a strong inner marriage. Then she was once again faced with a situation in which a strong father figure demanded what she could not honestly give. Although she stood to her NO, she became ill. She knew then she was not free of the father complex. She realized she was dangerously undermined by a negative inner marriage between her shadow and judgmental animus. The resulting paralysis is clear in the following passage from her journal.

> It is as if I were in two places at once. I feel as if my life is just beginning, as if everything I ever hoped for is now possible, but I am fifty years old and suddenly I fear that the dream I had for myself may have been the wrong dream. Doors are opening that I never imagined were there; other doors are closing. It's as if two currents of my life miraculously came together. Without knowing how I got here, I have arrived. The secret dream I never dared to hope for is possible and everything I did that seemed a tangent is now included. I feel I am thirty, as if my life is just beginning and yet I cannot take what I need for myself. What makes a decision most difficult is that, although I have worked hard to be where I am, I feel I am not worthy. When I see that I can have what I love, I am terrified. I feel selfish. The real issue—the right door to walk through—is lost in a myriad of rational reasons why I cannot have what is necessary to my soul. By some miracle I am standing in my own kingdom, but I cannot claim it. Is it because of my neurotic unworthiness? Or am I afraid to take the responsibility for being who I am? Or is it that the current that is carrying me to some unknown destiny, I comprehend, but only vaguely trust?

Jane holds in her hand the key to the life she has worked so hard to gain. Why, then, does she use the phrase, "by some miracle," to explain her success? It seems she cannot accept her own empowerment. She lays all her labors at the feet of another authority. Without quite realizing it, Jane is in the grip of the very father from whom she has worked so long to release herself. Through hard work she has forged the key that can release her from the prison cell of her father complex, but she cannot turn it in the lock. Jane, therefore, has to look very carefully at who, in her unconscious, is responsible for the "miracle." She may not yet be ready to open her spiritual eye. What she calls a miracle may still be her magician father holding her in thrall. Or even worse, when she does turn the key, her father's laughter may greet her on the other side of the door. The spiritual eye can open only when, in contact with her own masculinity, she is able to confront such possibilities creatively .

Lyn, who has also focused on the balance of masculine and feminine energies in her life, has a very different shadow marriage from Jane's. Through body/soul work she brought new life to her feminine matter, but then her positive mother complex became overconfident and smothered her creative masculinity; thus she now has a shadow marriage between a mother and an impotent animus. She had a dream that, in her words, "called for the redemption of a whole new layer of unconsciousness."

> My friend Sue's husband is in the hospital for a heart transplant. His foreign doctors cannot communicate well, but I realize they are not at all sure he will survive. Sue is taking no responsibility for her share in his illness. I cried and cried.

Associating with the dream, Lyn wept again.

"Sue is a negative mother. When she and David met seven years ago, David was an innovative leader at the university. He was respected for his ideas and his capacity to put them into action. Sue was committed to her spiritual journey through her body. She is convinced that institutions destroy people, that words and ideas block out inner truth. She imagines a fantasy Utopia in which she and David perfect themselves, two lonely pioneers. Now David rarely speaks. He resigned from his position. He can't find a new one. He takes no responsibility for anything. Sue can't see that she has broken his heart, that he loved the university, loved ideas and loved to articulate his thinking. She can't see that he is being destroyed by her fantasy. If I say anything, she takes that 'holier than thou' attitude toward me. It's straight power.

"I don't know about these foreign doctors. I can't communicate with them because they don't speak very good English, but I know they aren't sure the transplant is going to work.

"What does this mean about me? Sue is my shadow. I have to look at how I am unconsciously betraying my masculinity. How is my shadow destroying her inner man's soul? How is she taking his heart out of his work and silencing him? I weep for my shadow, her unconscious destructiveness. She can only be redeemed through love of the human condition. That love is born in the grief we experience for what the evil witch has unconsciously done to our bodies, and how we have perpetuated that destruction on ourselves, those we love and the Earth. The witch mother is not strong enough to take responsibility for the destruction she wreaks on others, but here the dream ego perceives the heart-broken masculinity."

For years before she had this dream, Lyn had worked at integrating the power-driven mother, especially in relation to her attitude toward sexuality which, she felt, had contributed to her husband's impotence. Having resolved that impasse, she was now faced with that same witch mother in relation to her own creative masculinity.

At the time of this dream, Lyn's focus was still on body/soul work, opening her body to Sophia and the love that could redeem the evil witch. She was reluctant to articulate what was happening in her body. She did not realize that she was overcompensating, putting blinders on her Eros (relatedness) and not seeing what that narrowness was doing to her Logos (discrimination). By separating them, by not allowing the flesh to become Word, she was taking the heart out of her masculinity. The "foreign doctors" cannot communicate well; therefore, the dream ego cannot understand what is going on.

The dream seems to be suggesting that having worked so long to contact the healing that is going on in her feminine body (represented by Sue in the dream), Lyn needs now to look at what is happening to her masculine side. Perhaps she needs to find a way for him to give voice to his new heart in the world around her. Like many women, Lyn is loathe to articulate, at the level of consciousness, the power of the unconscious working in her body, even though she recognizes in this fear the ancient body/spirit split.

The motif of the heart transplant is not uncommon in contemporary dreams. Does it suggest that in this leap from evil witch mother to Sophia, the old heart is not strong enough? Does this leap from personal possessiveness to an open heart through which love flows require a new heart? Will that heart be strong enough to pump with a new concept of love? Conscious of that leap on the feminine side, is the masculinity now able to illumine that consciousness with a new articulation of "the Word became flesh"? Maybe the first step is to teach our "foreign doctors" to speak better English, by which I mean, maybe we have to try to articulate the transplant process more clearly, bring it more fully into consciousness. When the witch mother is able to give the articulate innovator his freedom, the bride is at least putting the first stitches in her wedding dress.

The killer aspect of the witch power is ferociously embodied by Ursula in D.H. Lawrence's *The Rainbow*. While this is a man's description of the deadly power of the unconscious feminine, women listen to the passage with a knowing glint in their eyes.

> She stood for some moments out in the overwhelming luminosity of the moon. She seemed a beam of gleaming power. She was afraid of what she was. Looking at him, at his shadowy, unreal, wavering presence, a sudden lust seized her, to lay hold of him and tear him and make him into nothing. Her hands and wrists felt immeasurably hard and strong, like blades. He waited there beside her like a shadow which she wanted to dissipate, destroy as the moonlight destroys a darkness, annihilate, have done with. She looked at him and her face gleamed bright and inspired. She tempted him.
>
> And an obstinacy in him made him put his arm round her and draw her to the shadow. She submitted: let him try what he could do. Let him try what he could do. He leaned against the side of the stack, holding her. The stack stung him keenly with a thousand cold, sharp flames. Still obstinately he held her.

And timorously, his hands went over her, over the salt compact brilliance of her body. If he could but have her, how he would enjoy her! If he could but net her brilliant, cold, salt-burning body in the soft iron of his own hands, net her, capture her, hold her down, how madly he would enjoy her. He strove subtly, but with all his energy, to enclose her, to have her. And always she was burning and brilliant and hard as salt, and deadly. Yet obstinately, all his flesh burning and corroding, as if he were invaded by some consuming, scathing poison, still he persisted, thinking at last he might overcome her. Even, in his frenzy, he sought for her mouth with his mouth, though it was like putting his face into some awful death. She yielded to him, and he pressed himself upon her in extremity, his soul groaning over and over.

She took him in the kiss, hard her kiss seized upon him, hard and fierce and burning corrosive as the moonlight. She seemed to be destroying him. He was reeling, summoning all his strength to keep his kiss upon her, to keep himself in the kiss.

But hard and fierce she had fastened upon him, cold as the moon and burning as a fierce salt. Till gradually his warm, soft iron yielded, yielded, and she was there fierce, corrosive, seething with his destruction, seething like some cruel corrosive salt around the last substance of his being, destroying him, destroying him in the kiss. And her soul crystallised with triumph, and his soul was dissolved with agony and annihilation. So she held him there, the victim, consumed, annihilated. She had triumphed: he was not any more.[2]

This Medusa energy that can seize a woman and make her want to "lay hold of" a man and "tear him and make him into nothing," is the very energy that can seize hold of her own masculinity and make it impotent, "the victim, consumed, annihilated."

Men have good reason to associate this cold, fierce, corrosive side of the dark feminine with seductive evil, destructive matter. Trapped in Medusa, a man's anima is locked in the dark cave. His soul is "dissolved with agony and annihilation." So also is the woman's soul and with it her creative spirit.

One aspect of the dark cave is the unconscious body, frozen as an iceberg, without personal feeling, made rigid by stress and driven-

---

[2] D.H. Lawrence, *The Rainbow*, pp. 319-320.

ness: work harder, achieve more, get money, gain power, drink more, smoke more, eat more, have more sex. Any male or female existing in a frozen body (symbolized in dreams by freezers, snow scenes, and impenetrable glass) is Medusa's victim, gradually turning self and loved ones into stone. Nothing has personal, feeling value. All the senses are partially closed down because to open them is to open a volcano.

But that inert Medusa energy can transmute into empowerment. If we dare to travel down the bridge from head to body, we may find our soul in the darkness and we may find the questions which will quicken her, opening every cell as we bring her into consciousness. Body becomes embodiment, sight becomes insight. Sophia, wisdom in the body, begins to move through soul. Soul experiences herself as part of Shekinah, the light in creation, the Bride of God. Matter, instead of being a dark cave, becomes the revelation of God's beauty. The heart becomes the bridal chamber where soul that lives in time and space opens to spirit that is detached from life and death. There Bride and Bridegroom love.

Without the consciousness of Sophia's wisdom illuminating not only our body, but the body of creation, we lack the crucial connection to our own feeling. We judge with our minds and forget we have hearts, lungs, spleens and bowels. Then we fail to temper our winged spirit with human limitations. Without embodied soul, spirit cannot manifest through human feeling. It flies like an angel with no place to land, archetypal energy that merely swoops through, leaving the body a burned-out shell demanding whatever perverted solace it can find.

A disembodied woman is vulnerable to invasion by Medusa. If, on the other hand, she commits herself to embodiment, she will experience the agony of the thaw as her molecules awaken to the pain of past and present. In this agony of physical and psychic transition, she may not be able to receive male penetration. As she becomes acquainted with the outcast Magdalene buried in her own tissues, her perfectionist madonna comes off her pedestal and, stones or no stones, forgives herself and the rejected beauty within. In their embrace, they become one radiant human woman, no better, no worse, than she was born to be. "Home" becomes her body which accepts suffering as a necessary part of her soul's yearning to know herself. If physical intercourse is resumed when this union takes place, body and soul may open together to divine feminine energy and the woman will know that her sexuality will never again be in Medusa's power. Her body is part of the Grail through which Sophia and her divine partner make themselves known.

This embrace is poignantly imaged in the following dream.

> I am sitting alone in the gods [the upper balcony] of an old theater, listening to Mahalia Jackson—huge, joyous, suffering Mahalia, full of love and simple faith, walking on the earth with her heart wide open. From the bottom of her anguished soul, she sings, "His eye is on the sparrow/ And I know He watches me."
>
> My insides quiver as her voice rolls into me. I know I am going to burst out sobbing. A long, thin me, jumps up, runs down flight after flight of stairs, up the aisle and into her arms. She has a golden ball in her hands. There the two of us are, embracing and laughing and crying with joy, and the ball between us in the air.

This dream literally transformed Jeannie, the dreamer. As she related it, she was again "crying with joy." The opposites came together. The transcendent Self, imaged in the golden ball, broke down the stone wall of her either/or world.

Jeannie was an anorexic who aspired to the perfection of the gods. What had begun as dieting had gradually moved into a living death. Having cut her body off from food, she had cut herself off from the conviviality that goes with sharing food, fun, friends. As time went on, her body cut her off from sexuality, health and the tremendous vitality that was naturally hers. Her desire for a perfect body was compounded by an equal desire for a perfect spirit, and her love of Christ, coupled with a strong positive father complex, tricked her into the arms of a demon lover luring her away from life. She found herself with the gods, alone.

Everything Jeannie had so fiercely rejected in herself she saw in the dream in Mahalia Jackson. Far from being repulsed by Mahalia's size, she loved her immense capacity to laugh, cry, love, sing her faith with her heart wide open.

"Her body is the right size for her soul," Jeannie said. "Any woman that can make me know that God keeps His eye on the sparrow, makes me know that I belong in the universe. I am not alone. Singing with her breaks open the floodgates of my heart. I love the woman I was. I love the clown, the cook, the singer, the lover, the believer—I love them all. Dear God, what a long way down those stairs—around and down, around and down, down the long, long dangerous run—right the way down my spine from head to tailbone."

Jeannie had been working for four years with dreams and body/soul work. Loneliness, not the fear of death, had forced her into analysis. She called it "the loneliness of the patriarchy." Her efficiency, her strength, even her love, had been mere posturing. Underneath she knew that she "could feel [herself] closing down as intimacy opened." The long run down required her to face her own lies.

"I went through the hole in my soul whenever I tried to be soft and spontaneous," she said. "I put up the wall and pretended. I despised the perfect disguise as much as I hated my instinctual cravings. Without food, I was too weak to crave anything. My body gave up and the complex that I loved blinded me with Light."

Jeannie spent hours writing in her journal, bringing to consciousness her false ideals, separating out the image that was projected onto her from the authenticity of her own Being, separating out the complex from the true Light.

Having held the tension in body and soul for so long, and having felt the surrender in the dream, Jeannie quickly perceived the golden ball as the Self manifesting through the Black Madonna. She contemplated the ball in her own sacred temple and for the first time experienced her own subtle body as a jeweled goblet radiating light from within. To strengthen the Grail, and to keep her personal ego related but not identified with it, she ritualized the sacrifice of her false ideals. In that ego surrender, the terror of loneliness in the arms of the demon lover transformed into love in the presence of Christ. She accepted herself as a woman greatly loved, and capable of great loving.

The tyrannical masculinity that virtually destroyed Jeannie's frail femininity, forcing it toward an inhuman ideal utterly devoid of feeling, is an image of themselves that many women experience as they struggle to succeed in a world from which they are partially excluded. To come down out of the gods and embrace Mahalia Jackson would either destroy them or transform them. Viewed in the larger context of contemporary America, Mahalia Jackson as an image of the Black Madonna is a transformer which we as a culture are still afraid to embrace, even though we may suspect that it is essential for our survival.

Allowing a mature Eros to permeate inner and outer masculinity is one of our biggest tasks. Repeatedly, men have wept in my office, saying, "I thought everything was fine. I don't know what I did. I do not understand her." And women have wept, saying, "When I trusted him most, he left. I do not understand him."

The gap is in the feeling value. In the Chinese symbol of the inner marriage, the yang carries some yin, the yin some yang. Masculinity is tempered by the feminine, and vice versa. Disciplining masculinity that takes its superiority for granted demands as much strength and vigilance as training a wild horse that's never known a harness. And we dare not use a whip that will ultimately break its spirit.

A man walked into my office one day, pale, sick with exhaustion. He had just come from chairing a meeting which he had anticipated would proceed with its usual logic and efficiency. Instead, he had been confronted with feeling issues. "I tell you," he said, "if men ever get into their feeling, it's going to kill them."

This man was a thinking type whose feeling had been stamped underfoot all his life. There was good reason for his overwhelming anxiety, as he felt the shuddering volcano in his abdomen. Many women on their journey to consciousness have been trying for years to release their volcano with some civilized restraint. Men are beginning to realize they too have a volcano.

Sometimes in my lectures, while I have been trying to explain why women are so devastated by men's behavior, men have walked out. Afterward I have had the opportunity to ask them why they left. "I have a situation like the one you described in my own life," said one. "I can't resolve it and I can't endure knowing how she feels." Confronting their feeling can throw men into unconsciousness, often with severe body symptoms.

I am not suggesting the gap will ever be totally bridged. The two sexes have their own mysteries that must be respected. However, the degree of wounding in men and the resultant loss of feeling can no longer be shoved aside. Heart attacks are the number one killer in our society. As consciousness develops, the body will act as donkey for only so long. Men as much as women need to know that their soul is grounded in their own loving matter. "This is who I am. Every cell in my body tells me this is of value to me—not to my persona, to me." That is the container whose feeling can be trusted because it is grounded in reality.

Constructing a grail to receive the masculine light is just as difficult for men as for women. Robert is a man with a magnetic, charming persona; he writes and he acts.

"I'm not a method actor," he said "I don't live the part. I work through technique, come at it from the outside. I never know what I'm going to hit on the inside, but whatever I hit I use to refine the role I am playing. I'm more conscious of the role than the person behind it. If often strikes me as amazing that the audience is not aware of this.

"I often feel I'm on the wave of the audience's emotion, like a wind surfer with the wind blowing from the audience. I'm often aware of manipulating them, though I've never been accused of this. A performance never gives me great satisfaction. It feels like a trick. Whatever was there dissolves with the applause. There's nobody home. The anima that is present in the dream is never there for me in performance. Performing has nothing to do with soul."

Struggling to come to grips with his inner suffering, his sense of "nobody home," Robert had the following dream:

I am in a very large, narrow, old-fashioned iron bathtub with legs. It is white and the interior is sculptured like a Greek frieze. It looks like a sacred object, a place of initiation. There is not much water in the bathtub, but as soon as I stretch out in it, the water overflows. A stern figure whom I recognize as the principal of the arts college I first attended is watching me disapprovingly. I am determined that the water will not overflow again. As soon as I stretch out, however, the water spills on the floor.

"There, you've done it again," snaps the principal.

This time I recognize why it happens. When I stretch out, my feet force the water to one end of the bathtub and then it overflows. I am relieved to have resolved the problem, though I see that my explanation does not resolve the principal's anger.

I get out of the bathtub and realize that I am now expected to clean it. I look for the Dutch Cleanser, but I am told not to use it. I find a small brush and start scrubbing. It is very hard to clean because of all the crevices in the sculptured design. A woman is cleaning with me. I recognize her as a girl who was with me in the first six grades in school.

"I've been to London and New York," she says "and now for some reason I've come back here and I'm cleaning the bathtub."

In associating with the dream, Robert remembered the girl with astonishment and a big smile. "Once when we were playing hide and seek," he laughed, "we hid in a garage in front of a parked car. I sat on the bumper. She sat down beside me and kissed me. She was the first girl who ever kissed me. I haven't thought about her for years."

Robert is like many dreamers who, when they dream of their first love, wonder why they are dreaming of that sweetheart now. Suddenly their body is animated, their smile slightly embarrassed. They look away, imagining the photograph they worshiped as an adolescent. "She was a goddess," men whisper, "a god," women laugh.

Indeed, these are the right words. Those first arrows that shoot from our young souls are carrying our purest projections. They carry love, trust, hope and all our childhood faith in divine union. Concentrating on that first projection can give us a very good image of our inner partner. It will be immature, but the potential is there.

That figure often appears in later dreams as the *frater mysticus* (brother) or *soror mystica* (sister) in the alchemical bathtub.

That first love warrants careful consideration. In recognizing what was projected then, we can often see the same projection recurring in every serious relationship. Part of the projection is neurotic; part is a genuine yearning for the Beloved. The projection itself may become a betrayer—in a man, the maiden in the tower; in a woman, the rescuing knight. If not recognized as projections, these inner images become the ultimate betrayers of oneself. We cannot look to another human being to complete our soul process. The inner marriage is a divine marriage, the outer marriage a human one.

Robert recognized the old-fashioned tub as "a sacred object, a place of initiation."

"Even in the dream," he said, "I can't understand why, with so little water in the tub, it overflows when I push my feet. The fact that I figured out a logical reason isn't enough. I know there is a deeper reality that this logical reason doesn't touch. I'm trying to establish an equilibrium so the waters will be still, but the waters are being disturbed so something must be wrong. Not being able to stretch out is not a satisfactory answer. The only answer to that question has nothing to do with the literal feet, but the standpoint. I do try to take a standpoint in the tub—one of overflowing, a spontaneous overflow from the unconscious. While that is a standpoint, it is not a container. The dream is telling me I have to prepare the tub, but that can't be done with Dutch Cleanser—a practical standpoint.

"As long as I stick to a shallow view of things—which I identify with conventional society—I have at least a pseudo-identity, an identity that comes with fitting into an accepted mold, aping the attitudes of conscious reality. So long as I did that at college I seemed to be able to get along. As soon as I stretched out, expanded to embrace new possibilities and unconventional ideas, the floodgates, which I think of as conventional reality, gave way and life seemed almost limitless. All the repressed world overflowed from the unconscious. In college there wasn't room for that, at least I didn't think there was. If the bathtub is the place of birth, then I'm struggling to take a very shallow view of it, as if my initiation is to be into the conventional world. That's why there's so little water. Changing all this has nothing to do with rational reason. It doesn't change anything. The principal is still angry. My dream ego is not satisfied.

"The nitty gritty is getting down to the embossed figures on the inside of the tub—the archetypal images. That involves the anima, not the stern disapproving father. My feeling goes with me to New York and London when I go to art galleries, concerts, museums, but what I'm looking for now is not there. She comes back now to the first stab at initiation—the first kiss. Preparing the container together would exclude the disapproving father and presumably allow for stretching forth. Then the overflow would have a very different meaning. 'My cup overfloweth,' far from being a merely spontaneous eruption of the unconscious in free associations, would be as in the twenty-third psalm—Grace.

"Instead of the disapproving principal, The Lord as my Shepherd would lead me beside the still waters. That is an image of equilibrium between conscious and unconscious; in other words, the tub would contain the waters of initiation with me in it. I would become the container of the waters."

In meditating further on the dream, Robert remembered his mother's stories about her pregnancy with him. It had been very difficult and when he was born he emerged feet first. His mother had yearned for a girl and his father had not wanted another child at all. Thus he was born into the arms of a disappointed mother and a rejecting father. He escaped from that impossible reality by moving into the archetypal world of art, music, theater.

As Robert grew up, his mother overcompensated for his father's withdrawal. In the quarrels that ensued, Robert identified with his mother, all the time trying to create a bond between his parents. His wholeness was projected into their relationship. In building his container, Robert became aware of contrasexual and transvestite fantasies, as well as a homosexual shadow. Women whose fathers were alienated from *their* fathers must also be conscious of this kind of shadow in their masculinity.

The dream suggested to Robert that if he was to emerge from the trauma of his birth and redeem his alienation from his father, he and his anima must prepare the baptismal font for a second birth. The image of the font brought back an association of the one time in his childhood when he could remember feeling close to his father. Attempting to do "the most forbidden thing," he purposely spilled the holy water from the holy font in the church. When he told his parents, his father made the most astonishing statement Robert had ever heard: "Come with me." For the first time in his life he felt they were father and son, "a most unusual situation for us to be in." They went to the priest's house. The priest opened the door. Then Robert heard an even more astonishing statement, "My son has come to apologize." Robert had never heard his father refer to him as "my son." He did as he was told. The priest accepted the apology.

As father and son walked home together the child felt a strange sense of elation. "One person walked to the priest's house, another came back," Robert said. "I had faced the forbidden action and it was redeemable."

This association suggests that Robert, in deliberately spilling the holy water and then admitting it, was unconsciously assuming responsibility for his unwanted birth and the guilt he felt as an unwanted child whose very existence separated his parents. Children who carry this guilt will unconsciously commit criminal acts until their parents or the law courts confront them. They feel they should not be here and invent ways to become invisible, at the same time committing antisocial acts that repeat the birth trauma. They need to be found out, admit their crime and thus be released from it. When the trauma is finally confronted, the "crime" is brought into consciousness and they no longer have to be criminals. Instead of feeling they should not be here and assuming roles that make them invisible, they can realize they are not to blame for their parents' failed marriage. They can take the responsibility for their own lives and leave their parents to theirs.

It is that possibility that emerges in this dream. Robert may give birth to himself from clean water. The feeling value that he projected onto his audience, both in the theater and in life, leaving "nobody home," is now in the tub with him. The spiritual birth may come about through celebrating the bond between him and his anima, not through the cold perfection of the archetypal world imaged in a Greek frieze, but through the love that can bring new feeling to the frieze, through meticulously scrubbing on the nitty gritties of relationship within and without.

If the rebirthing is to be recognized, it is essential in the reading of the dream to recognize the archetypal character of the images and the necessity for Robert to bring to those images the value he could not bring to the roles he played on stage or the scripts he had written. It is here that the analyst's role is crucial. The dreamer's associations—the baptismal font, the spilling of the water, the walk with the father, the priest—all must be related to the dream. Just going with the images, without consciously feeding the associations into the dream, can leave the dreamer disconnected from the vital energies that can heal the trauma. Far from simply dreaming the images on, as one might observe a film over which one has no control, the dreamer needs a conscious ego to facilitate the connections. Otherwise, the anima will stay in London or New York or a pleasure dome of glass. The creation of the vessel that will receive the lance calls out for the virility of the lance. They cannot be separated one from the other.

In this chapter, the wise virgins have been scrubbing their lamps, filling them with fresh oil. They know neither the day nor the hour wherein the bridegroom comes.

Cradle Thoughts	Virgin Thoughts
If I do it right, I'll be accepted.	I won't have this relationship at the expense of my own reality.
Femininity means subordinate, mindless, vague. Men don't like my femininity except in bed.	I cannot leave these untruths hanging around. I've got to be straight. I've got to know my freedom so I can make my own choices. I reject the old labels.
I am playing the role of a grown-up woman in order to hide the little girl I really am. I fear being found out.	I'm brave. Brave also means being nervous.
I have to have a man. I feel I am nobody without a man to love me, and my body goes dead without sexuality.	I try to discover which cross God gives me and when I create my own. It is difficult to act without discernment and hard to live without intimacy. Still, I have to ask myself if I ask too much of life, whether I should concentrate on giving rather than the returns.
I might as well shut up. I put out a good idea, I'm ignored. A man puts out a silly idea, he's heard.	It's taken years to nurture my little girl into maturity. I am now ready to express who I am in every way—my voice, my body, my clothes, my values.
I find myself wanting to return to the baby pool. Then all my needs will be met. There are lots of other babies in the pool.	If you're looking for a symbiotic relationship, any boundary is annihilation.
I am afraid of freedom. I expect nothing, therefore I am never disappointed.	Nobody has been able to kill my dream. Not parents, not army officers, not Viet Nam.
Sometimes I refuse to suffer. I choose Scotch on the rocks.	After the death and rebirth, we don't promise ourselves roses, do we?

Are you looking for me? I am in the next seat.
   My shoulder is against yours.
You will not find me in stupas, not in Indian shrine
   rooms, nor in synagogues, not in cathedrals:
not in masses, nor kirtans, not in legs winding
   around your own neck, nor in eating nothing but
   vegetables.
When you really look for me, you will see me
   instantly—
you will find me in the tiniest house of time.
Kabir says: Student, tell me, what is God?
He is the breath inside the breath.

—Robert Bly, *The Kabir Book.*

It is true that the unknown is the largest need of the
intellect, though for it, no one thinks to thank God.

—Emily Dickinson, *Letters.*

The greatest and most important problems of life are all in a certain sense insoluble. They must be so because they express the necessary polarity inherent in every self-regulating system. They can never be solved, but only outgrown. . . . This "outgrowing" . . . on further experience was seen to consist in a new level of consciousness. Some higher or wider interest arose on the person's horizon, and through this widening of his view the insoluble problem lost its urgency. . . . What, on a lower level, had led to the wildest conflicts and to panicky outbursts of emotion, viewed from the higher level of the personality, now seemed like a storm in the valley seen from a high mountain-top. This does not mean that the thunderstorm is robbed of its reality, but instead of being in it one is now above it.

—C.G. Jung.

7

The Bridegroom

Give me a fish,
I eat for today.
Teach me to fish,
I eat for a lifetime.
—Chinese proverb.

Mythically speaking, this book has explored the wilderness in and around the Fisher King. T.S. Eliot's poem, *The Waste Land*, published in 1922, indelibly expressed the consciousness and conscience of this wilderness in the twentieth century. It is a time when we all have searched in vain for a way out of the spiritual dryness that has desiccated Western civilization.

Eliot ends his poem with "Shantih, shantih, shantih,"[1] the formal ending of an Upanishad, comparable to "the peace that passeth understanding." Is the very presence of the foreign words suggesting that our Western tradition no longer contains within itself the power of regeneration? Is the shaping of the fragments of the poem which Eliot has "shored against [his] ruins"[2] a desperate, perhaps futile, attempt to order a chaos which is no longer redeemable?

Sometimes in working with the dreams that appear in this book, and the many more that do not, I have been assailed by the thought that they too may be "a heap of broken images," shored up against the inevitable ruin of our collapsing civilization. Then I find hope in Perceval as a symbol of modern masculinity. Perceval, at the beginning of his journey, is able to imagine the Grail Castle; that is, his consciousness briefly connects with his unconscious. At the heart of that vision, he intuitively feels his life's task, though he does not

---

[1] *The Waste Land*, line 433.
[2] Ibid., line 430.

consciously perceive it. Without that perception, he does not ask about the Grail and the lance which could bring healing to the wounded Fisher King and his lands. His sin is not so much in doing wrong as in not being conscious of the effect of his actions on other people. His lack of emotional empathy shelters him from the conflicts that lead to manhood. But he is still young; he has the potential to connect consciously with the feminine values that can rejuvenate the sterile king and his apathetic, but frenzied, kingdom.

In working with the wounded king image in dreams, it is important to keep in mind the peeling of the onion. The layers of the personal complex that have to do with the father surround the archetype of God. Therefore, while at one level we are sloughing off the outworn attitudes we have introjected from our personal father and the masculine side of our mother, we are at the same time activating deeper levels which our parents inherited from the collective. At the core of the onion is the archetypal image of God. At every level we are struggling with the nature of the unconscious, what Jung calls "extreme conservatism, a guarantee, almost, that nothing new will ever happen."[3] He is quick to add that paradoxically the unconscious is "a creative factor, even a bold innovator."[4]

As the social organization of Earth has moved from tribe to nation to empire, smaller loyalties have had to give place to larger. Now we are leaping into a global village, a leap which is demanding a mutation in consciousness. Dream sequences dealing with the old king usually begin by requiring the dreamer to differentiate the known authority figures, discard the parental home and car, throw out the accumulated baggage. Sorting out what is of value and what must be let go is an agonizing task, as anyone who has closed a home forever knows. Clutter Clubs that function according to the Twelve Step program of Alcoholics Anonymous are being organized to support people who are paralyzed by anxiety when they attempt to throw out

---

[3] "Some Aspects of Modern Psychotherapy," *The Practice of Psychotherapy*, CW 16, par. 61.
[4] Ibid., par. 62.

their clutter. They cannot advance because they cannot stop dragging their burden of the past. (These addicts often dream of the old queen, a concretized mother who is their security.)

The need to discriminate between individual and parental values often activates dreams of riding buses and trains, symbolizing movement on well-worn grooves laid down by society. If and when the train or bus takes off into the woods, the dreamer feels suddenly alone, facing the loss of the known tracks the collective provided. The void threatens. Is the God of mother and father there? Is anything there? Where, what, who is God? Here the real hero faces the unknown for unknown reasons. The individual now has to connect with the inner laws, the inner love. That is the Grail Castle.

The Fisher King is king of the Grail Castle which, according to the Celtic conception, was either an island in the water or beneath it. In primitive groups, the king embodies the divine spirit of the tribe which is dependent on his psychic and physical health for its fruitfulness. Psychologically, the king represents a symbol of the Self (the god within) incarnate in a human being and the society he rules. In *Mysterium Coniunctionis,* Jung explores the mystery of the ritual killing and renewal of the king as it manifests in alchemy:

> It will not have escaped the reader how primitive the idea of God's ageing and need of renewal is. . . . A similar idea appears in the Grail tradition of the sick king, which has close connections with the transformation mystery of the Mass. The king is the forbear of Parsifal, whom one could describe as a redeemer figure, just as in alchemy the old king has a redeemer son or becomes a redeemer himself (the lapis [stone] is the same at the beginning and at the end). Further, we must consider certain medieval speculations concerning God's need of improvement and the transformation of the wrathful God of the Old Testament into the God of Love in the New: for, like the unicorn, he was softened by love in the lap of a virgin.[5]

Commenting on the need for the renewal of the concept of God in an evolving society, the authors of *The Grail Legend* write:

---

[5] *Mysterium Coniunctionis,* CW 14, par. 375.

The dominant attitude of consciousness is only "right" when it accords with the claims of both consciousness *and* the unconscious. Only then can it combine their opposing tendencies into unity. If, on the other hand, the ruling attitude is either too weak or incomplete, the "life is consumed in unfruitful conflict." But if the old attitude of consciousness is renewed through its descent into the unconscious, then from the latter there emerges a new symbol of wholeness which is as son to the old king. As we know, Perceval is elected to be the "son" in the Grail legend, but in the beginning this process of transformation is somehow arrested so that the old king cannot die nor can Perceval relieve his suffering.[6]

The king is sick because consciousness and the unconscious are split apart; therefore, the psychic life of his country has stagnated. In one story, the relics are lost and prosperity cannot be regained until they are found. The lance symbolizes *"the human capacity for continually being able to discern what is essential in the latent symbol of God,* and this enables the symbol increasingly to dispense its inexhaustible, life-giving, spiritual strength to humanity."[7] The lance aims at the center. The Grail contains what is at the center. Psychologically, the relics symbolize the possibility of new life emerging from the old symbols. Similarly, when the God-image has crystallized into a dead stereotype in collective consciousness, the psychic values represented by the relics hidden in the depths of the unconscious are the very values that can transform and rejuvenate the outworn concepts.

Suffering and fishing are often connected to the treasures in the depths. In a Jewish tradition, for example, at the end of the Age of Leviathan, the Angel Gabriel will catch a "pure fish" which will be eaten by the righteous. Their eating of the flesh of the Leviathan is redemptive. "At the very time the Messiah comes, this messianic fish will be partaken of."[8] The Fisher King is fishing for something to redeem him. Perceval becomes that redeemer. Healing the king is the

---

[6] Emma Jung and Marie-Louise von Franz, *The Grail Legend,* p. 192.

[7] Ibid., p. 97 (italics in original).

[8] Ibid., p. 198.

goal of the quest and healing lies in the images that bring water to the desert.

The story of the Grail grew out of the ritually and sacramentally sterile world of the eleventh and twelfth centuries. Readers who are interested in the similarities between that epoch and our own will find the discourse in Emma Jung and Marie-Louise von Franz's *The Grail Legend* extremely valuable in elucidating symbols that arise in contemporary dreams. With reference to our evolving theme of the inner marriage, the legends make clear that the Grail serves the lance, even as the lance serves the Grail. The Grail (as the inner feminine) is raised to a consciousness that is the penetration of the lance, even as the penetration of the lance is the raising to consciousness of the Grail. The one is present in the other; the two are in consciousness indissoluably linked. In the loss of that organic, life-giving connection between masculinity and femininity resides the sterility of the Fisher King and the wasteland over which he presides.

As we work our way through the ruined majesty of Eliot's poem, we become Perceval asking the question which he at first failed to ask: Whom does the Grail serve? In other words, how are consciousness and the unconscious connected? Through the evocative power of the images and rhythms, our whole soul is called into creativity, creativity that is at once the question and the answer—the inner marriage at work.

Eliot's poem, like the Grail, serves as the spiritual opening through which its readers receive the light of the lance. The very structure of the poem constellates an awakened reader, a reader gradually becoming aware of his or her own regenerative power. Working in a subliminal manner—all the more forceful for being subliminal—is the process of the healing of the Fisher King within the concentrated reader, a process that, in the best poetry, is always going on.

The same process is present in dreams. Any series of images, if carefully perceived, gradually reveals the presence of a pattern in its fragments. Moreover, the individual patterns, at a deeper level, become a collective pattern addressing the recurrent psychic concerns which define the spirit of an age. No poet, I suggest, better articulates the concerns of our age than Eliot. The "heap of broken images" that make up this book may perhaps be read as yet another footnote to *The Waste Land* in its attempt to participate in increasingly urgent action: the healing of the Fisher King—our own and that of the collective. Having gathered together various images of ravaged masculinity, I will in this final chapter discuss some images of the emerging bridegroom who is king of what appears to be, not a restored domain, but a new one.

Elaine is in mid-life, married, with adult children. When she had the following dream one year ago, she was in the process of finding new life for herself, personally and professionally.

> A king was dying. He had a disease in which he was rotting away. Pieces of his flesh were falling to the floor. His young son, about eighteen years old, loved his father and wanted to be close to him so that pieces of rotten flesh fell onto his left shoulder and back. The council of men said it must be washed off with iodine. This the boy did not do.
>
> The king was escorted to his bed, dressed in crown and stately robes. The Queen Mother stood at his side and called the boy into the room. The boy took his father's gloved hand with a jewel at the cuff and said, "Father, I love you so much. You have taught me to feed and take care of the puppies so that they will grow to be loyal guardians."

Elaine was crying so hard as she dreamt that she woke up. "I'm grieving for my own father's death by suicide twenty-nine years ago," she said. "The emotions which I was unable to deal with then are resurfacing through hypnosis. But the dream also relates to the tremendous shift I feel inside." Her knowledge of fairy tales and myths gave Elaine an understanding of what the death of the king meant and she could feel the rotten flesh of her repressed emotions falling off her as the values that had chained her to obsolete attitudes transformed. The royal characters also suggest a collective upheaval foreshadowing the immense social revolutions now taking place throughout the world. The rotting king, appareled in his crown and robes, enacts a ritual as he moves to meet his death.

He is accompanied by the Queen Mother, in alchemy the mother of the gods through whom renewal takes place. It is she who calls her eighteen-year-old son, the Perceval figure, to the dying king where the son acknowledges his love, and the gift he has inherited from his father for his ongoing life.

When the council of men told him to wash off the rotting flesh with iodine, he refused. Iodine is an antiseptic, a superficial way of cleansing the surface of a wound. The boy chooses to own the rotting flesh of his father, to take on the shadow of the patriarchy as his own responsibility.[9] Dismissing it with surface cleansing does not resolve the deeper wounding. In the presence of the mother, the containing vessel within whom the transformation can take place, he recognizes the positive side of his heritage. His father has given him a deep connection to his instinctive nature, the psychic source of renewal. Although that connection is still in the puppy stage, he has learned how to nurture those instinctive impulses so that they can become the loyal guardians of the threshold.

Dogs, or statues of dogs, still stand at the gateway of many households. On medieval monumental brasses, they are engraved at the feet of their dead masters. Mythically, they are the guardians between life and death, between the known and the unknown. They are an intuitive bridge between conscious and unconscious, connectors to the psychoid level of the psyche. Dogs are invaluable to those who love them, because their love is total and they mirror their master's inner world, a world with which the master may have lost touch. Experiencing the dog's responses, the human being makes the inner connection. They are like us, but other, a step toward the humanization of wild instincts. In dreams they often act as guides through the underworld.[10] The father has given the son the potential to go into

---

[9] For further discussion of the shadow in contemporary society, see Robert Bly, *A Little Book on the Human Shadow.* Bly is well known for his work with men in forest retreats, attempting to reconnect with "the wild man" within.

[10] A detailed study of the psychological meaning of the dog appears in Eleanora Woloy, *The Symbol of the Dog in the Human Psyche.*

the depths of his own instincts in order to create an organic kingdom in which he, as the new king, will be empowered by new spiritual values embodied in his own virility. This inestimable gift gives the masculine the connection between lust and love.

A crucial question needs to be asked: Why is the son eighteen years old? Associating with the dream, Elaine remembered that at eighteen she left the restrictions of her family to go to college.

"For the first time, I was free," she said. "I fell in love with my professor, an incredible love. The last year at college I spent all my time in his office learning to play chess and to love Lao-Tzu. I cut myself off from my peers and gave away my real masculine energy to my professor. I transferred it from my father to this beloved man. I was still giving it away when I went to medical school and fell in love with my husband. I got married, had my children and then relied on my identity as a mother. I could own myself as a mother. That carried through the early years of my marriage. When my children left, I fell into depression. I had to go out and claim my masculinity in order to do anything. I felt paralyzed. Real masculinity is not interested in copying the old king parading his empty power in robes and crown. Real masculinity is interested in genuine empowerment grounded in the instincts. To find that, I am going back to claim what was arrested at eighteen.

"Nurturing the puppies for me is being in nature. My father gave me the gift of loving the land. Every April he had a man come with a horse, not a tractor, to plow our garden. It was a numinous experience for him to see the furrows being turned over. That first dandelion of spring he brought to my mother as a lover. He breathed in the perfume of the fruit blossoms. That was my terrible confusion: all his sensitivity and then his drinking, with his violence and abuse of my mother. That sensitivity was the point of his wounding and the point of my healing.

"At the time of the dream I was wiped out with fatigue. I am finding new strength through being in nature. I totally forget time when I go to the woods and just follow deer trails in the fresh snow. I'm finding new rituals through Native American Indians. My body has changed its shape. I've lost my mother fat. My ground in my body is strong."

When we rediscover the young boy who was struck down in ourselves, it is easy to sentimentalize him, to hold onto the dream he never had the chance to live. Reconnecting with him evokes gutwrenching grief. Some modern movies are lancing the pain of that arrested boy for both men and women. In *The Dead Poets Society,* for example, who can forget the steel blue eyes of the patriarchal father murdering the last hope in the beseeching eyes of the son fighting for the freedom to live his own life? Who can forget the colluding mother helplessly standing by, powerless to think or act from any center in herself? Sentimentalizing him is as killing as denying his reality. Men and women have to honor this young man in themselves, in their partner, and in their children. Honoring him does not mean rejoicing in his return and coddling him into the warm nest from which he can never escape. Women dare not mock the mother-bound sons of the patriarchy all the while using the wily feminine intrigues that make men pageboys rather than kings. Although "I am not your mother," may shock some men into consciousness, relentless inner work has to be done if the son is to be free.[11]

The death of the old king may appear in dreams as the death of a patriarchal father or brother, or the death of a head of state. When the traditional conscious attitude loses control, it leaves behind grief, joy, relief, often combined with extreme anxiety. Without the security of the old ways, our sentimental attachments are undermined, our once cherished convictions ravaged by iconoclastic attacks. The Virgin may give birth to a tiger, a bull may lust after a young woman, body memories may break their dams. Such dream images seem outrageously bizarre, funny, sacrilegious, and the emotions that accompany them can be terrifying. The ego has to muster all its strength to hold a detached position, watching the action and at the

---

[11] See Jung, "The Dual Mother," *Symbols of Transformation,* CW 5, pars. 464ff, and M. Esther Harding, "The Sacrifice of the Son," *Woman's Mysteries,* chapter 14.

same time participating in the feelings released. This is the descent into the chaos of the maternal matrix where death may be transformed into new life. Going through the death, however, releases the fear of annihilation. The depression can be so deep that dreams are not retrievable. Then the body has to rest until the energies of nature can reconstruct the foundations that can no longer be taken for granted. For dreamers who have been cemented into stereotypes, it is a very dangerous time that requires immense patience and courage. For those who are accustomed to trusting dream imagery, however grotesque it may appear, it is a time of challenge and adventure as they try to assimilate into consciousness what is happening in the depths of the unconscious.

Mary had reached that time in her life. During six years of analysis, many changes had taken place. Her children having grown up, she still enjoyed being a housewife, but in addition she had ventured into a secure job outside the home. Her sexuality had flowered as she had never experienced it before and, while her husband at first enjoyed their new-found passion, his own emerging instincts brought with them a resentful young boy. A smoldering depression seduced him into heavy drinking and he became increasingly abusive toward his wife, verbally and physically.

"I was beginning to take a conscious attitude," Mary said, looking back over their relationship. "That provoked the negativity. I wasn't willing to play the vacant-eyed role any longer. I ceased to be a little girl, but I knew I did not want to lose Phillip. For a long time I had been questioning the life we were living. That disturbed him, made him feel insecure because he wanted to control the relationship. At first I was perfectly willing to have it that way. I was willing to be victim. I sensed that we were too close, but only rarely did it bother me. I didn't want to look at what we were involved in.

"Then I realized I had to take a stand. I had to confront him with his drinking. I'd stabbed at it for quite a while. This time I made it. I made it quite clear that I was not going to go on being victim. I was not going to live the wasted life we were living, going nowhere but toward disaster."

The night of the confrontation Mary had the following dream:

Phillip and I are walking along the sidewalk. I'm carrying a long, living yellow fish wrapped in shrink wrap. Through the wrap I am aware of sharp scales which have not been removed from the smooth yellow flesh. Phillip complains that the fish is a dangerous children's toy.

Once in the house I attempt to remove the shrink wrap. This is a difficult process and Phillip seizes the fish, saying that the only way to handle it is to wring its neck. He proceeds with the neck wringing. The fish turns into a man. Phillip violently attacks him, tossing him about, severely wounding him. The man is bleeding and badly beaten but he makes no attempt to defend himself.

At first I actually help Phillip in the attack. Then with dawning awareness, I refuse to take part in the violence. When Phillip realizes I will no longer help, he tosses the man aside. I look at the victim of our violence. Looking directly into my eyes, he says, "I knew you would save me." I am looking into the face of Christ.

Discussing this dream three years later, Mary said:

"The sidewalk is the collective way. Phillip and I tried to live like suburbanites. Our values were all the wrong values for us—achievement, social success, money. There we are walking along a collective route carrying a symbol of the Self with its golden flesh squeezed into a plastic bag. There was no room for it in the environment. The sharp scales are those parts of me I hadn't yet dealt with. They were still rough and dangerous underparts of me that were attracted to violence and being the victim of violence, the shadow parts that constellate the demonic side of the Self.

"I don't know about the fish being a dangerous children's toy. Perhaps it has something to do with Phillip's attitude toward analysis. Perhaps the shrink bag also has to do with analysis. Phillip thought analysis should be playful and creative, icing on the bread of life. He never wanted to look at the negative side of things. When I actually found my voice, actually stood up to him that night, I was tremendously threatening to things as they were. He hated my growing independence. He feared what the analysis was doing to his little girl. I guess he feared too where the Self was taking me. The fish is a content of the unconscious and Phillip's way of dealing with it was to wring off its body and stay in the head. Intellect separated from heart. Now *there's* a dangerous toy.

"I have to take responsibility here too. My own negative masculinity did not want me to work on the process of individuation. Neither outer nor inner man welcomed that side of the Self. Nor could either face reality. My inner man did not think much of body work. Only later was I astounded when I realized how it threw me into the truth of my feelings.

"At that time the fish was too big for the dream ego to deal with. Fear makes me collude with Phillip in attacking the man. But even in the dream, consciousness dawns. The ego refuses to collude any longer, and chooses to support the man. He makes no attempt to defend himself. Fighting is not his way. He wins by looking me straight in the eye. I can't even begin to describe the feeling of looking into those eyes—so clear, so deep. It was as if I had always known them, known them forever. That's what stays with me. It was like a bond that could never be broken—was there, is there, always there.

"I stopped being a church-goer years ago. I rejected the dogma and the conventional forms. I came to a completely different understanding of Christ through my dreams. Now he is a living reality within, a wholeness that holds the warring opposites together. He is the potential, a melding of all the various potentials. I know him. I love him.

"That dream came exactly when I needed it. It has been a guiding light in my psyche all through the anguish of our separation and my trying to find my own feet."

Mary had once dreamed of a hummingbird, flying at darting speed—busy, busy, busy, putting things into its nest—too busy to notice a praying mantis in the bottom of the nest. This is a superb image of a workaholic so galvanized by her own busyness that she fails to see the danger at the very center of her drivenness. This is typical behavior for a daughter of the patriarchy. In devoting herself to the ideals which she has learned with the efficiency she has mastered, she flies in her frenzied tiny perfection around the very core of her downfall. She allows her devotion to a good cause to blind her to the intuitive voices that warn her that her femininity is flying into its own destruction. Her charming, seductive partner—inner and outer —undermines her loyalty to her feminine Self. Whether that manifests as intellectual idealism violating a soul that craves relationship, or as an actual man seeking to possess her body as a prize to be won, she victimizes herself in innocently, ignorantly, colluding with the power principle.

Mary is a father's daughter. Therefore, so long as she submitted, inwardly and outwardly, and did not step onto the path of her own individuation, her father complex was benign. It owned her. On the very night that she decided to stand to her own truth, the full power of the demonic energy in that complex attacked, determined to separate her from her inner bridegroom. In life, her husband fought; in the dream, her own identification with negative masculinity at first colluded in the destruction.

The bridegroom first appears in this dream as a fish. Mary's blossoming sexuality was bringing new life; thus, the fish coming out of the deep waters of the unconscious brings with it instinctive and spiritual energies still merged together. The fish symbolizes the incarnated wisdom that comes through suffering life's realities in the flesh. Attempting to wring the head from the body constellates the deeper reality symbolized by the fish—the Christ figure.[12] Then the negative masculinity attacks more violently. Power battles with empowerment. The dream ego, however, instead of falling into the unconsciousness of rage or escape, is strong enough to stay conscious. It is strong enough to counter the partner—inner and outer—who would cut her off from her inner reality, and strong enough to look into the eyes of love. The fish becomes the transcendent figure whose love can release the dreamer from the father complex.

Unquestionably, this transition causes immense problems for one's human partner. Great sensitivity is required to deal with the

---

[12] See Jung, "The Sign of the Fishes," *Aion,* CW 9ii, pars. 127ff.

overwhelming sense of abandonment a man feels when "his" woman recognizes her inner bridegroom, unless, of course, he has discovered his inner bride. Projections carry real energy, and when the god or goddess projection is withdrawn, something vital is lost, at least temporarily. The inner marriage is creative, and when the woman goes off with her creative masculinity to write, or the man to his music, the partner feels forsaken. Allowing the relationship to evolve, through dialogue, patience and mutual consideration, is the only way through the crisis.

Phillip chose not to allow his marriage to evolve. He found another woman. Thinking back to the time of his leaving, Mary said:

"I loved Phillip. He was the only man I ever loved, perhaps the only man I will ever love. Had I not loved him it would have been all right to go on pretending or just to break up. In the beginning I had no substance in the relationship. When I began to find it, he ran away. When a woman loves a man, she wants him to know her reality, as she wants to know his. Both are then free to look at their own shadows. That means being human. By breaking free, I was offering Phillip freedom. But life was a power game for him—a romantic power game that kept him running away from reality. He could not accept freedom. Creative as he was, he had no receiver for his soul when he was drunk. He loved his soul when he was creating, and he couldn't face the fact that he was killing her."

In Mary's dream, the unconscious, the fish and the Christ figure are closely related. Since Christ becomes a very important symbol in this phase of the work, we must ask what Christ symbolizes. To understand what Christ means psychologically, we need to discard preconceived ideas and prejudices. Whether we call ourselves agnostic, atheist, Buddhist, Jewish or Christian—by whatever name, the component in the psyche represented by the word Christ appears in dreams if the process is working. In alchemy this component was known as the *filius regius,* son of the king, renewal of life. When the the dominant ego attitudes, symbolized by the king, are no longer expansive enough to contain what is evolving in the unconscious (although the ego may be so busy it is quite unaware of anything disruptive mustering its forces), or when the heart is no longer involved in the ego's concerns, then the king may be forced to dissolve in the queen. Consciousness dissolves in what feels like the chaos of the creative matrix.

In the psychic agony that ensues, the ego becomes aware of its impotence, and gradually surrenders to a power mightier than itself. (Members of Alcoholics Anonymous know through experience the significance of this surrender.) The capacity to surrender is undermined in contemporary society because the fear of the feminine has left the dogmatic ego without contact with that inner resource. So long as the creative feminine remains unconscious, it is projected, and the yearning for something more becomes concretized in greed, lust, power. Negative passions feeding on themselves can permeate a culture as well as a personality.

Reason cannot abolish the conflict. Growth is natural. It will happen either creatively or destructively. If destructively, two hundred pounds becomes three hundred, one lake poisoned becomes many, millions spent on nuclear defence become a nation's way of relating. If the old-fashioned, rigid attitude can surrender to the potential in the unconscious, the inner marriage takes place. The fruit of that union is the *filius regius,* the son, the new ruling dominant within which masculine and feminine are united. The new consciousness is not only conscious, but is conscious that it is dependent on a higher power. The independent attitude of the old king that believed will power was sufficient to take him toward progress and liberation is now perceived as inflated and arrogant. When the new king is born, the ego acknowledges the spiritual authority that transcends egohood. Paul says it succinctly: "I live; yet not I, but Christ liveth in me."[13]

By whatever name we call the new king, he is intimately connected to the feminine in a union of androgynous masculine and androgynous virgin. As in the Chinese image of totality, the yang has within it the yin, the yin has within it the yang. Although the word

---

[13] Gal.. 2:20.

virgin has been distorted in the interests of bourgeois morality, virgin is the word that carries the feminine strength of the androgyne. She is Sophia, Wisdom, mother, bride, Shakti, Shekinah. She is the love that radiates in, through and around the new king—enlightened matter opening to embody spirit. In their marriage, conscious and unconscious are united. Water is restored to the wasteland, the Fisher King is healed.

For many women, the discovery of the creative masculine involves a dream sequence that swings from encounters with intense light or swift winds to equally powerful encounters with chthonic passion. Spiritual intensity is reinforced at the physical level by dreams of sexual arousal. The dreamer may be passionately attracted to a lion with human eyes, to a bull or stag or leopard—all chthonic images of the Self. One dreamer found herself attracted to a wild Irishman who sometimes rolled in manure, but everything in her responded to his erect penis. Sometimes a group of lusty wild men arrive at the dreamer's door demanding entrance. Fearful but curious, the dreamer lets them in. They may be carrying candles in round holders, triangular crystals, or big round pizzas. For all their roughness, they are full of good humor and carry symbols of wholeness.

As a woman becomes aware of her own chthonic energy, she may feel herself resonating with the barbaric shadow energy of her father or mother. If she can own that destructive energy in herself, eat deeper of the apple of the Tree of Knowledge, she will no longer think of herself as sweet and innocent. Then her unconscious, free of the repressed darkness, can release its full light. The intensity of her sexuality is deeply connected to both the negative and positive sides of her chthonic power. At an even deeper level, her very survival is quickened by that power. If she can connect to the survival energy in the lowest chakra, and through meditation send its roots deep into the center of the earth, feel herself solidly planted, then that grounding becomes the necessary base for the Light which she is capable of receiving. Stretching to her full stature, with feet firmly rooted in the earth and head receptive to the sun, her heart opens to the Tree of Life.

Each woman has her own dream images of maturing femininity being met by an unknown man, both more radiant and more chthonic than any man she ever knew. Often he gives her a gift—a pearl ring encompassed by a golden snake, a crystal bowl incorporating four candlesticks, a crowned serpent—always a gift beyond price. In the background there may be a spinning wheel, a revolving clock, a talking computer—some image that suggests the fulfillment of destiny. The dreamer has to be patient and alert, and eat the food that is being offered in the dreams.

Dreams of the approaching marriage often include purification rites. The initiant may have to go through a radical cleansing process, both in body and dreams. One woman, for example, who suffered from chronic constipation, dreamt that a long white tapeworm encased in a plastic bag was pulled from the rectum of a man, and smaller worms from the rectums of cats. Exquisite feminine rituals are enacted before the dream ego enters a huge city square, or simply a square in a vast field. In the center of the hallowed place is a tall cylindrical column or some other phallic monument. Sometimes the sacred ground is a mansion filled with light. Whatever the image, that secure place becomes Home, the place where soul and Self meet, the Home that is the heart of the new order.

Without that Home, we would be in perilous danger in the new kingdom—babes lost in the woods. We would not be able to distinguish between the voices in our dreams. The voices of the evil side of the unconscious can be so alluring that they seduce us toward our doom. Trust and patience and finely tuned discernment, combined with good honest doubt, gradually establish the inseparable bond.

Few of my analysands or friends have actually experienced a dream of the sacred marriage. Those who have are still in the process of assimilating what occurred. Perhaps, as in the ancient mystery rites, the marriage should be veiled in silence. Its beauty and passion are the secret of a life lived in love.

As I participate in these journeys, the questions become more numerous, more complicated. As one of my analysands said in the midst of her own inner earthquake, "One thing this work does is give us the courage to spiral down, down, right down to the spiritual core to ask the one question worth asking: What does life mean?" Essentially, that is Perceval's question: Whom does the Grail serve? That is not an intellectual question when we come to a crossroads where the little life our ego controls is shattered by a larger reality.

Catherine had worked very hard to create a meaningful life. She had a good marriage, a fulfilling career, grown children who were making their way in the world. She had done the creative things that keep a harmonious balance in a home—entertaining, gardening, decorating. After several years of analysis and body work, a different kind of energy began to stir. Whereas she had expressed her creativity in tangible, concrete ways, the new energy drew her into spirit, into ideas and images that were breaking the fetters of physical laws.

Trying to express this new creativity demanded a greater self-discipline than Catherine could maintain.

"I had to learn that happiness beyond the ordinary boundaries required a formidable discipline," she said. "I had to learn to stay with something and see it through, not abandon it when the initial enthusiasm waned. I had to stretch and wait for further guidance when I felt blocked. I had to develop a new confidence in myself in order to stand to my convictions, even in the face of opposition and criticism. I had to find the ability to take positive action to defend and protect what was important to me. It was the creative force of spirit that I needed to find, spirit creative enough to break the rigid laws that say this is how it must be done. My maturing femininity required a new masculine partner—a creative force of spirit and ideas that could stand and hold, and take positive action to defend living laws that penetrated to new life. I had always tried to measure up to the old law. Now I was discovering within myself another law that was committed to my soul, to my husband as a whole man—a commitment of heart strong enough to break the self-righteous patterns."

Then she began having dreams with recurrent blue images—nymphs with blue eyes, a blue-eyed kitten, an immense blue vein creating an underground circuit. One day she found herself looking into the blue eyes of a man whom she had never seen before, and "out of the blue" she was caught up in a powerful obsession over which she had no control. Fires she had never known before flared into dangerous heat. The innocent little girl whose garden was suddenly too small was being pushed out by forces in the unconscious. "Who am I? What am I doing? Is this really me?" Such questions rang in her head, and every bell in her resonated with, "Yes, it is, Yes, Yes."

Extraordinary coincidences brought the two together in places where neither would ordinarily be. Repeatedly Catherine decided never to see him again, and repeatedly Fate contrived another meeting. She became fearful of going out because these chance encounters created such chaos, and fearful of turning in because, in spite of her devotion to her husband, she had dreams of the other man. The unconscious was forcing her to look at everything that was not acceptable about herself in her marriage, and everything she had always found unacceptable in others. In an effort to try to get some perspective on the conflict, Catherine wrote in her journal:

> I have become totally obsessed with this man. I can't understand it, because it just came out of nowhere. And I don't even like him very much.
>
> I tell myself I have fallen into an animus projection—that I see in him my own inner, unintegrated man. I tell myself what a good marriage I have, how much I love my husband. I tell myself to stop it, that I am having a midlife crisis. I tell myself a lot of things, but nothing helps.
>
> It gets worse. I am thinking about him practically every moment of the day. I don't have as good an appetite as usual. I wake up in the night. I feel guilty like Hell. I feel ridiculous.
>
> I follow John [her husband] around like a puppy. I think about telling him what is happening. I think it might help me if I could just say, "Look, I've become totally obsessed with this man I don't even know. I think about him all the time, I can't get him out of my mind."
>
> But I don't. I am afraid. I am afraid that I will hurt him. I am afraid that he will interpret the fact that I am so wrapped up in another man as a betrayal of the heart. I don't think he would ever forgive me for that. Not really, not in the depths of his soul.

I also think how I would feel if our roles were reversed, and it was John whose thoughts were no longer with me, but with another woman. I know the jealous shrew who lives in a dark place within me would rise up with all her wrath and venom to destroy him, her, me, everything.

I don't believe John could ever understand or forgive what is happening because he believes that we have control over matters of the heart. He believes that these things don't happen to people who really love each other. I used to believe that too.

I get worse. I try working harder. I try meditating. I try to understand.

No matter with what reason or logic my mind tries to combat what is happening, it is totally useless. My feelings simply march on like the Pied Piper, gathering more and more followers, until everything inside me has left its previous position and is all caught up in a holy crusade. Every day the army in me gets stronger.

I know I am losing. I know my mind can no longer help. I hold onto John physically. I try to absorb his love for me through my body. I sleep fitfully, clinging to him, always touching him, sometimes just with a toe, desperate, afraid.

In the fieriest heat of the conflict, Catherine had the following dream.

I am in the water, in the sea, very, very far from shore, so far I cannot see it. An enormous wave comes behind me. I feel it coming and take a big breath. The wave rushes over me with overwhelming power and I am carried along under it. Just as I can no longer hold my breath the wave releases me and I emerge. I am close to the shore, but still not there. Somehow, because of my absolute devotion to Marlowe's *Faust,* I am released from my struggle and no longer have to get to the shore. I have been delivered.

For Catherine, the story of Faust had particular meaning. She had always empathized with Faust, a man whose longing to experience all of life exceeded his ability. Faust had glimpses of what was possible, but he was unable to actually *live* what he felt. By agreeing to sell his soul to the devil, Faust dared to refuse the boundaries that were prescribed for him. He yearned to live *all* of life, and was willing to sacrifice his immortal soul in order to do so.

Catherine too had had glimpses of a life beyond her own experience. She had yearned for a deep soul connection with her husband. She felt there were areas of herself that she dared not know; she sensed a deeper creative part of herself that she could not express.

Consciously, Catherine was powerless to stop the wave from the unconscious. Its forward-striving thrust was breaking the too-perfect balance that she and her husband had found in adjusting to each other, one crooked complex dovetailing with another, smothering growth. The dream indicates that she will not be drowned, but she will endure a fearsome resolution. She is delivered, born out of the water, because she is true to Marlowe's *Faust*.

Catherine knew that in Marlowe's play God did not take pity on Faust. She preferred Marlowe's version to Goethe's because, in her projection, God was unforgiving. There could be no redemption. Yet, in the dream, Catherine's absolute devotion to Marlowe's *Faust* frees her from going to the shore, and she is delivered. Clearly there is a paradox at the center of this conflict. What seems to be damnation is, in fact, redemption. In working through this life or death contradiction, Catherine allowed herself no rationalization, no self-pity. Daily she wrote in her journal straight statements of where she believed she was. According to the old order she was disobeying what she believed to be the word of God, "Thou shalt not commit adultery," and all the other thou-shalt-nots.

"In breaking the old moral code," she said, "I felt I was damning myself. What I was doing was wrong, irreparable. On a deeper level, I knew that going against that old code was, in fact, my redemption. I discovered I was obeying an inner law, more potent, more demanding than any collective law. The more I know myself as a woman, the more my values are coming out of my own experience. The stronger my creative masculinity becomes, the more I can risk breaking with the past. The more too I can discern my guilt as a rejection of my own soul, a way of not accepting what is. I am clear. I will take responsibility for who I am."

The near-perfect marriage became an empty shell. Because Catherine projected an unforgiving god onto her husband, she was afraid to tell him what was happening. He felt cut off, alienated, powerless to reach her. Meanwhile, her inner law began to tell her that acting out sexually with the other man had to be sacrificed to what was meant to be a soul connection. On the night she determined to make the sacrifice, she had the following dream:

> My dog is struggling on the floor. He is dying, but he is trying desperately to get up on my lap. I take him in my arms and, in spite of his frail body, he tries to get up-on his hind legs as if to connect more closely to me. His crying becomes my sobbing. As he dies, he transforms into a radiant baby boy with golden red hair. I awoke shaking with grief.

For nine months, Catherine had known that she had surrendered to the wave, that she was too far out ever to return to the same shore. In her commitment to all of life, she found a love strong enough to forgive her own shadow and compassionate enough to forgive other human beings seventy times seven.

Having owned her passionate nature, she also acknowledged the necessity of sacrificing it in that particular relationship in order to bring the new-found energy into her marriage. That sacrifice manifested in her dream as her beloved dog in the throes of death, understanding and loyal to the end. The transformation of the dog into the radiant baby boy—instinct into love—happens because the soul has endured the conflict of the opposites to the breaking point. Fully aware of the cost of the sacrifice to the body, at the same time totally committed to what is essential to the soul, ego desire surrenders to a higher power, the heart bursts open, every cell of the body is suffused with divine love. The entire personality transcends its former boundaries. New life is born. What felt like death becomes the travail of birth.

When Catherine was finally able to tell her husband what had happened, the marriage went into a serious crisis. But John was not the unforgiving god Catherine had projected onto him. In his therapy he too found the strength to deal with the truth. Both committed themselves to a vision of what their marriage could be, and day by day they allowed their new relationship to evolve.

Crucial to this evolution is the realization that the inner partner is not the same as the outer partner, and so long as the inner divinity is projected onto the outer human creature, there can be nothing but illusion, confusion, disappointment and despair, to mention but a few of the heartaches flesh is heir to. While our relationship to the inner bridegroom will influence our outer relationships, he is the presence that accompanies us in our inner journey to totality. Our outer partner shares the earthly path.

Discriminating between the two can be a humbling and releasing experience. I remember the first time I saw my husband without a projection. We had been married twenty-five years. It was early morning. I had awakened cranky and discontent. I was sitting in the living room drinking my coffee, thankful for silence. Then he decided to get up and make his own breakfast. I saw him in the kitchen trying to break an egg into a single little egg poacher. He was in his old Black Watch housecoat, his two spindly legs sticking out the bottom. "I deserved better than this," I thought. But as I watched him patiently cutting his bread, there was something about the concentration of his hand on the loaf that caught a lifetime in a moment. "He's still here," I thought. "I'm still here. We're in this little box on the seventeenth floor in a place called Toronto with a crazy world out there. Whatever life is, we've walked our parallel paths together. God knows, I've made him suffer, and he's made me suffer. But we're here. Neither of us has given up the search." I respected him. Whatever the mystery is that holds two people together exploded through my heart. Aware of my old housecoat and not so thin legs, I knew that human love and divine love are of the same essence.

"Do you want some more coffee?" he asked.

"Yes," I said.

Many people are in the death throes as the old order collapses on our planet. Like Catherine, they feel that some serpent has brought knowledge into the Garden of Eden. The old order based on innocence and unthinking allegiance to an outer authority is giving way to a new order based on questioning, experience and inner truth. The strength to undergo the dismemberment lies in the connection between the soul and the spirit—the Grail and the lance. Out of that union comes the image that can guide us when our feet no longer know where to go. Some understanding of the ancient mysteries that map the subtleties of the psychic process can give us enough courage to keep us walking toward the sacred marriage.

Among the myths that are particularly helpful in understanding the union of instinctual and spiritual energies—a union fraught with power and powerlessness in both men and women—is the Egyptian myth of Isis and Osiris, the twin brother and sister who are also the royal husband and wife. Osiris is a systematic, sensitive king who is murdered by his brother Set, who symbolizes the many aspects of insatiable lust that freeze the energy in matter. Osiris, then, is at the mercy of his physical body, imaged as a coffin floating down the Nile. Releasing Osiris from the dictates of his physical body is the task of Isis. When she finds the casket, she throws herself on her dead lover's body in a paroxysm of love. Set finds the body, cuts it into fourteen pieces and scatters them over the countryside. Isis finds thirteen parts which she magically puts back together, but the fourteenth part, his penis, she cannot find. Through the intensity of her love, she creates an *image* of what is missing and that consecrated image becomes phallos through which she conceives a son.

The consecrated image of the phallus is phallos.[14] Phallos is not simply an erect penis. Phallos, as distinct from phallus, does not belong to the physical body. It belongs to the resurrected body which is the body of spiritual desire, like the heavenly Jerusalem. Isis is the mother and bride of phallos. When she unites with her own desire, she creates the child of her desire. What was a phallus—power, erection—becomes phallos—love, resurrection. Through her love, her masculine energy is regenerated, empowered through spirit. When the dismembered body (dismembered through lust for power) is reconstituted through her love—the divine feminine becoming the mother of the divine masculine—she unites with that phallos and brings forth the divine boy. The whole body is animated in the spiri-

---

[14] See Eugene Monick, *Phallos: Sacred Image of the Masculine,* pp. 13ff.

tual body. All life is eroticized when soul and spirit meet. The pre-figuration of this conscious process is imaged in the womb of their mother, where Osiris and Isis sexually unite.

In the ancient world, women were custodians of the mysteries. The mysteries of Isis were enacted in her shrine but the culmination of the rites was the moment when the initiant, having experienced the full range of lust and passion, became the god, Osiris, whose potency (creative spirit rather than will to power) was raised from the dead through the love of the goddess.[15]

The bridal robe of Osiris was radiant and worn only once; the many-colored veil of Isis was worn for other religious ceremonials. The difference between the robes suggests both the difference between the god and goddess and their inherent unity—the veils of nature charged with the glory of the spirit. To blind eyes and deaf ears, nature is matter to be raped by a phallus in whatever form it takes—bomb, gun, missile. The massacre of matter is the massacre of the feminine in whose womb, in whose womb only, we can experience passion powerful enough to release spirit that bodies forth love through every living thing.

The wanderings and efforts of Isis in her yearning to find Osiris are similar to those of Psyche in her yearning to be reunited with Amor. In the Eleusinian Mysteries, the secret in the winnowing basket and the awakening in the cradle echo with the secret of the Annunciation and the cradle of Bethlehem. The union of the inner feminine with phallos is the inner marriage which is imaged, when psychologically understood, as the androgyne. The child born of that union is the new personality.

Phallos symbolizes the desire for union with one's own creative power. The literalization of that desire becomes penis worship that projects creative power onto the male, reducing feminine creativity to biological reproduction. The male, by virtue of the penis, becomes the sole source of new life. Impregnation then depends upon sub-

---

[15] See Marie-Louise von Franz, *A Psychological Interpretation of the Golden Ass of Apuleius.*

mission to the male will. Motherhood in the literal sense becomes the ultimate expression of the creativity of the woman.

In the symbolic world, phallos, as distinct from physical phallus, is created through surrender, an archetypal feminine energy whether in men or in women. In our culture, the word surrender strikes terror, as Mary and Catherine discovered. Difficult questions arise: How can I give up my ego and still hold the focus? How can I concentrate and give up at the same time? Are you asking me to tear out my backbone? Surrender is a conscious act of letting go, the sacrifice of ego desire so that imprisoned energy can be transformed into new life. A seed must die, be buried in the earth, in order to bear fruit. In the Christian myth, Mary surrenders to phallos; within her receptive womb God is conceived in his human form, and from it he is born. Phallos in its relation to the feminine embodies the androgynous nature of God.

Jung discusses the incestuous nature of the sacred marriage at length. In "The Psychology of the Transference" he writes:

> Incest symbolizes union with one's own being. It means individuation or becoming a self, and because this is so vitally important, it exerts an unholy fascination . . . as a psychic process controlled by the unconscious, a fact well known to anybody who is familiar with psychopathology.[16]

In contemporary society, incest is coming increasingly into focus. In interpreting dream images of incest, however, we need to be mindful of their possible symbolic nature. To interpret a dream of incest concretely when it is, in fact, part of a "psychic process controlled by the unconscious" can cause needless suffering outwardly and confound the process inwardly. In the self-destructive and murderous literalism of our time, caution and careful consideration are necessary to protect the psychic reality. The treasure at the core of our father and mother complexes is often revealed in incestuous im-

---

[16] *The Practice of Psychotherapy,* CW 16, par. 419. See also Jung, "Symbols of the Mother and of Rebirth," *Symbols of Transformation,* CW 5, pars. 300ff.

agery that symbolizes our connection with our richest source of creativity.

Borne on the wave of the sea, Aphrodite-Venus was created from the cut-off phallus of her ravaging father. Redeeming the phallus from the darkness of lust, greed, drivenness, is the task of the conscious feminine in both men and women. In the process of sacrificing ego desire, at the breaking point the feminine surrenders to divine love. Paul on the road to Damascus was assailed by something unplanned, unpredictable, coming to him as light. Surrender and the conception of phallos are virtually simultaneous. Here is the moment of true virginity—the feminine one-in-herself—divine femininity uniting with divine masculinity. The fruit of that surrender is the radiant divine child, strong enough to transcend the obsolete Herods who seek to kill him, and creative enough to move life into a different reality.

That renewal can happen only when the old king has experienced the full range of his lust and found himself unfulfilled. By lifting the veil of Isis—reconnecting with the unconscious—he realizes that what he sees with his physical eyes is but a garment hung over the real. The real is the divine love that reaches out to greet him.

In *Four Quartets,* written twenty years after *The Waste Land,* T.S. Eliot calls this moment of apprehension "the point of intersection of the timeless/ With time":

> The hint half guessed, the gift half understood, is Incarnation.
> Here the impossible union
> Of spheres of existence is actual,
> Here the past and future
> Are conquered, and reconciled,
> Where action were otherwise movement
> Of that which is only moved
> And has in it no source of movement—
> Driven by daemonic, chthonic
> Powers. And right action is freedom
> From past and future also.[17]

---

[17] "The Dry Salvages."

Bringing together the worlds of timeless and time, spirit and matter, is the problem of the Grail King who "corresponds to an *imago Dei* [image of God] that is suspended, suffering, on the problem of the opposites."[18] Perceval's task is to incarnate the god-image on a deeper and more conscious level. His task is to take God off the cross.

The Grail King in most of us is also suspended, his feeling and ideals not grounded in his body. He is the mother-bound masculine who renders himself impotent because his infantile yearning for a Paradise he thinks he deserves blinds him to the Moment. He is, therefore, a victim escaping from matter, or a rebel fighting against it without a standpoint of his own. His healing depends on Perceval's capacity to go into the feelings and passions buried in his unconscious, and endure the fires of incarnation—empowered through embodiment. For centuries he has been cut off from his own matter, from what has been considered the dark, serpentine feminine side of himself. His renewal comes from below through union with the instinctual, ecstatic side that brings the passion of the body and the passion of the spirit into harmony. Attempting to transcend his own nature has not worked. Nature herself is beginning to rumble. Our very survival depends upon spirit embracing embodied soul.

Seeing the eternal in the transitory has traditionally been the occupation of saints. Now many dreamers are envisaging daily scenes permeated with inner reality. Their inner vision transforms their outer relationships. Sometimes they dream they are in a class being taught by a wise old woman or man. They are learning to take immense leaps over deep chasms. Sometimes their inner partner is radiant, also learning. Something unpredictable, absolutely new, is stirring from below, something quite different from the unpredictable that traditionally has come from above. Is Kore in danger of rape? Is Persephone strong enough to be ravished?

"Right action is freedom/ From past and future." Our responsibility is to the present, to the images that guide us, to the two energies

---

[18] *The Grail Legend,* p. 298.

that together are love. "The gift half understood" shimmers within the following dream.

My beloved and I are partners in a creativity contest to see who can make the most original object. Playfully, board by board, we build a small, sturdy boat.

"What shall we use for a sail?" he asks.

"It has to be silk," I say.

We talk and kiss each other and try to think of a sail. I lie in the boat with my head by the mast. Suddenly, I've got it. So has he. He kneels beside me and weaves my long blonde hair into a golden sail. A quick gust fills it. My beloved grabs the rudder and we are carried out into a sunlit sea. I don't know if we win the contest. Nothing matters except that I love him and he loves me and we both love the water and the wind. I am the sail, he is the rudder. In our little craft we are borne by the Holy Spirit over the eternal sea.

Constantin Brancusi, *The Kiss.*

Bibliography

Arnold, Matthew. "Stanzas from the Grande Chartreuse." In *The Poetical Works of Matthew Arnold.* Ed. Humphrey Milford. London: Oxford University Press, 1945.

Beckett, Samuel. *Endgame: A Play.* New York: Grove Press, 1958.

Blake, William. *The Selected Poetry and Prose of William Blake.* Ed. David Erdman. Garden City: Doubleday, 1965.

Bly, Robert. *A Little Book on the Human Shadow.* New York: Harper and Row, 1988.

_____. *The Kabir Book.* Boston: Beacon Press, 1977.

Boyle, Jimmy. *A Sense of Freedom.* London: Canongate Publishing Ltd. and Pan Books Ltd., 1977.

Cardinal, Maria. *The Words To Say It.* Trans. Pat Goodheart. Cambridge, MA, Van Vactor and Goodheart, 1983.

Chesterton, G.K. "The Donkey." In *The Oxford Book of English Verse, 1250-1918.* New ed. Ed. Arthur Quiller-Couch. New York: Oxford University Press, 1940.

Corbin, Henry. *Spiritual Body and Celestial Earth* (Bollingen Series XCI:2). Trans. Nancy Pearson. Princeton: Princeton University Press, 1977.

cummings, e.e. *Poems 1923-1954.* New York: Harcourt, Brace, 1954.

Dante. *The Divine Comedy.* Trans. Thomas G. Bergin. New York: Grossman Publishers, 1969.

Dickinson, Emily. *The Complete Poems.* Ed. Thomas H. Johnson. Boston: Little, Brown and Company, 1960.

_____. *The Letters of Emily Dickinson.* Ed. Thomas A. Johnson. Cambridge, MA: Belknap Press, 1958.

Eliot, T.S. *The Complete Poems and Plays.* New York: Harcourt Brace, 1952.

Hamilton, Edith. *Mythology.* New York: New American Library, 1969.

Harding, Esther. *Woman's Mysteries: Ancient and Modern.* New York: Bantam Books, 1973.

Ingpen, Roger and Peck, Walter E., eds. *The Complete Works of Percy Bysshe Shelley,* vol. 7. London: Ernest Benn Ltd., 1926.

Jung, C.G. *The Collected Works* (Bollingen Series XX). 20 vols. Trans. R. F. C. Hull. Ed. H. Read, M. Fordham, G. Adler, Wm. McGuire. Princeton: Princeton University Press, 1953-1979.

_____. *Memories, Dreams, Reflections.* New York: Pantheon Books, 1961.

_____. *Nietzsche's Zarathustra: Notes of the Seminar Given in 1934-1939* (Bollingen Series XCIX). 2 vols. Ed. James L. Jarrett. Princeton: Princeton University Press, 1988.

Jung, Emma and von Franz, Marie-Louise. *The Grail Legend.* 2nd ed. Boston: Sigo Press, 1980.

Keats, John. "The Fall of Hyperion." In *English Romantic Writers.* Ed. David Perkins. New York: Harcourt Brace and World, Inc., 1967.

Kundera, Milan. *The Incredible Lightness of Being.* Trans. Michael Henry Heim. New York: Harper Colophon, 1985.

Laurence, D.H. *The Rainbow.* New York: Viking Press, 1961.

Merton, Thomas. *A Thomas Merton Reader.* Ed. T.P. McDonnell. New York: Image Books, 1974.

Miller, Alice. *For Your Own Good: Hidden Cruelty in Child-Rearing and the Roots of Violence.* New York: Farrar, Straus, Giroux, 1983.

Milton, John. *The Student's Milton.* Rev. ed. Ed. Frank Allen Patterson. New York: Apple-Century-Crofts, Inc., 1933.

Monick, Eugene. *Phallos: Sacred Image of the Masculine.* Toronto: Inner City Books, 1987.

Rilke, Rainer Maria. *Letters to a Young Poet.* Trans. Stephen Mitchell. New York: Vintage Books (Random House), 1986.

_____. *The Selected Poetry of Rainer Maria Rilke.* Ed. and trans. Stephen Mitchell. New York: Vintage Books, 1984.

Schaeffer, Susan Fromberg. *The Madness of a Seduced Woman.* New York: E.P. Dutton Inc., 1983.

Sharman-Burke, Juliet and Greene, Liz. *The Mythic Tarot.* New York: Methuen, 1986.

Sharp, Daryl. *The Survival Papers: Anatomy of a Midlife Crisis.* Toronto: Inner City Books, 1988.

Tardat, Claude. *Sweet Death.* London: Pandora Press, Unwin Hyman Ltd., 1989.

van Gennep, Arnold. *The Rites of Passage.* Chicago: University of Chicago Press, 1960.

von Franz, Marie-Louise. *A Psychlogical Interpretation of the Golden Ass of Apuleius.* Zurich: Spring Publications, 1970.

_____. *Shadow and Evil in Fairytales.* Zurich: Spring Publications, 1974.

Wolf, Fred Alan. *Star Wave.* New York: Macmillan Publishing Co., 1984.

Woloy, Eleanora. *The Symbol of the Dog in the Human Psyche.* Evanston, IL: Chiron Publications, 1990.

Woodman, Marion. *The Pregnant Virgin: A Process of Psychological Transformation.* Toronto: Inner City Books, 1985.

Wordsworth, William. *The Poetical Works of William Wordsworth.* Ed. Thomas Hutchinson. Rev. Ernest De Selincourt. London: Oxford University Press, 1960.

Yeats, William Butler. *Collected Poems of W.B. Yeats.* New York: Macmillan, 1959.

Index

220

Studies in Jungian Psychology
by Jungian Analysts

Sewn Paperbacks

New, recent and choice:

The Psychological Meaning of Redemption Motifs in Fairytales.
Marie-Louise von Franz (Zurich). ISBN 0-919123-01-5. 128 pp. $14

Alchemy: An Introduction to the Symbolism and the Psychology.
Marie-Louise von Franz (Zurich). ISBN 0-919123-04-X. 84 illustrations. 288 pp. $18

Descent to the Goddess: A Way of Initiation for Women.
Sylvia Brinton Perera (New York). ISBN 0-919123-05-8. 112 pp. $14

Addiction to Perfection: The Still Unravished Bride.
Marion Woodman (Toronto). ISBN 0-919123-11-2. Illustrated. 208 pp. $17 ($22 hard)

The Creation of Consciousness: Jung's Myth for Modern Man.
Edward F. Edinger, M.D. (Los Angeles). ISBN 0-919123-13-9. Illustrated. 128 pp. $14

The Illness That We Are: A Jungian Critique of Christianity.
John P. Dourley (Ottawa). ISBN 0-919123-16-3. 128 pp. $14

The Pregnant Virgin: A Process of Psychological Transformation.
Marion Woodman (Toronto). ISBN 0-919123-20-1. Illustrated. 208 pp. $17 ($22 hard)

The Jungian Experience: Analysis and Individuation.
James A. Hall, M.D. (Dallas). ISBN 0-919123-25-2. 176 pp. $16

Phallos: Sacred Image of the Masculine.
Eugene Monick (Scranton/New York). ISBN 0-919123-26-0. 30 illustrations. 144 pp. $15

The Christian Archetype: A Jungian Commentary on the Life of Christ.
Edward F. Edinger, M.D. (Los Angeles). ISBN 0-919123-27-9. Illustrated. 144 pp. $15

Personality Types: Jung's Model of Typology.
Daryl Sharp (Toronto). ISBN 0-919123-30-9. Diagrams. 128 pp. $14

The Sacred Prostitute: Eternal Aspect of the Feminine.
Nancy Qualls-Corbett (Birmingham). ISBN 0-919123-31-7. Illustrated. 176 pp. $16

The Survival Papers: Anatomy of a Midlife Crisis.
Daryl Sharp (Toronto). ISBN 0-919123-34-1. 160 pp. $15

The Cassandra Complex: Living with Disbelief.
Laurie Layton Schapira (New York). ISBN 0-919123-35-X. Illustrated. 160 pp. $15

The Ravaged Bridegroom: Masculinity in Women.
Marion Woodman (Toronto). ISBN 0-919123-42-2. Illustrated. 224 pp. $18

Liberating the Heart: Spirituality and Jungian Psychology.
Lawrence W. Jaffe (Los Angeles). ISBN 0-919123-43-0. 176 pp. $16

The Dream Story.
Donald Broadribb (W. Australia). ISBN 0-919123-45-7. 256pp. $18

The Rainbow Serpent: Bridge to Consciousness.
Robert L. Gardner (Toronto). ISBN 0-919123-46-5. Illustrated. 128 pp. $15

Circle of Care: Clinical Issues in Jungian Psychology.
Warren Steinberg (New York). ISBN 0-919123-47-3. 160 pp. $16

Jung Lexicon: A Primer of Terms & Concepts.
Daryl Sharp (Toronto). ISBN 0-919123-48-1. Diagrams. 160 pp. $16

Prices and payment (check or money order) in $U.S. (in Canada, $Cdn)
Add Postage/Handling: 1-2 books, $2; 3-4 books, $4; 5-8 books, $7

Complete Catalogue and 36-page SAMPLER free on request

INNER CITY BOOKS
Box 1271, Station Q, Toronto, Canada M4T 2P4